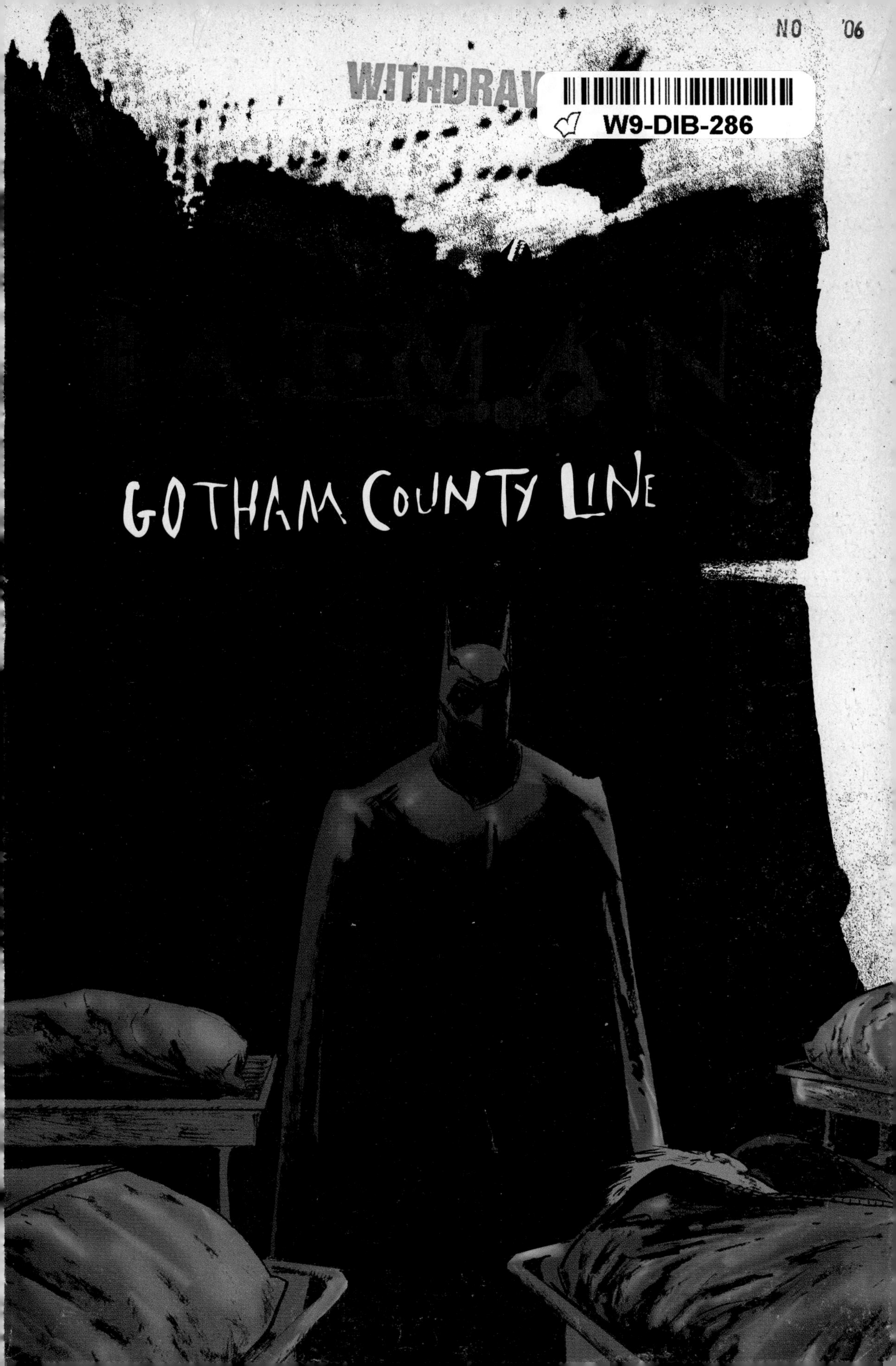
GOTHAM COUNTY LINE

GOTHAM COUNTY LINE

Steve Niles
Writer

Scott Hampton
Artist

Jose Villarrubia
Colorist

Pat Brosseau
Letterer

Batman created by Bob Kane

Special thanks to Angi Shearstone
for art assistance on book three.

DAN DiDiO Senior VP-Executive Editor JOEY CAVALiERi Editor-Original series
MICHAEL WRiGHT Associate Editor-Original series ANTON KAWASAKi Editor-Collected edition
PAUL LEViTZ President & Publisher GEORG BREWER VP-Design & DC Direct Creative
RiCHARD BRUNiNG Senior VP-Creative Director PATRiCK CALDON Executive VP-Finance & Operations
CHRiS CARAMALiS VP-Finance JOHN CUNNiNGHAM VP-Marketing TERRi CUNNiNGHAM VP-Managing Editor
STEPHANiE FiERMAN Senior VP-Sales & Marketing ALiSON GiLL VP-Manufacturing
HANK KANALZ VP-General Manager, WildStorm LiLLiAN LASERSON Senior VP & General Counsel
JiM LEE Editorial Director-WildStorm PAULA LOWiTT Senior VP-Business & Legal Affairs
DAVID McKiLLiPS VP-Advertising & Custom Publishing JOHN NEE VP-Business Development
GREGORY NOVECK Senior VP-Creative Affairs CHERYL RUBiN Senior VP-Brand Management
JEFF TROJAN VP-Business Development, DC Direct BOB WAYNE VP-Sales

BATMAN: GOTHAM COUNTY LiNE

DC Comics, 1700 Broadway, New York, NY 10019
A Warner Bros. Entertainment Company
Printed in Canada. First Printing.
iSBN: 1-4012-0905-X
iSBN 13: 978-1-4012-0905-6
Cover by Scott Hampton with Jose Villarrubia.
Logo design by Nessim Higson.

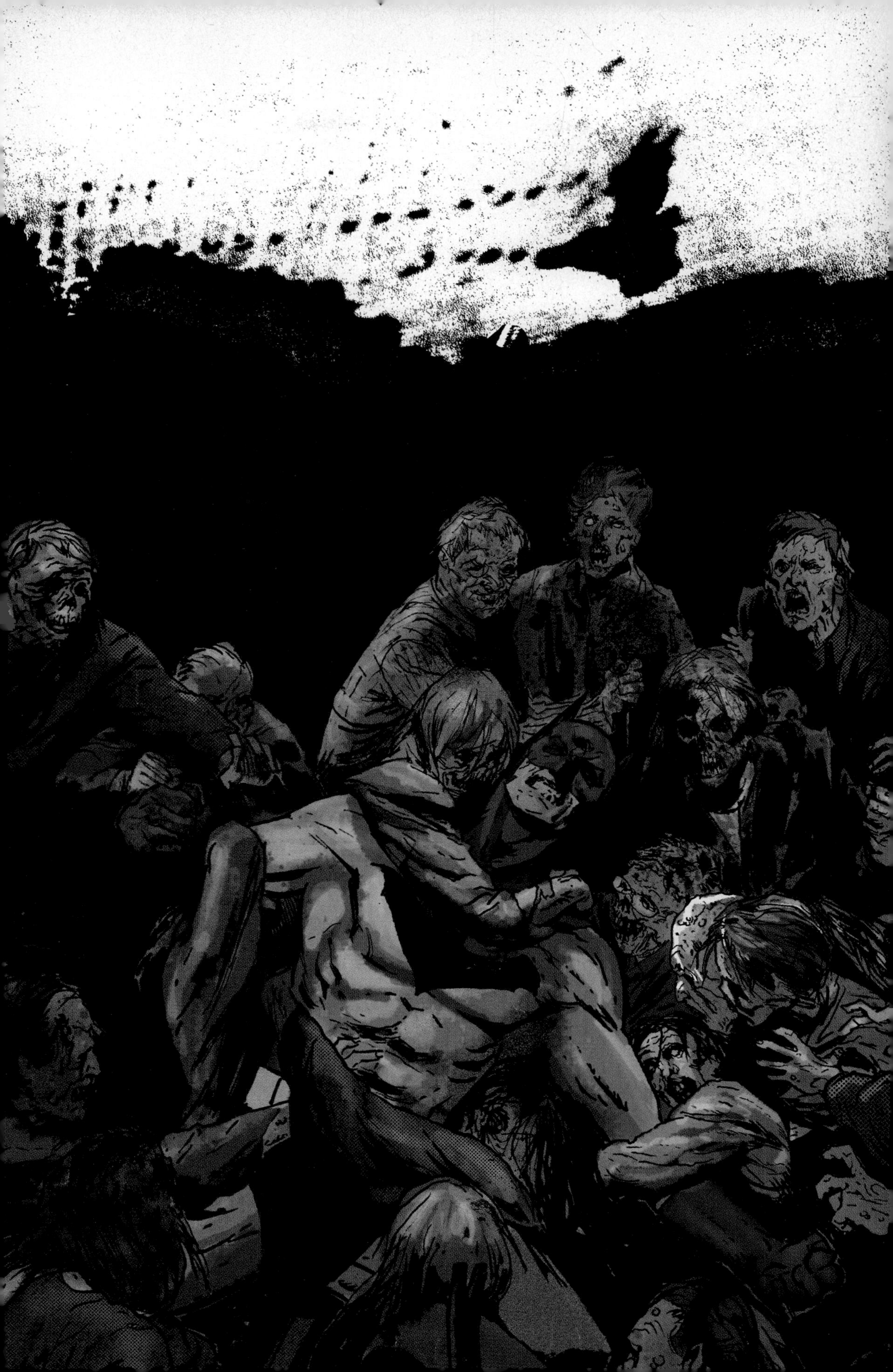

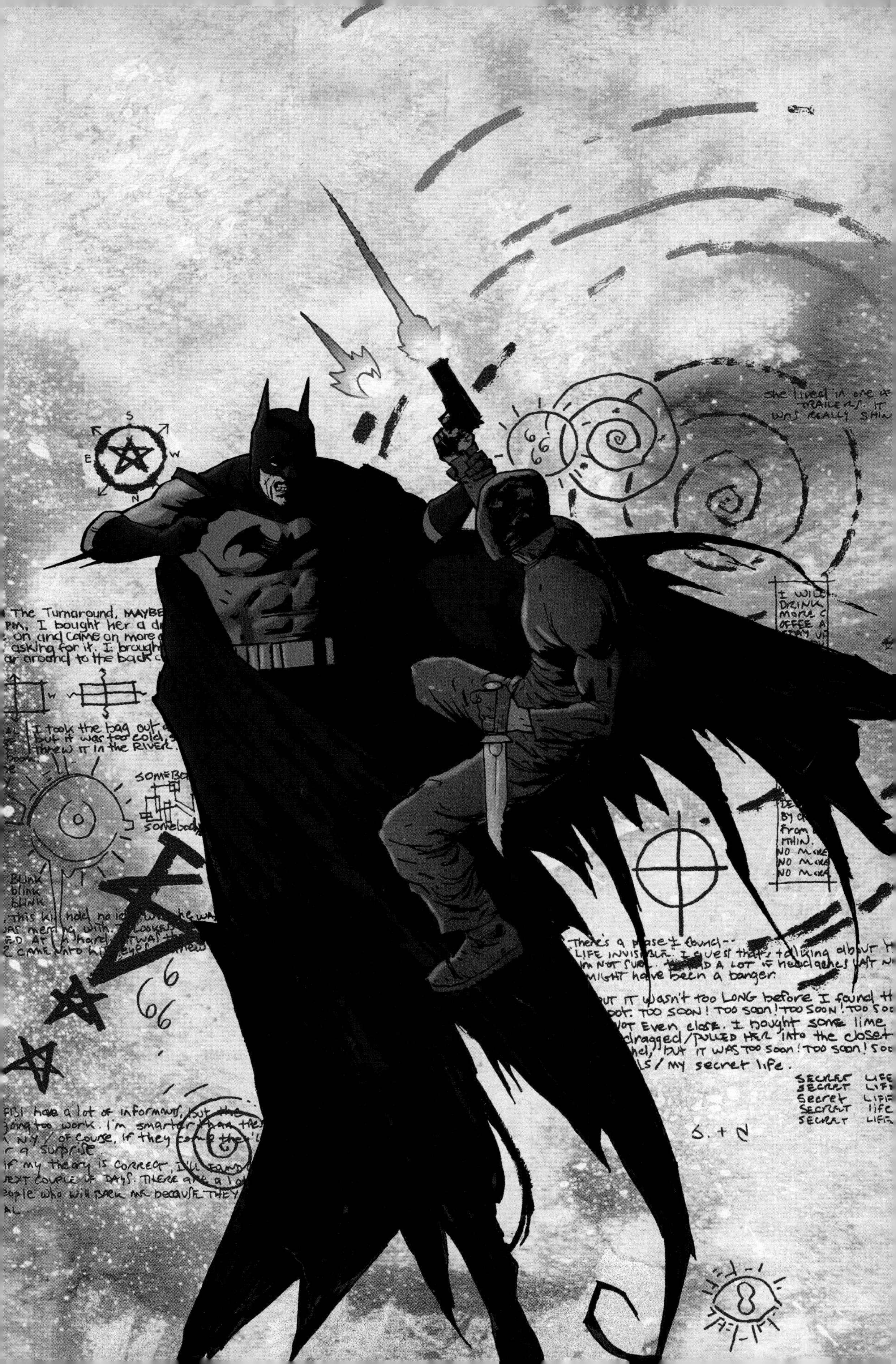

she lived in one of
TRAILERS. IT
WAS REALLY
The Turnaround, MAYBE
I took the bag out
threw it in the RIVER.
Blink
blink
NO MORE
NO MORE
NO MORE
There's a phrase I found--
MIGHT have been a banger.
TOO SOON! TOO Soon! TOO SOON!
dragged/PULLED HER into the closet
but IT WAS TOO Soon! TOO Soon!
my secret life.
SECRET
SECRET
Secret
SECRET
SECRET
66
66
66
If my theory is correct

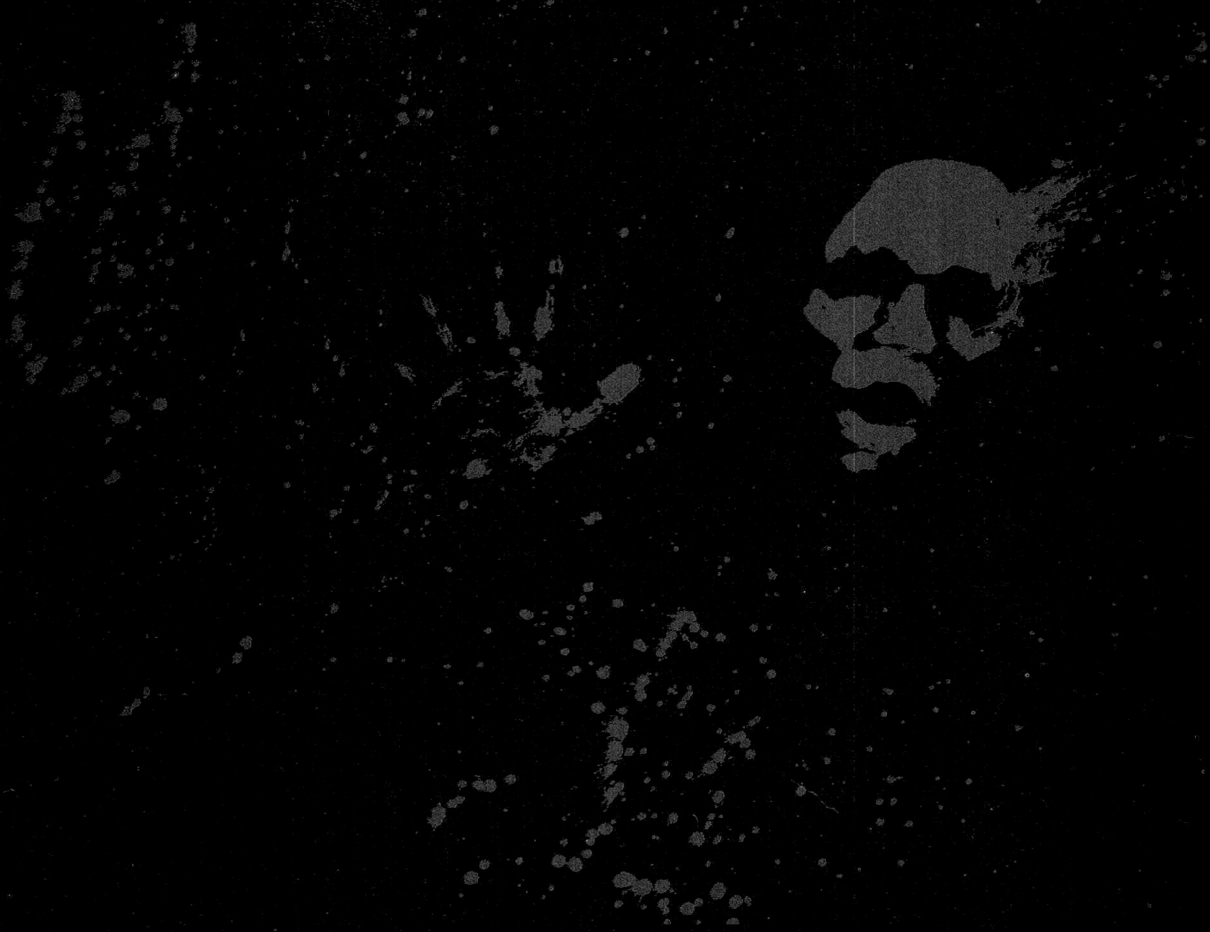

BOOK ONE:
THE OBVIOUS KILL

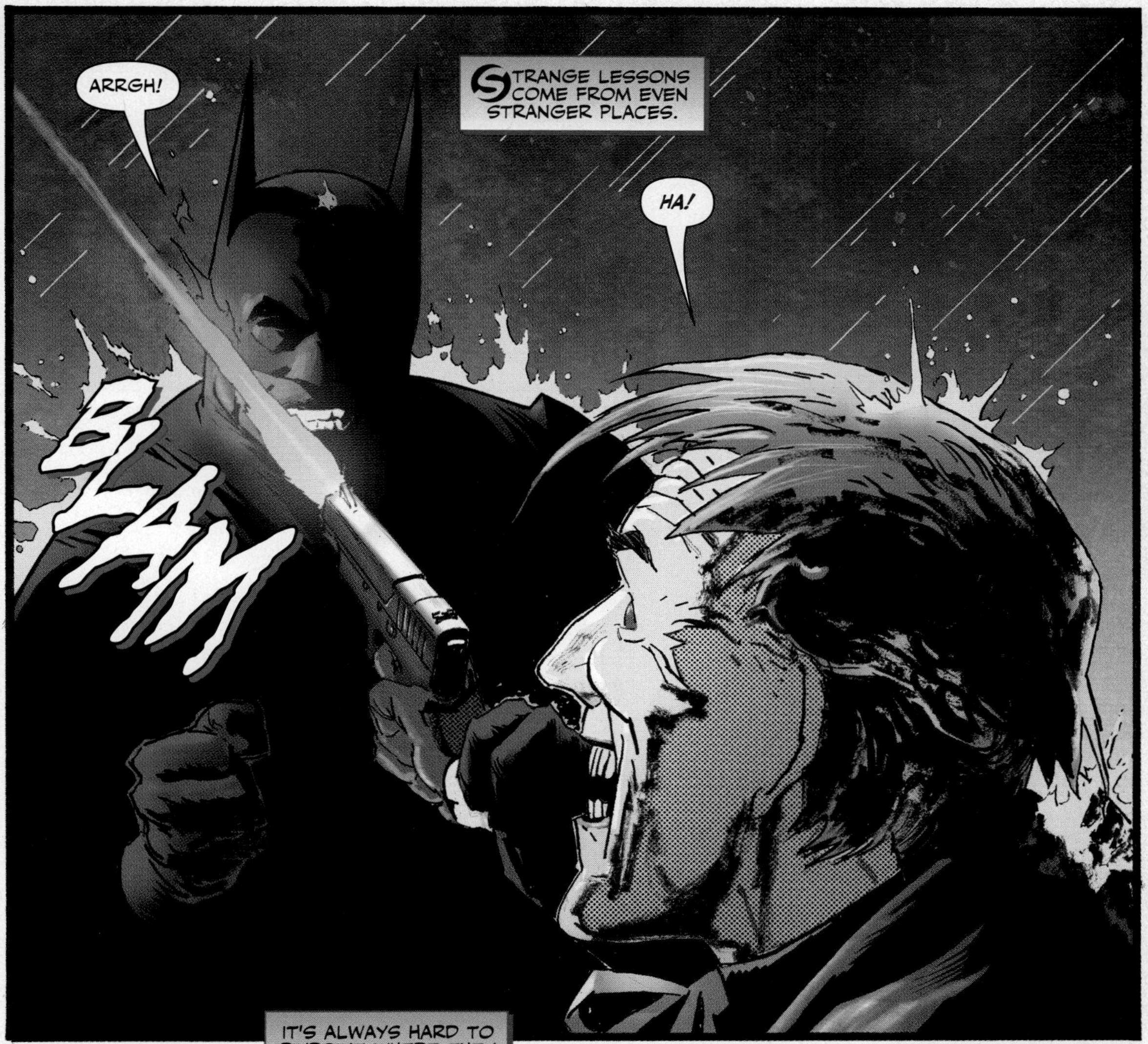
STRANGE LESSONS COME FROM EVEN STRANGER PLACES.
ARRGH!
HA!
BLAM

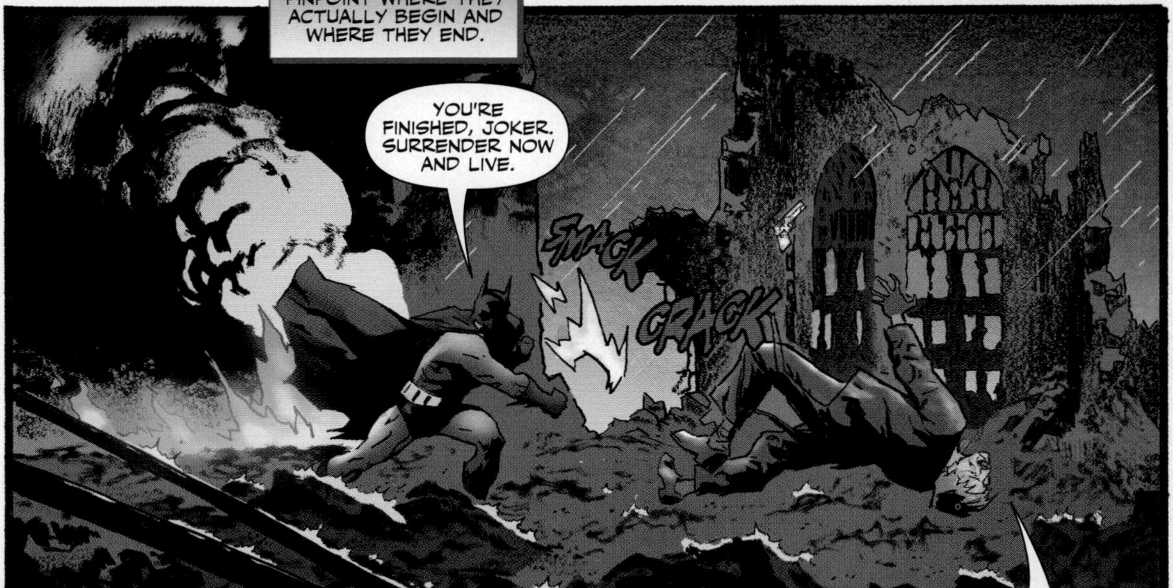
IT'S ALWAYS HARD TO PINPOINT WHERE THEY ACTUALLY BEGIN AND WHERE THEY END.
YOU'RE FINISHED, JOKER. SURRENDER NOW AND LIVE.
SMACK
CRACK
OH!

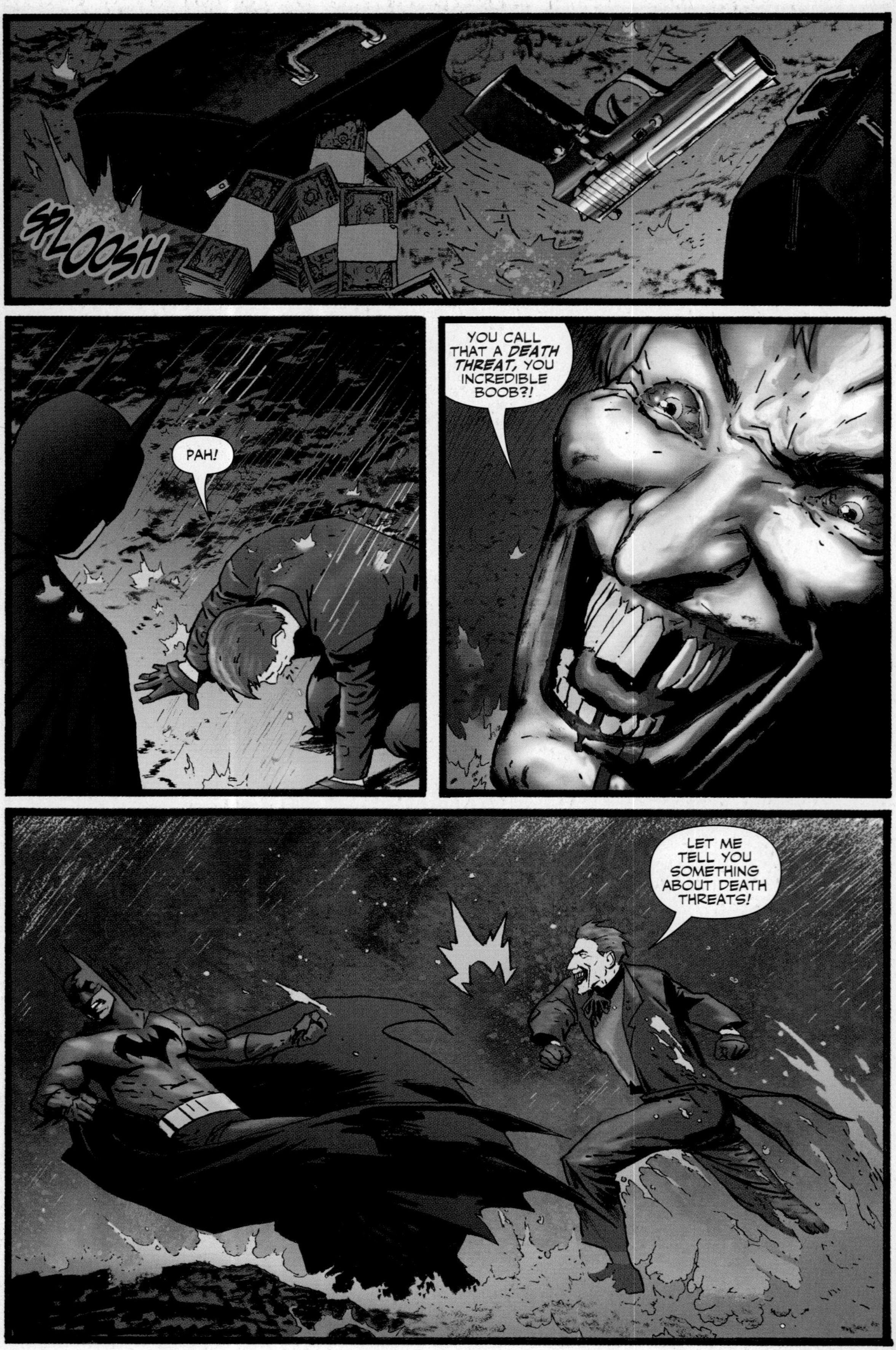
SPLOOSH
PAH!
YOU CALL THAT A *DEATH THREAT,* YOU INCREDIBLE BOOB?!
LET ME TELL YOU SOMETHING ABOUT DEATH THREATS!

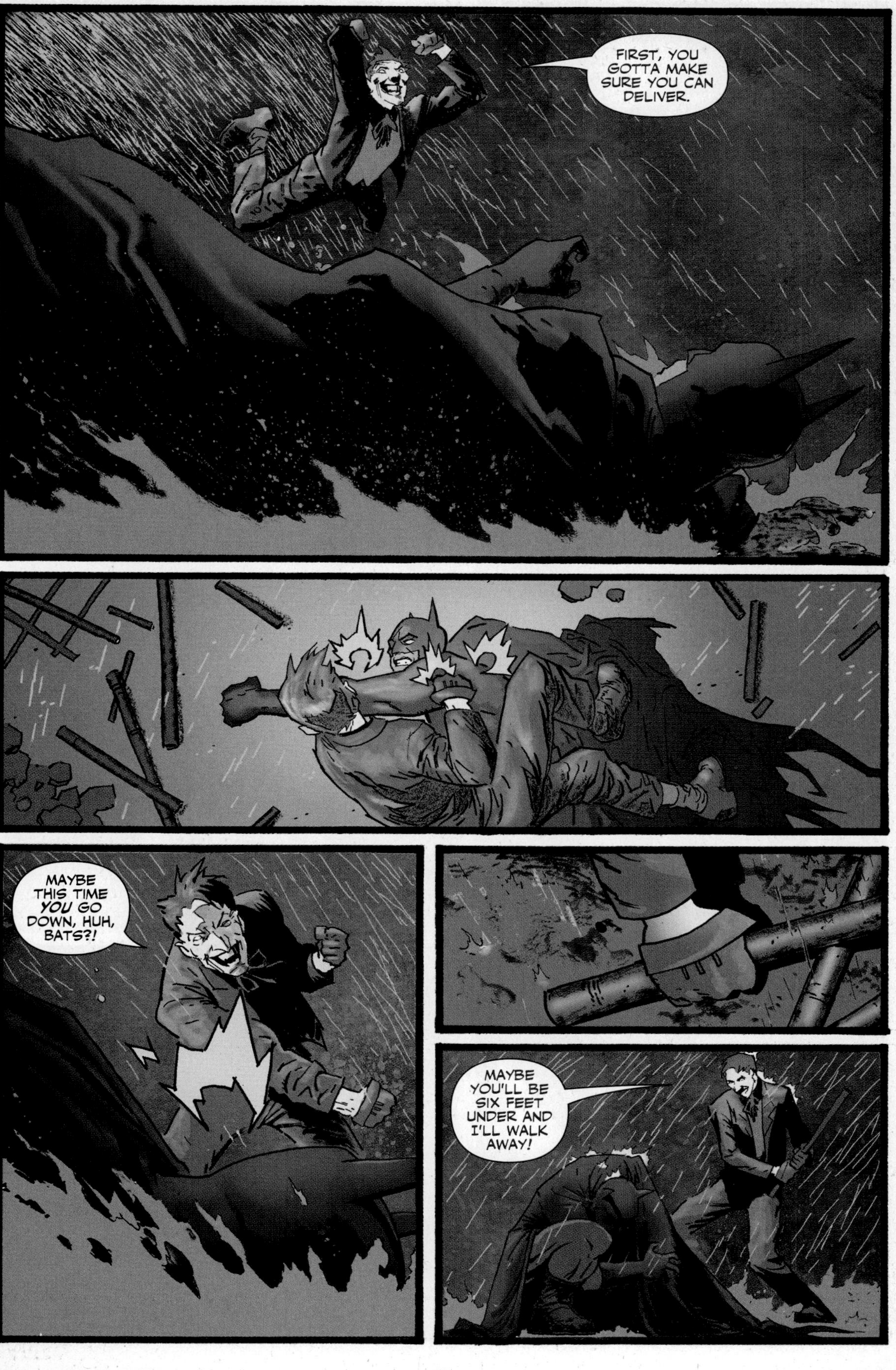
FIRST, YOU GOTTA MAKE SURE YOU CAN DELIVER.
MAYBE THIS TIME YOU GO DOWN, HUH, BATS?!
MAYBE YOU'LL BE SIX FEET UNDER AND I'LL WALK AWAY!

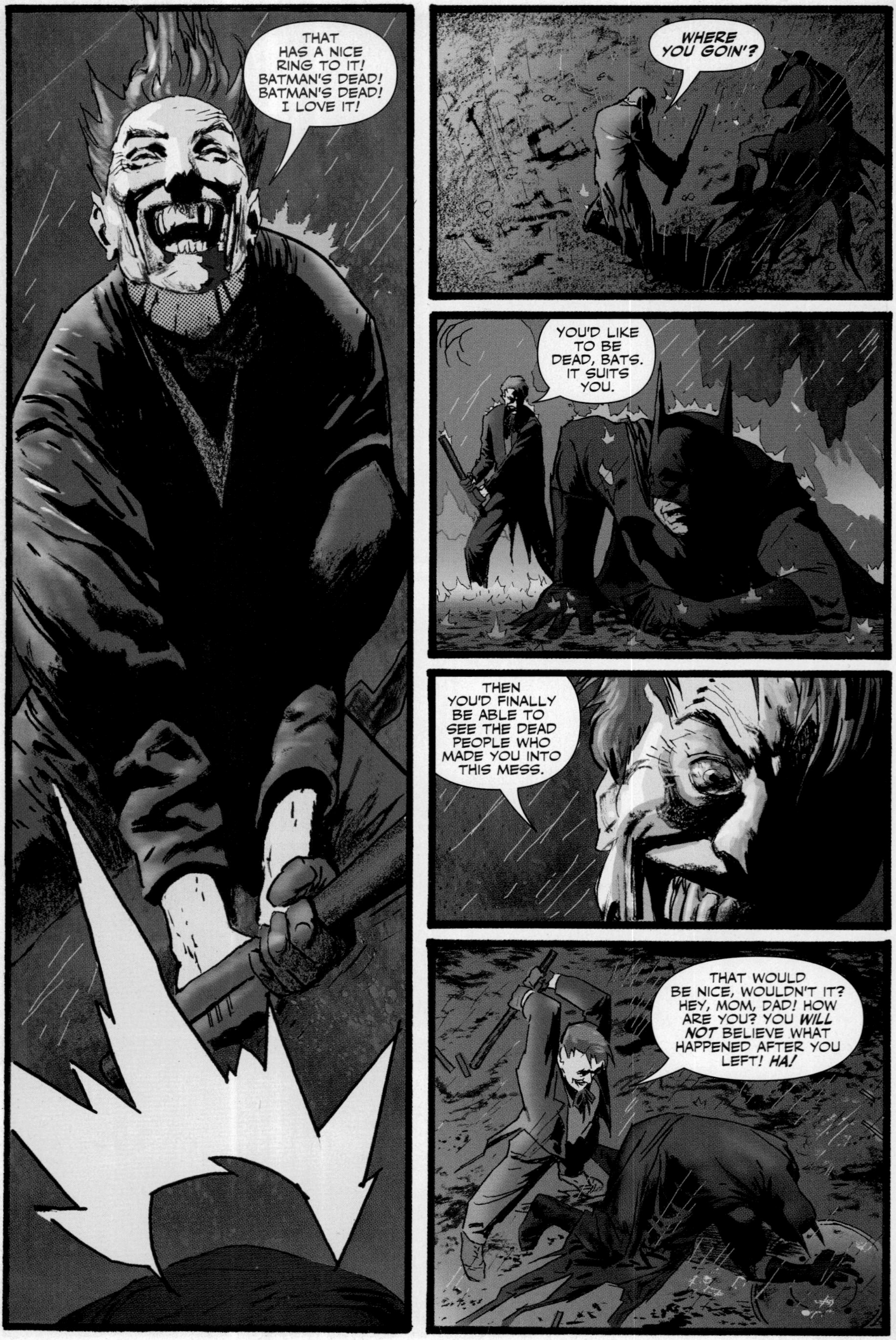
THAT HAS A NICE RING TO IT! BATMAN'S DEAD! BATMAN'S DEAD! I LOVE IT!
WHERE YOU GOIN'?
YOU'D LIKE TO BE DEAD, BATS. IT SUITS YOU.
THEN YOU'D FINALLY BE ABLE TO SEE THE DEAD PEOPLE WHO MADE YOU INTO THIS MESS.
THAT WOULD BE NICE, WOULDN'T IT? HEY, MOM, DAD! HOW ARE YOU? YOU WILL NOT BELIEVE WHAT HAPPENED AFTER YOU LEFT! HA!

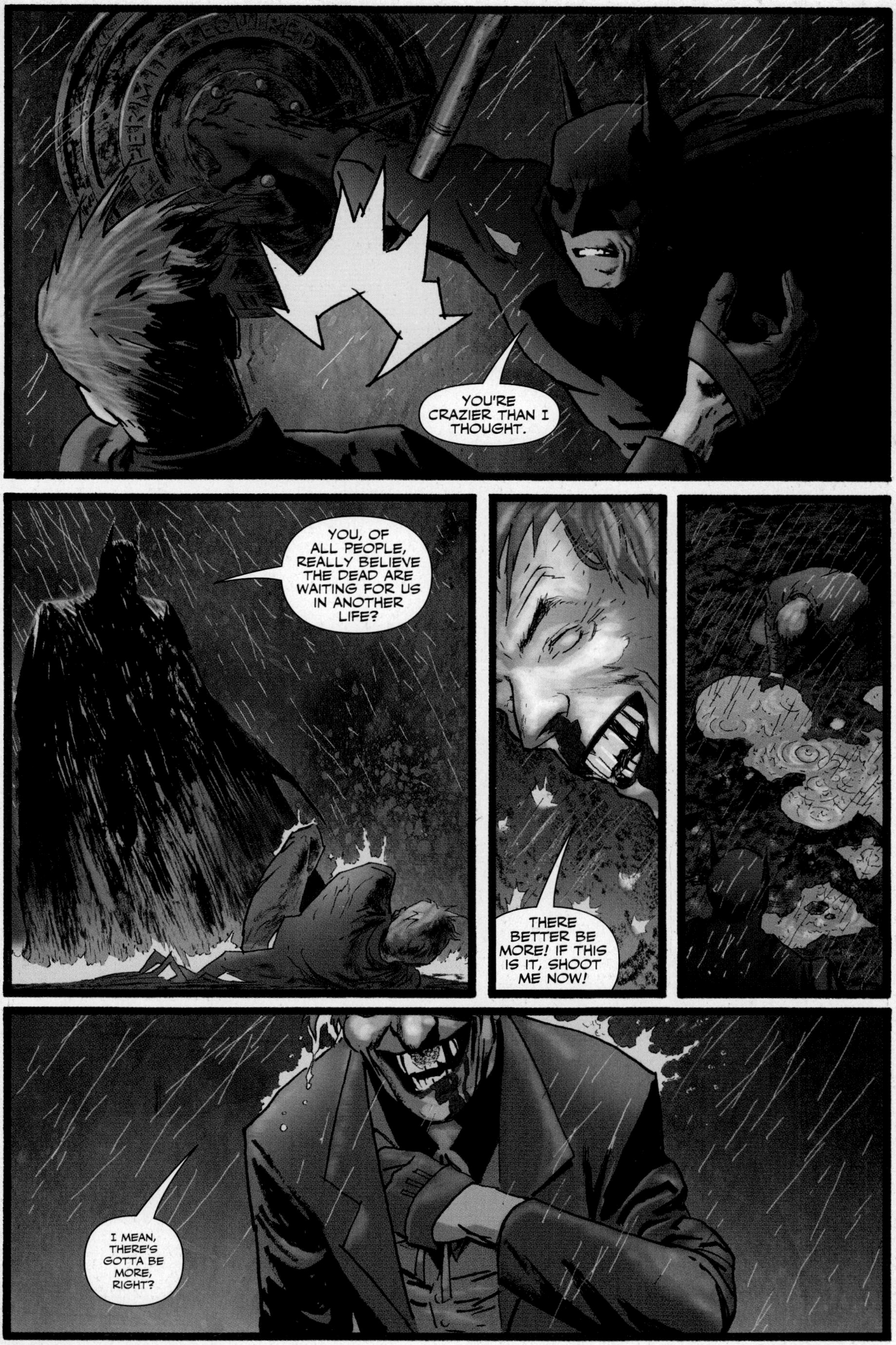
YOU'RE CRAZIER THAN I THOUGHT.
YOU, OF ALL PEOPLE, REALLY BELIEVE THE DEAD ARE WAITING FOR US IN ANOTHER LIFE?
THERE BETTER BE MORE! IF THIS IS IT, SHOOT ME NOW!
I MEAN, THERE'S GOTTA BE MORE, RIGHT?

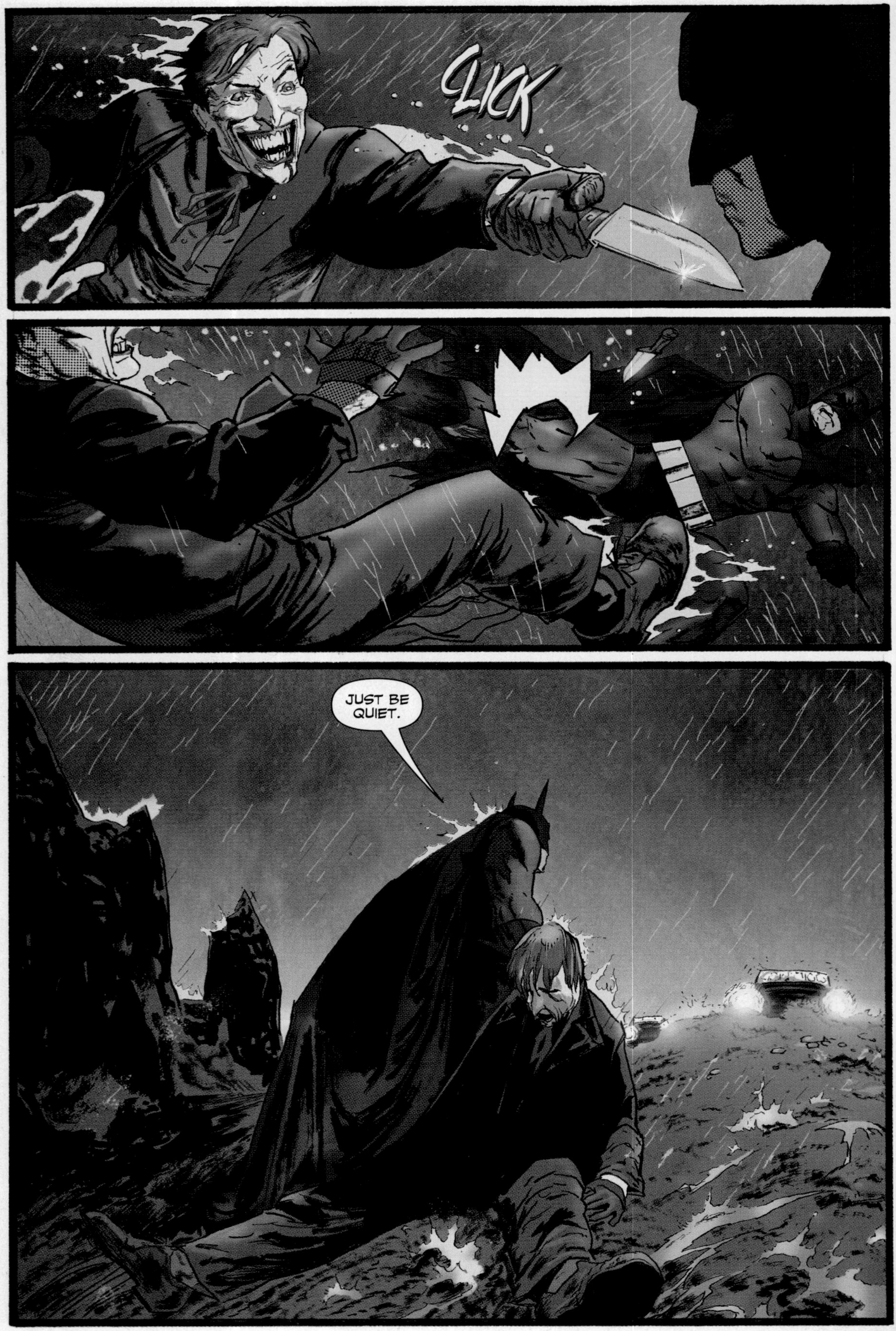
CLICK
JUST BE QUIET.

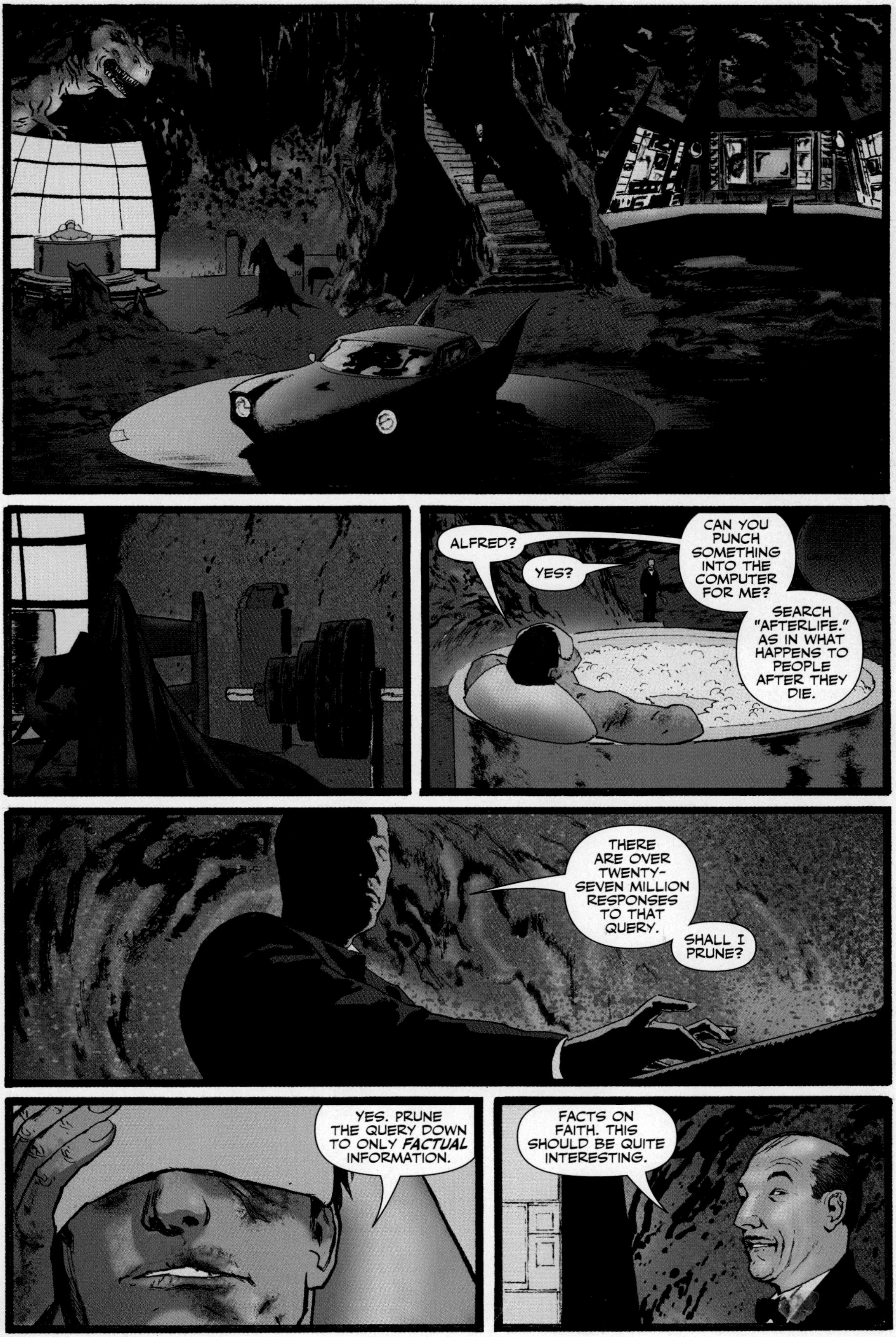
ALFRED?
YES?
CAN YOU PUNCH SOMETHING INTO THE COMPUTER FOR ME?
SEARCH "AFTERLIFE." AS IN WHAT HAPPENS TO PEOPLE AFTER THEY DIE.
THERE ARE OVER TWENTY-SEVEN MILLION RESPONSES TO THAT QUERY.
SHALL I PRUNE?
YES. PRUNE THE QUERY DOWN TO ONLY *FACTUAL* INFORMATION.
FACTS ON FAITH. THIS SHOULD BE QUITE INTERESTING.

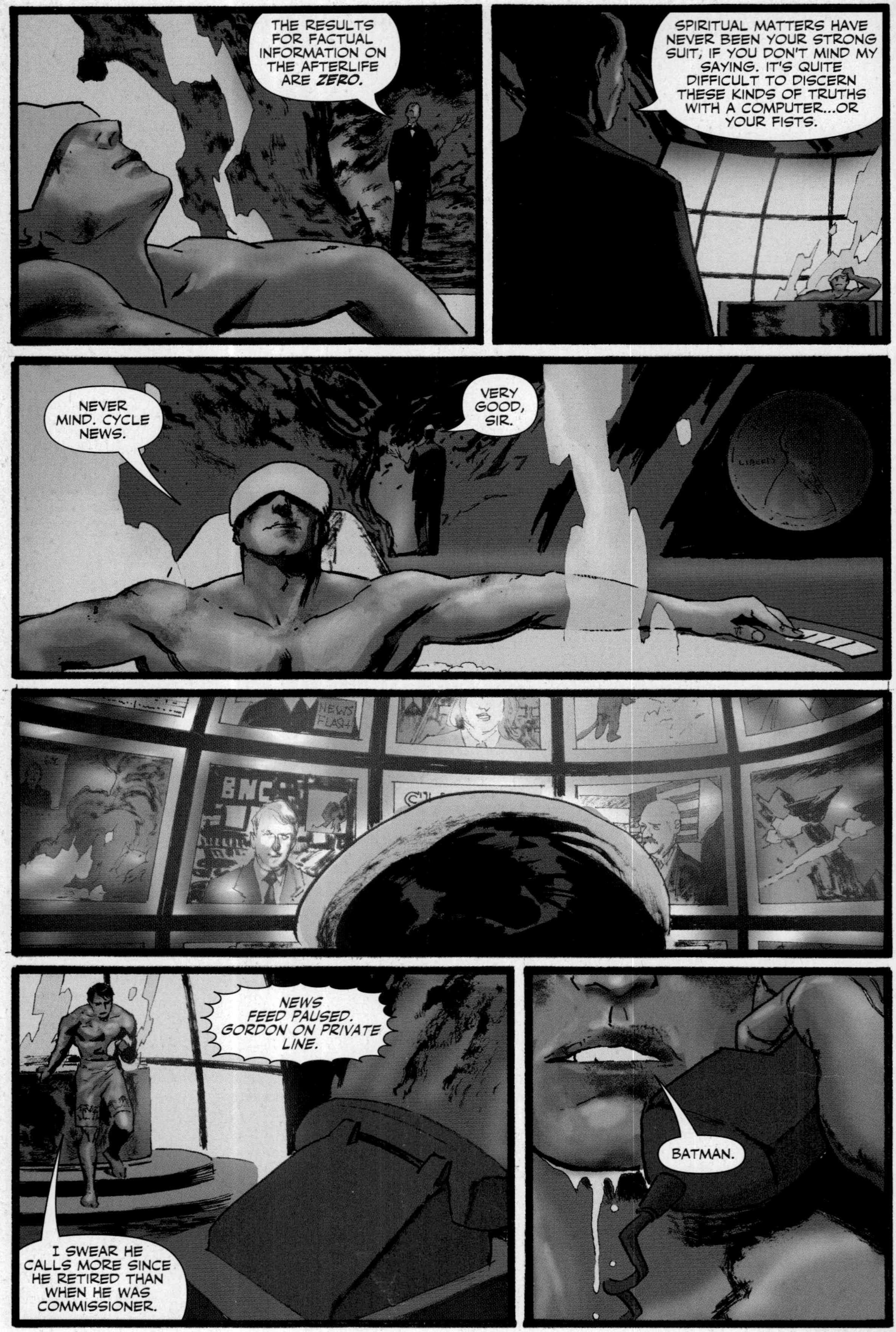
THE RESULTS FOR FACTUAL INFORMATION ON THE AFTERLIFE ARE ZERO.
SPIRITUAL MATTERS HAVE NEVER BEEN YOUR STRONG SUIT, IF YOU DON'T MIND MY SAYING. IT'S QUITE DIFFICULT TO DISCERN THESE KINDS OF TRUTHS WITH A COMPUTER...OR YOUR FISTS.
NEVER MIND. CYCLE NEWS.
VERY GOOD, SIR.
LIBERTY
NEWS FLASH
NEWS FEED PAUSED. GORDON ON PRIVATE LINE.
I SWEAR HE CALLS MORE SINCE HE RETIRED THAN WHEN HE WAS COMMISSIONER.
BATMAN.

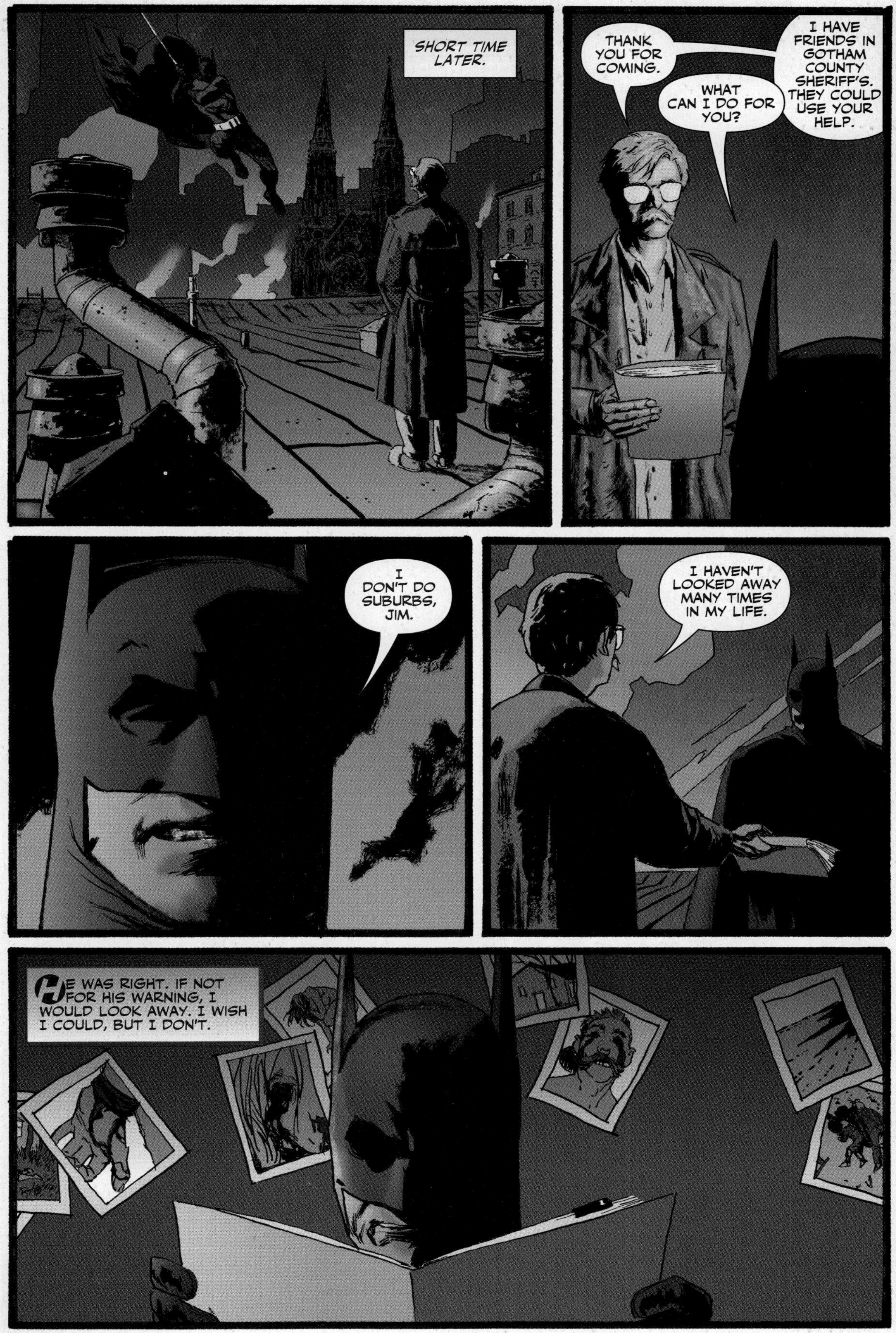

SHORT TIME LATER.
THANK YOU FOR COMING.
I HAVE FRIENDS IN GOTHAM COUNTY SHERIFF'S. THEY COULD USE YOUR HELP.
WHAT CAN I DO FOR YOU?
I DON'T DO SUBURBS, JIM.
I HAVEN'T LOOKED AWAY MANY TIMES IN MY LIFE.
HE WAS RIGHT. IF NOT FOR HIS WARNING, I WOULD LOOK AWAY. I WISH I COULD, BUT I DON'T.

THEY STARTED OUT AS ROBBERIES, SAME EVERY TIME: RESIDENTS WOKE IN THE MORNING AND THEY WERE CLEANED OUT. THEY NEVER HEARD A SOUND. G.C.S.D. HAD A SUSPECT, SOME JUNKIE. EVEN GOT A CONFESSION OUT OF HIM.

BUT?

THE ROBBERIES HAPPENED AGAIN, BUT--

INSTEAD OF THEFT, MURDER.

IT'S HAPPENING EVERY WEEK. FOUR WEEKS NOW SINCE THE KID WAS PICKED UP: FOUR FAMILIES DEAD.

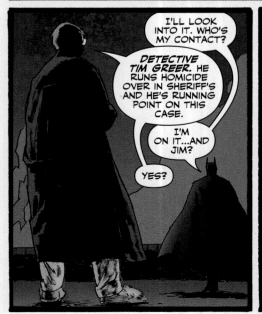

I'LL LOOK INTO IT. WHO'S MY CONTACT?

DETECTIVE TIM GREER. HE RUNS HOMICIDE OVER IN SHERIFF'S AND HE'S RUNNING POINT ON THIS CASE.

I'M ON IT...AND JIM?

YES?

NICE SLIPPERS.

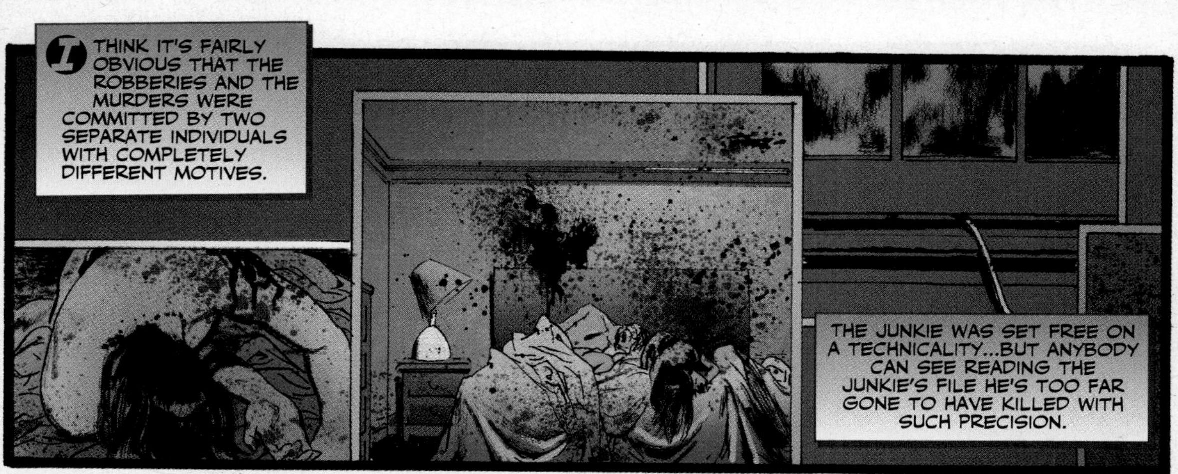
I THINK IT'S FAIRLY OBVIOUS THAT THE ROBBERIES AND THE MURDERS WERE COMMITTED BY TWO SEPARATE INDIVIDUALS WITH COMPLETELY DIFFERENT MOTIVES.
THE JUNKIE WAS SET FREE ON A TECHNICALITY...BUT ANYBODY CAN SEE READING THE JUNKIE'S FILE HE'S TOO FAR GONE TO HAVE KILLED WITH SUCH PRECISION.

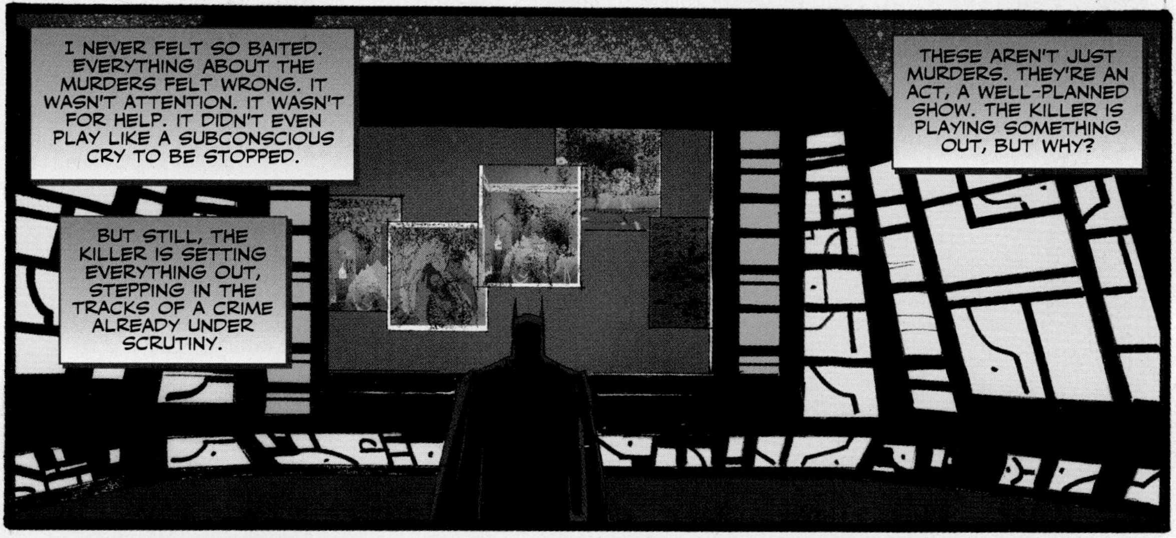
I NEVER FELT SO BAITED. EVERYTHING ABOUT THE MURDERS FELT WRONG. IT WASN'T ATTENTION. IT WASN'T FOR HELP. IT DIDN'T EVEN PLAY LIKE A SUBCONSCIOUS CRY TO BE STOPPED.
BUT STILL, THE KILLER IS SETTING EVERYTHING OUT, STEPPING IN THE TRACKS OF A CRIME ALREADY UNDER SCRUTINY.
THESE AREN'T JUST MURDERS. THEY'RE AN ACT, A WELL-PLANNED SHOW. THE KILLER IS PLAYING SOMETHING OUT, BUT WHY?

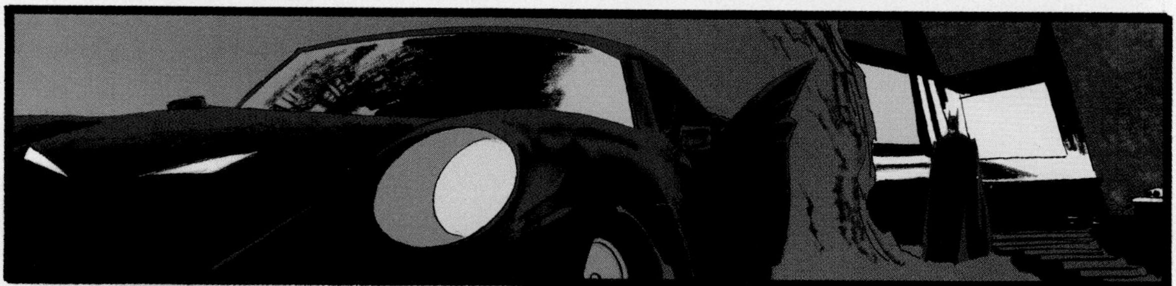

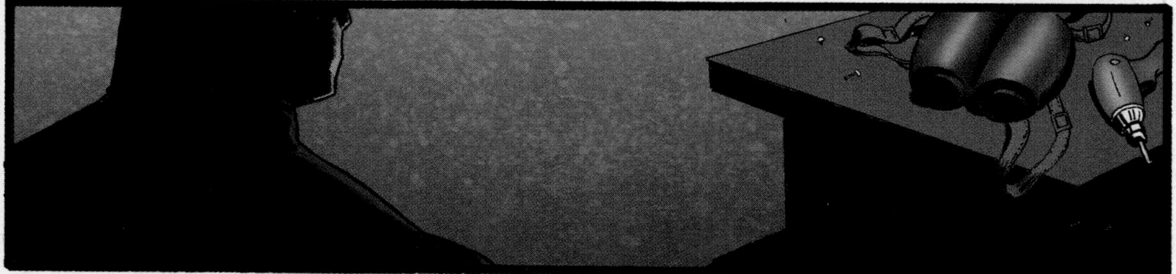

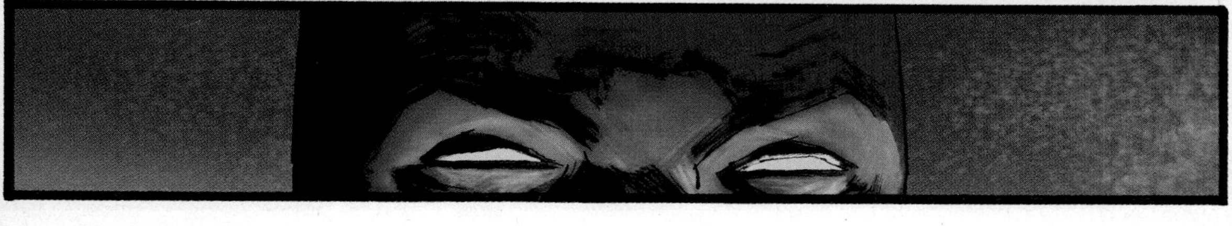

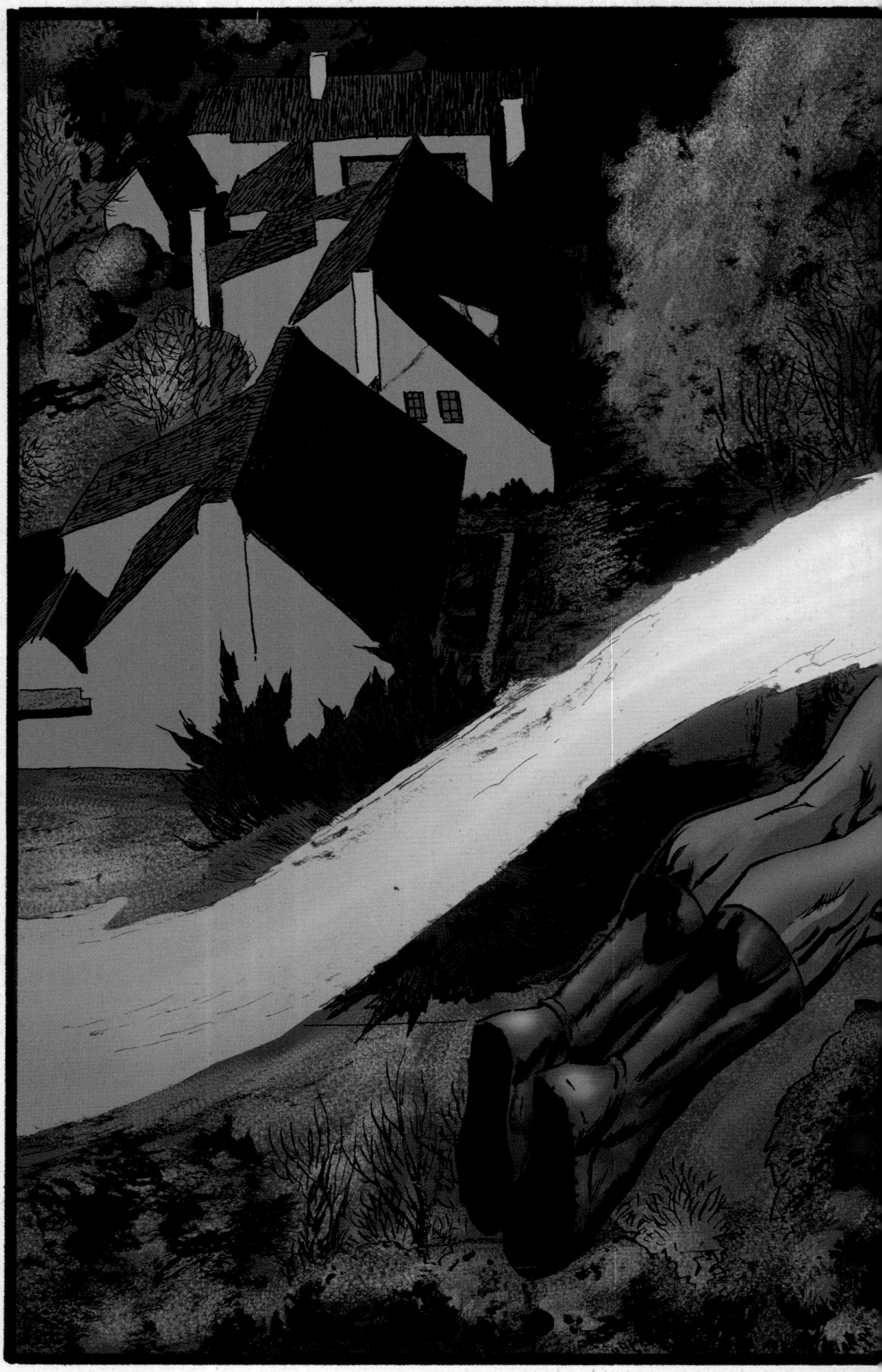

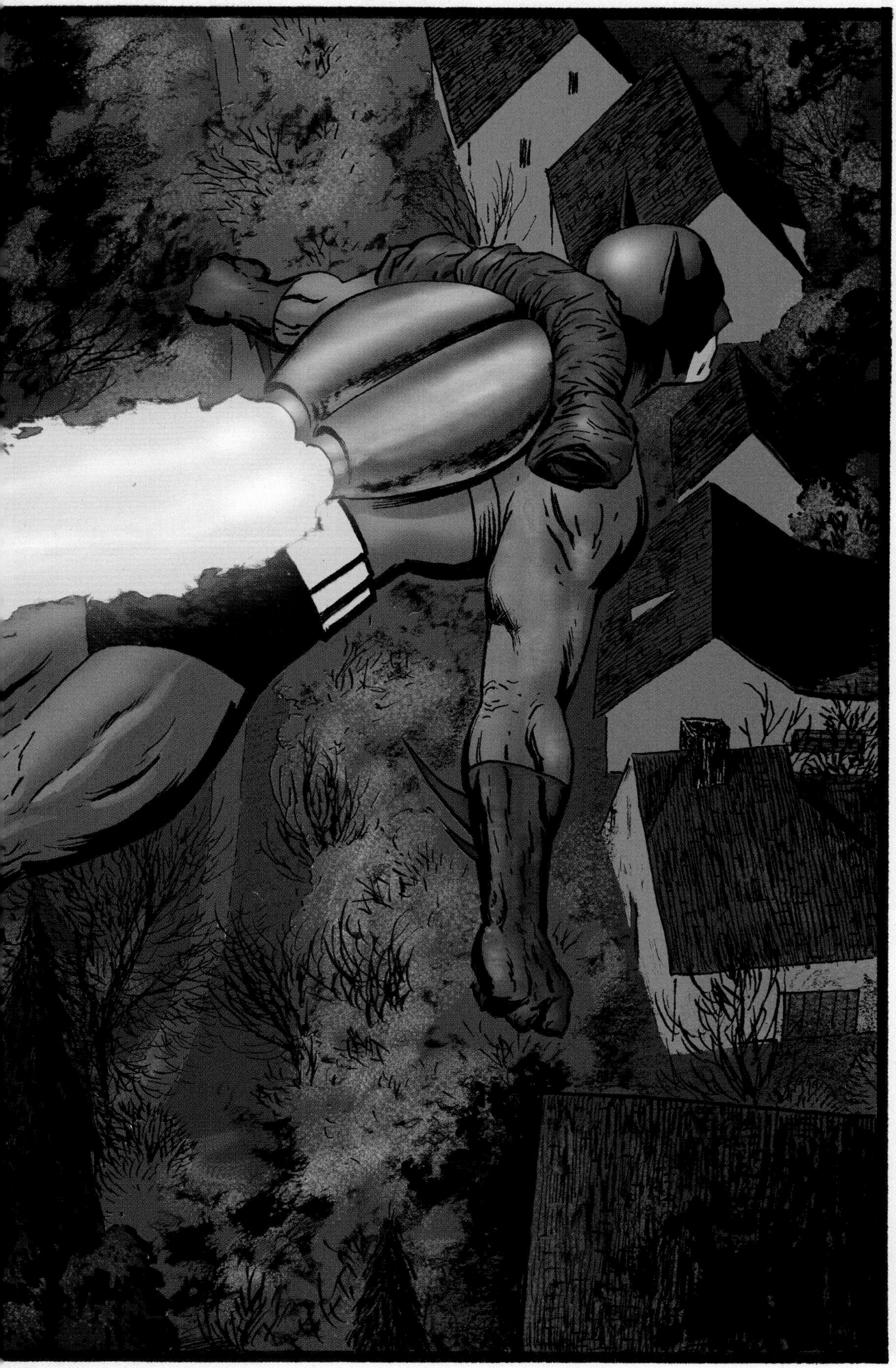

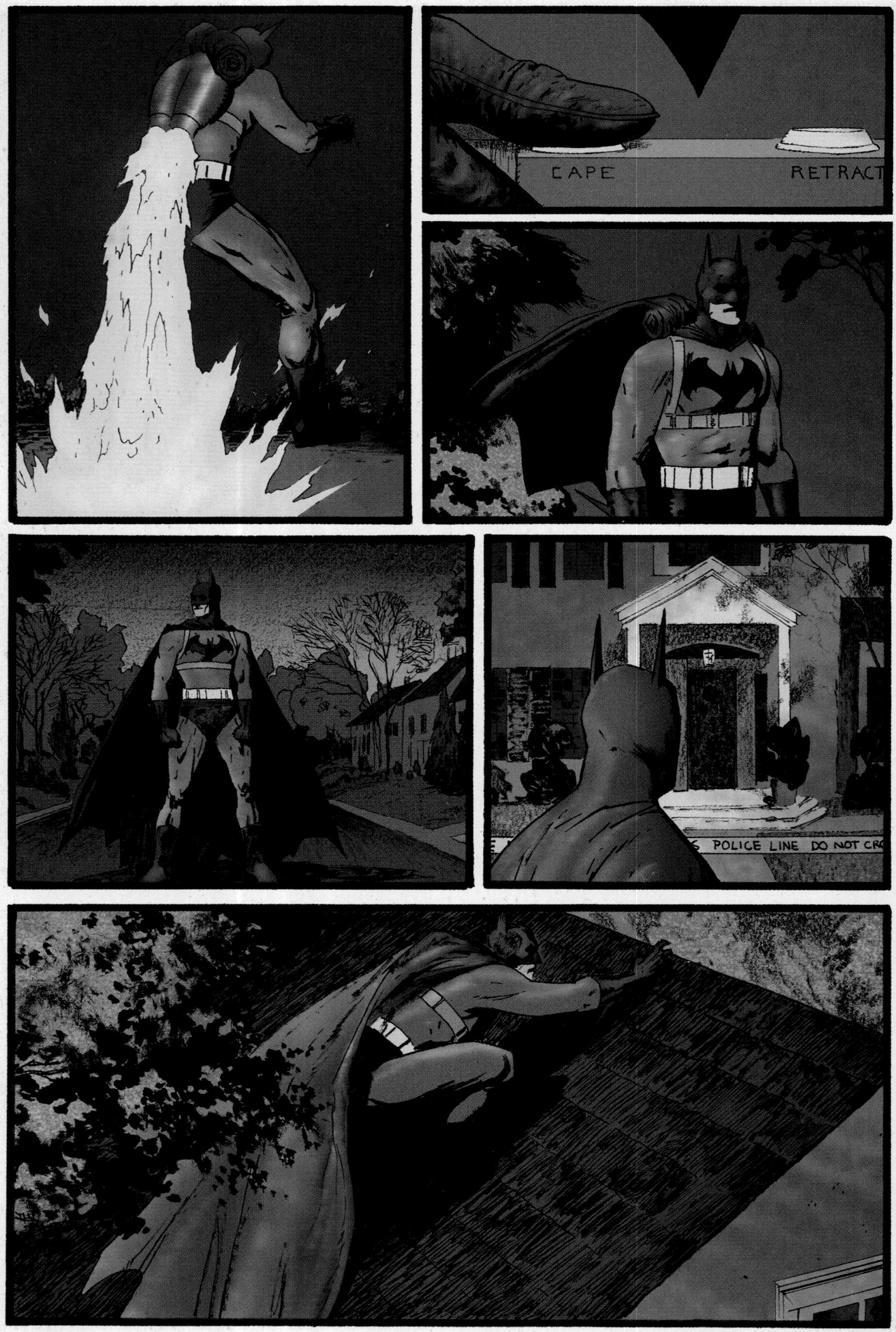
CAPE
RETRACT
POLICE LINE DO NOT CRO

GORDON'S PALS MISSED SOMETHING.

IT'S AN EASY MISS.

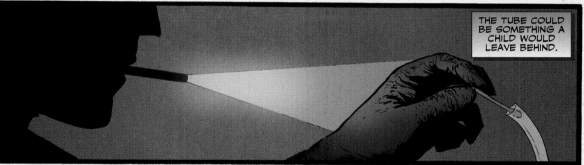

THE TUBE COULD BE SOMETHING A CHILD WOULD LEAVE BEHIND.

EVIDENCE:

BUT THEY SHOULD HAVE NOTICED THE UNIT'S POWER HAD BEEN CUT TO ALLOW THE TUBING TO PASS THE FAN BLADES.

THAT'S HOW THE JUNKIE CLEANED THEM OUT WITHOUT WAKING THEM AND MAYBE WHY THE KILLER DECIDED TO USE THE SAME METHOD.

TWO STRIKES FOR JIM'S FRIENDS.

POLICE LINE DO NOT CROSS POLICE LINE

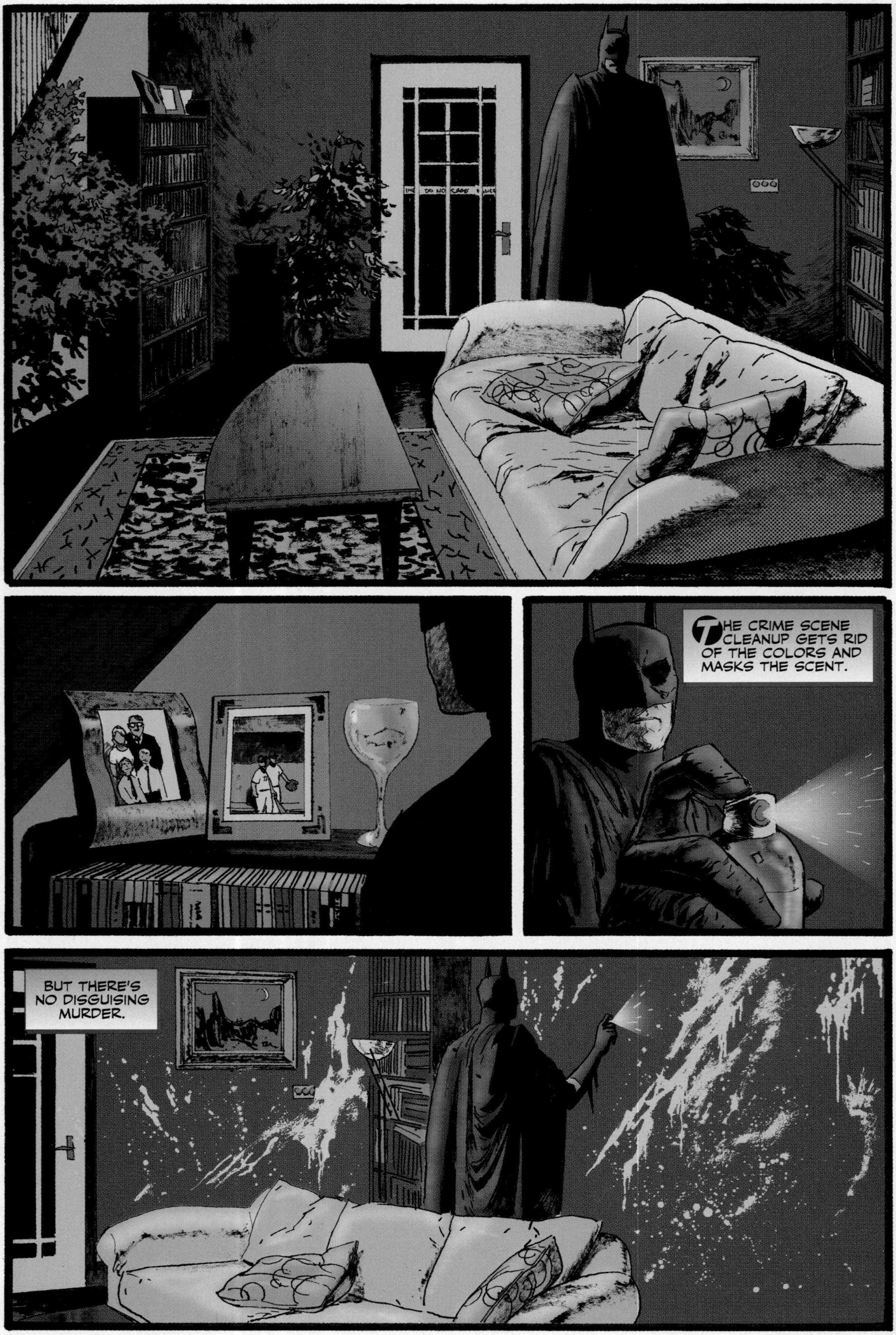
THE CRIME SCENE CLEANUP GETS RID OF THE COLORS AND MASKS THE SCENT.
BUT THERE'S NO DISGUISING MURDER.

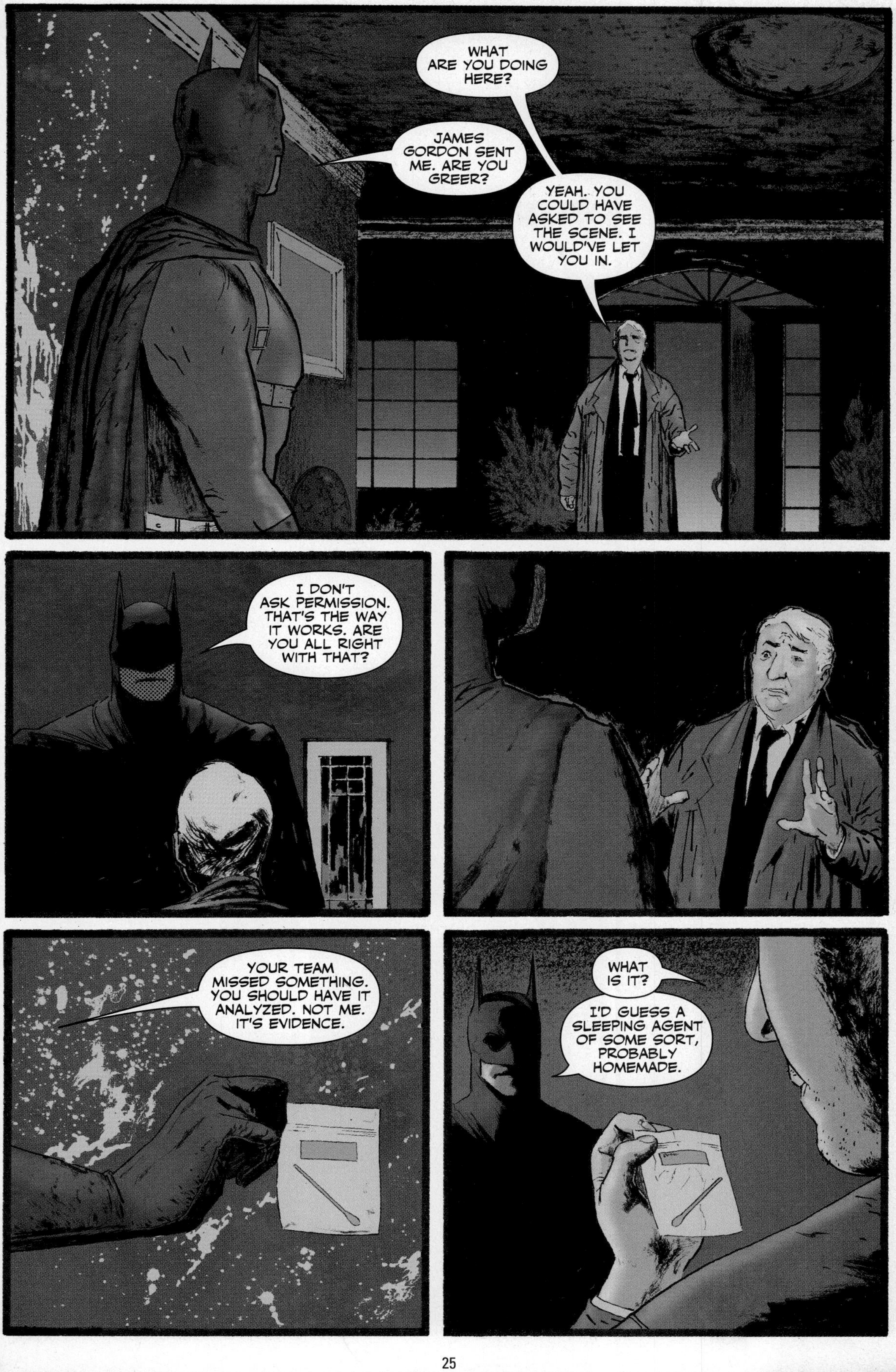
WHAT ARE YOU DOING HERE?
JAMES GORDON SENT ME. ARE YOU GREER?
YEAH. YOU COULD HAVE ASKED TO SEE THE SCENE. I WOULD'VE LET YOU IN.
I DON'T ASK PERMISSION. THAT'S THE WAY IT WORKS. ARE YOU ALL RIGHT WITH THAT?
YOUR TEAM MISSED SOMETHING. YOU SHOULD HAVE IT ANALYZED. NOT ME. IT'S EVIDENCE.
WHAT IS IT?
I'D GUESS A SLEEPING AGENT OF SOME SORT, PROBABLY HOMEMADE.

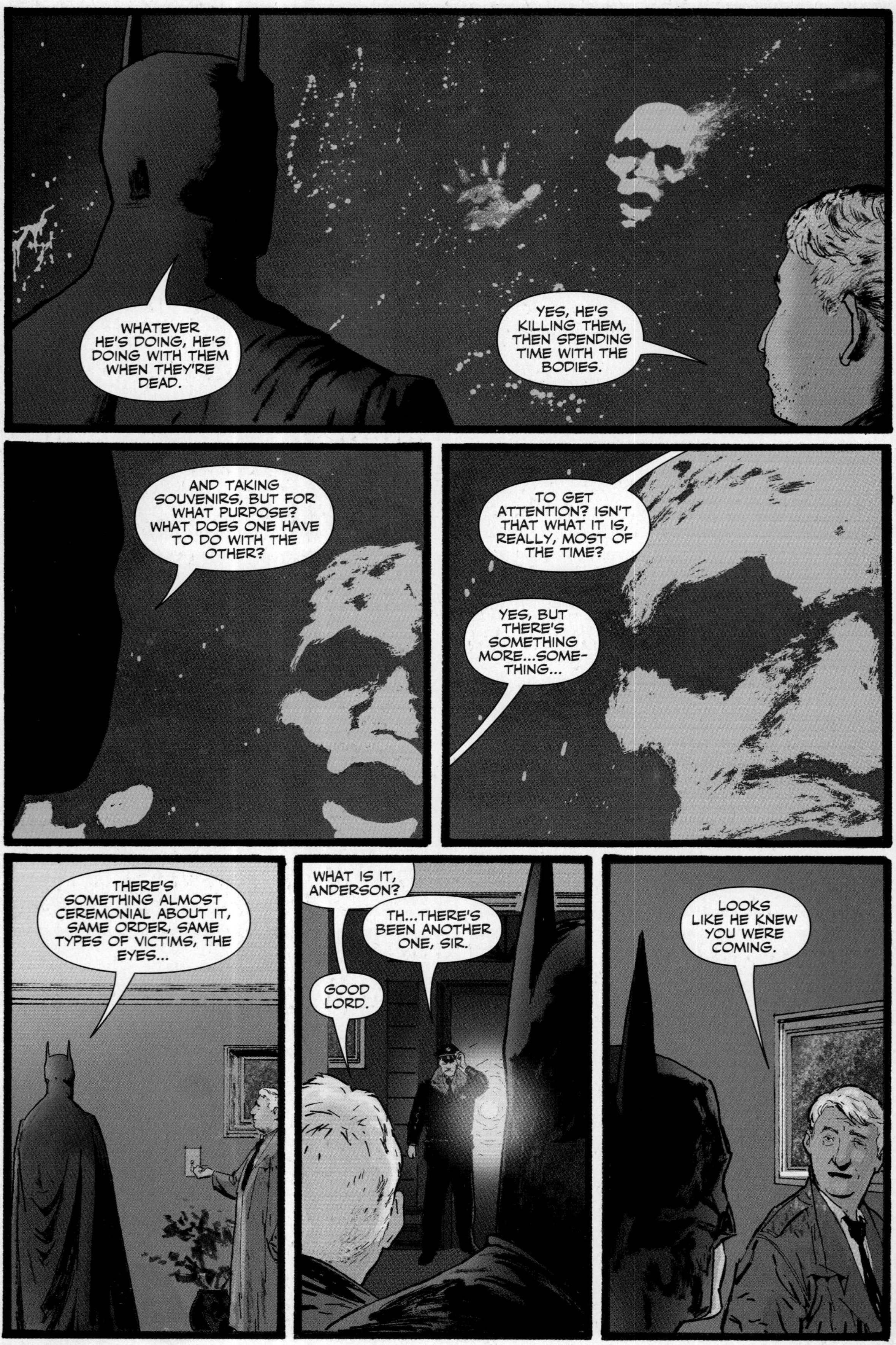
WHATEVER HE'S DOING, HE'S DOING WITH THEM WHEN THEY'RE DEAD.
YES, HE'S KILLING THEM, THEN SPENDING TIME WITH THE BODIES.
AND TAKING SOUVENIRS, BUT FOR WHAT PURPOSE? WHAT DOES ONE HAVE TO DO WITH THE OTHER?
TO GET ATTENTION? ISN'T THAT WHAT IT IS, REALLY, MOST OF THE TIME?
YES, BUT THERE'S SOMETHING MORE...SOME-THING...
THERE'S SOMETHING ALMOST CEREMONIAL ABOUT IT, SAME ORDER, SAME TYPES OF VICTIMS, THE EYES...
WHAT IS IT, ANDERSON?
TH...THERE'S BEEN ANOTHER ONE, SIR.
GOOD LORD.
LOOKS LIKE HE KNEW YOU WERE COMING.

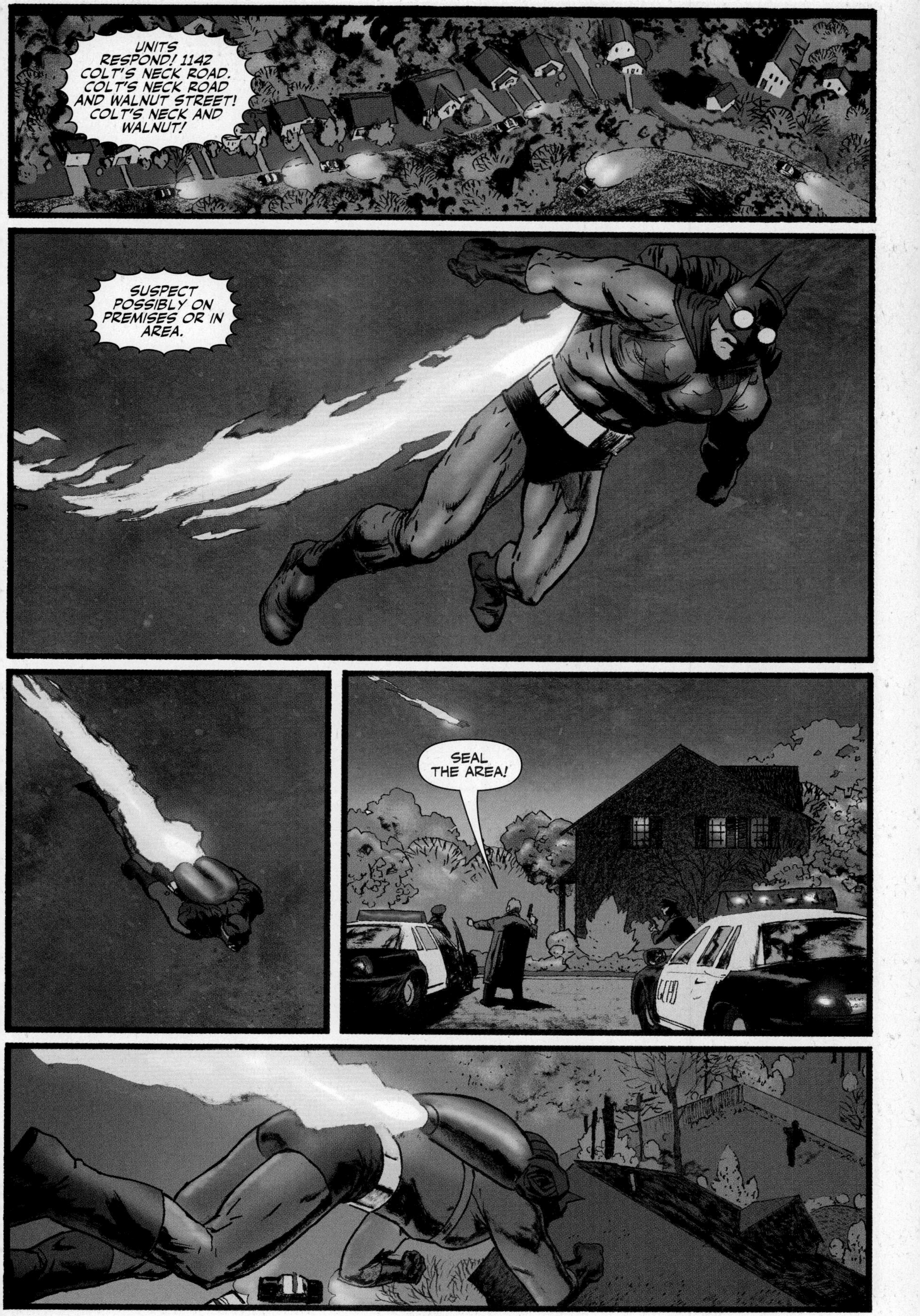
UNITS RESPOND! 1142 COLT'S NECK ROAD. COLT'S NECK ROAD AND WALNUT STREET! COLT'S NECK AND WALNUT!
SUSPECT POSSIBLY ON PREMISES OR IN AREA.
SEAL THE AREA!

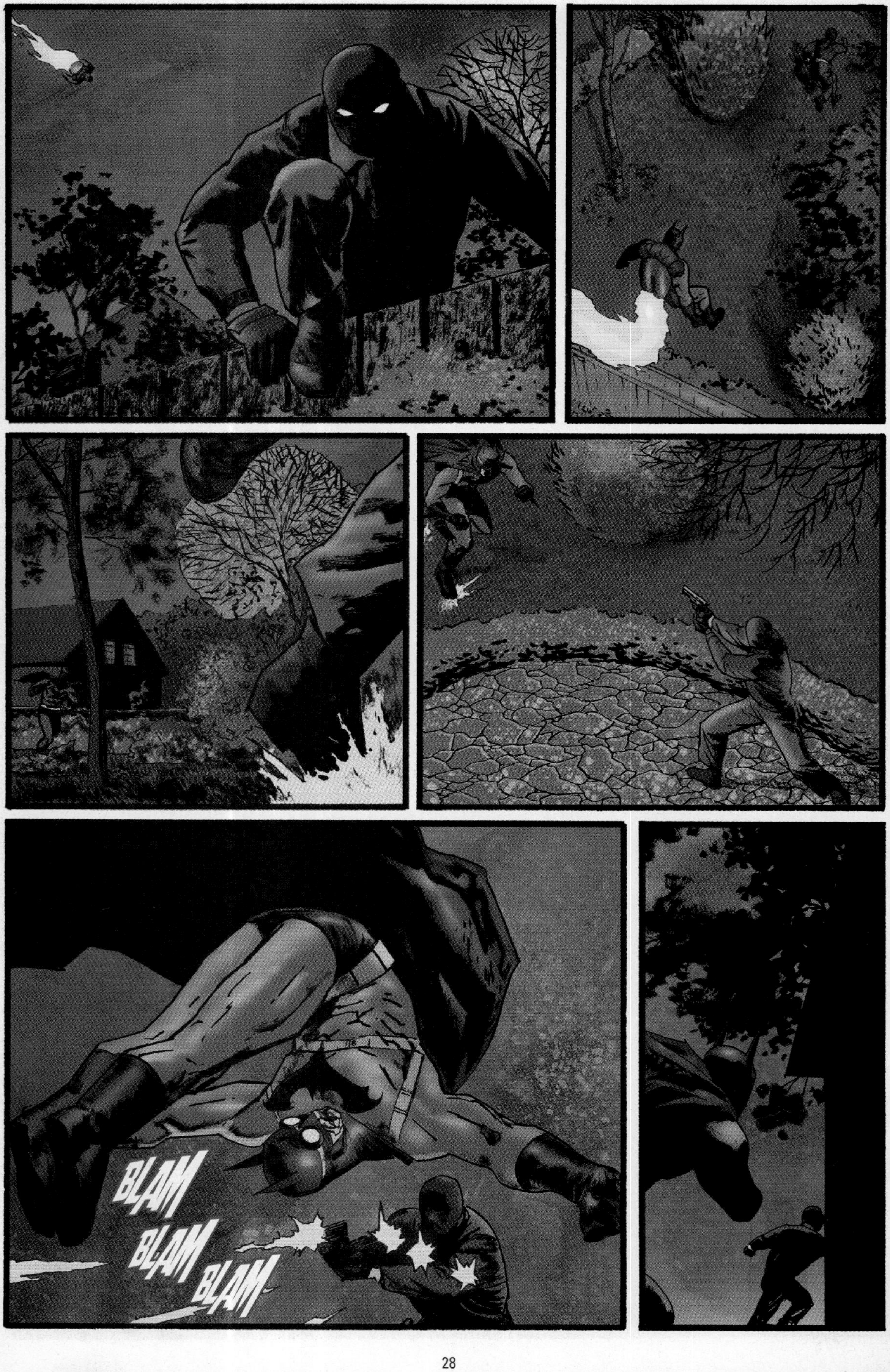
BLAM
BLAM
BLAM

HEY, MISTER, LOOK OUT.

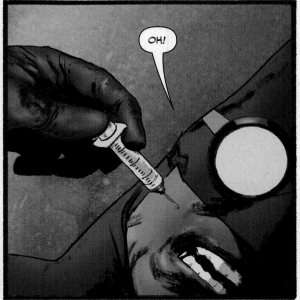

OH!

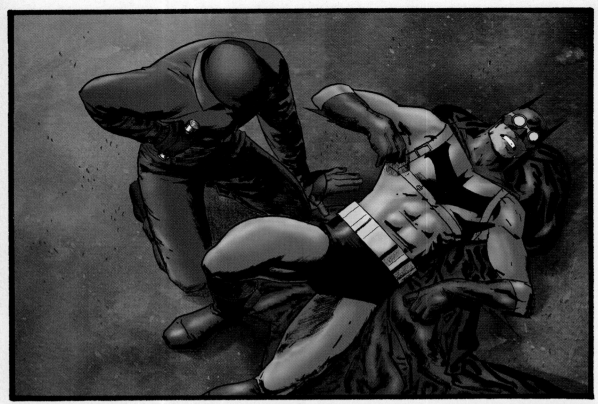

REST NOW, VIGILANTE.

IT'S NOT TIME FOR US TO MEET JUST YET.

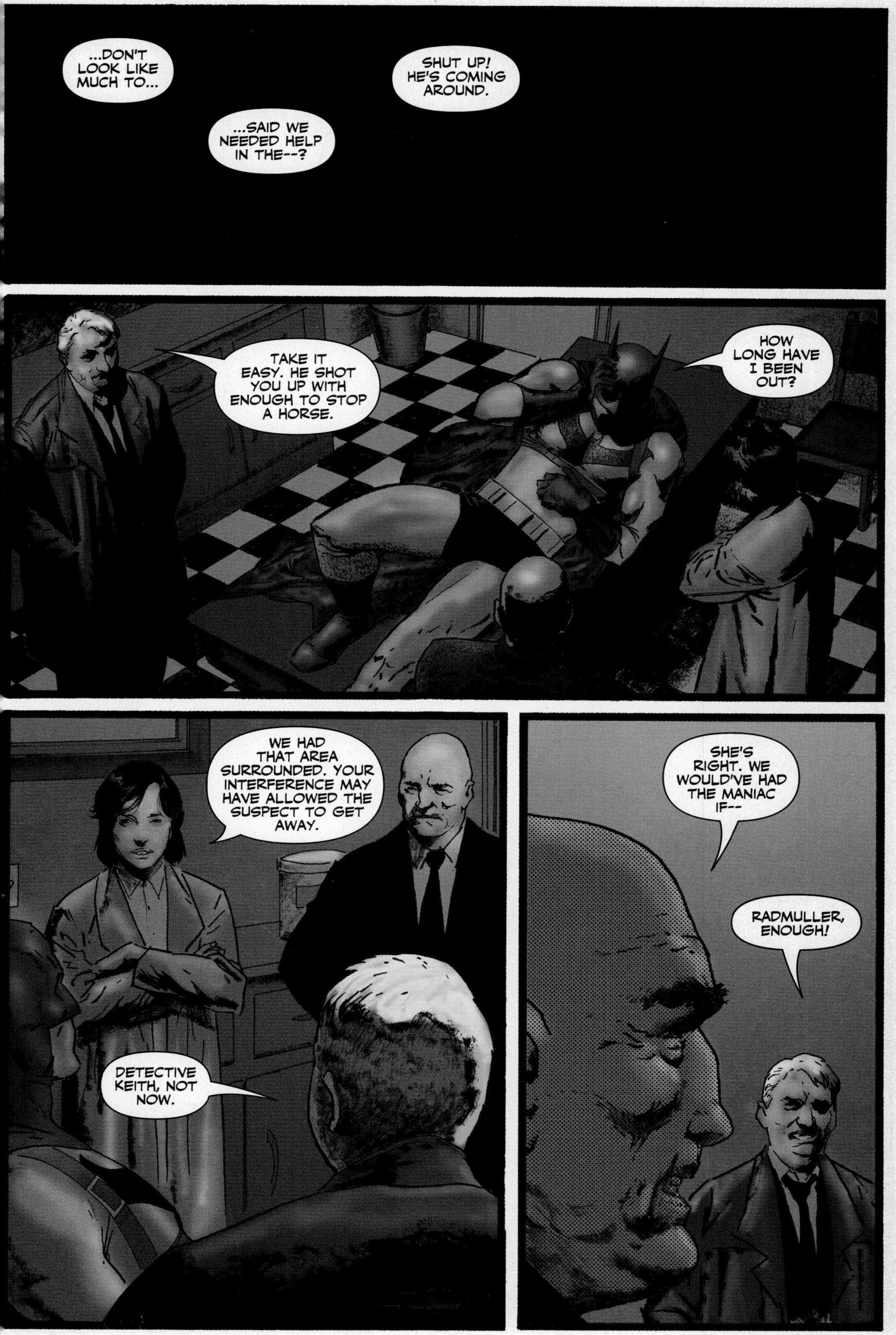
...DON'T LOOK LIKE MUCH TO...
...SAID WE NEEDED HELP IN THE--?
SHUT UP! HE'S COMING AROUND.
TAKE IT EASY. HE SHOT YOU UP WITH ENOUGH TO STOP A HORSE.
HOW LONG HAVE I BEEN OUT?
WE HAD THAT AREA SURROUNDED. YOUR INTERFERENCE MAY HAVE ALLOWED THE SUSPECT TO GET AWAY.
DETECTIVE KEITH, NOT NOW.
SHE'S RIGHT. WE WOULD'VE HAD THE MANIAC IF--
RADMULLER, ENOUGH!

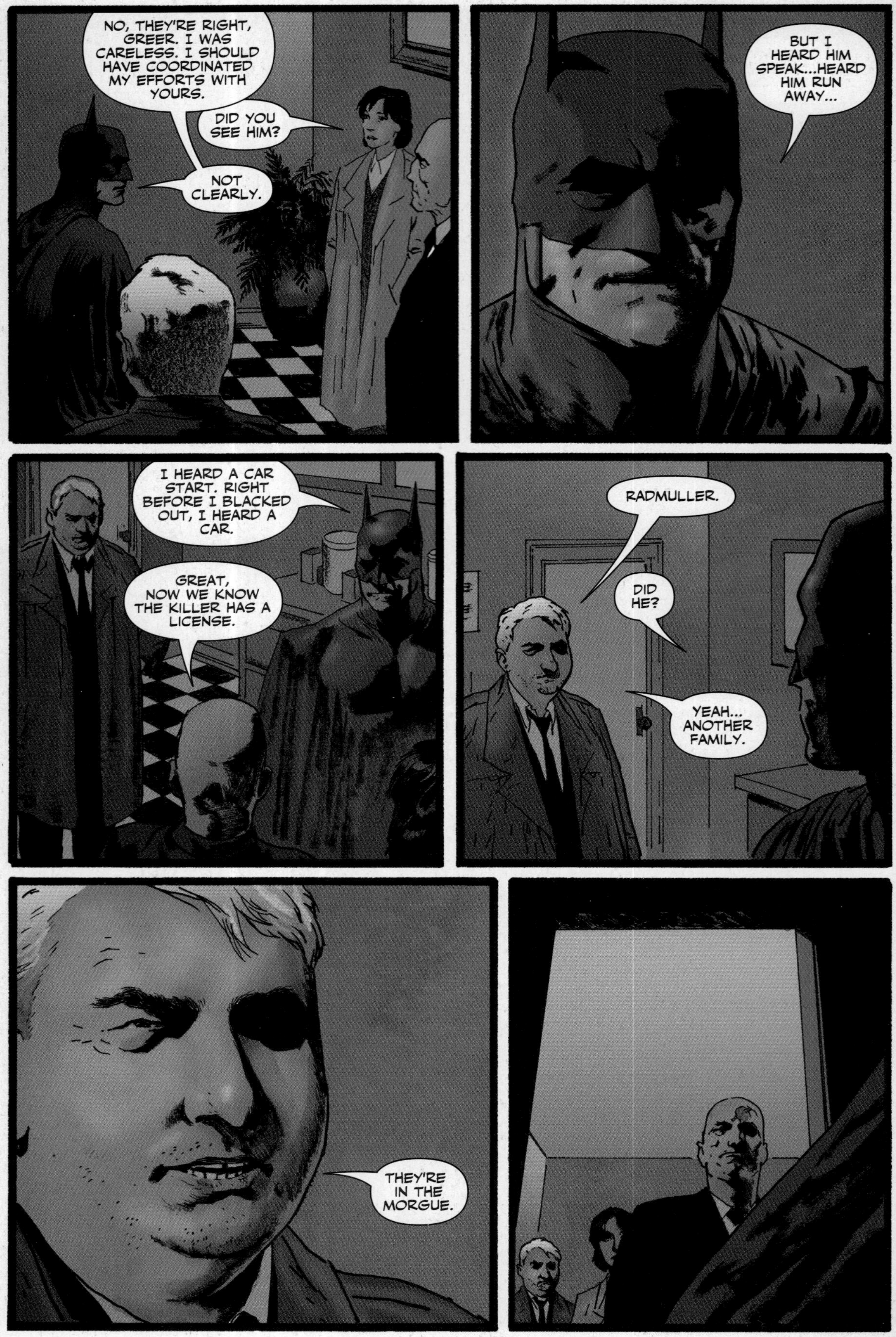
NO, THEY'RE RIGHT, GREER. I WAS CARELESS. I SHOULD HAVE COORDINATED MY EFFORTS WITH YOURS.
DID YOU SEE HIM?
NOT CLEARLY.
BUT I HEARD HIM SPEAK...HEARD HIM RUN AWAY...
I HEARD A CAR START. RIGHT BEFORE I BLACKED OUT, I HEARD A CAR.
GREAT, NOW WE KNOW THE KILLER HAS A LICENSE.
RADMULLER.
DID HE?
YEAH... ANOTHER FAMILY.
THEY'RE IN THE MORGUE.

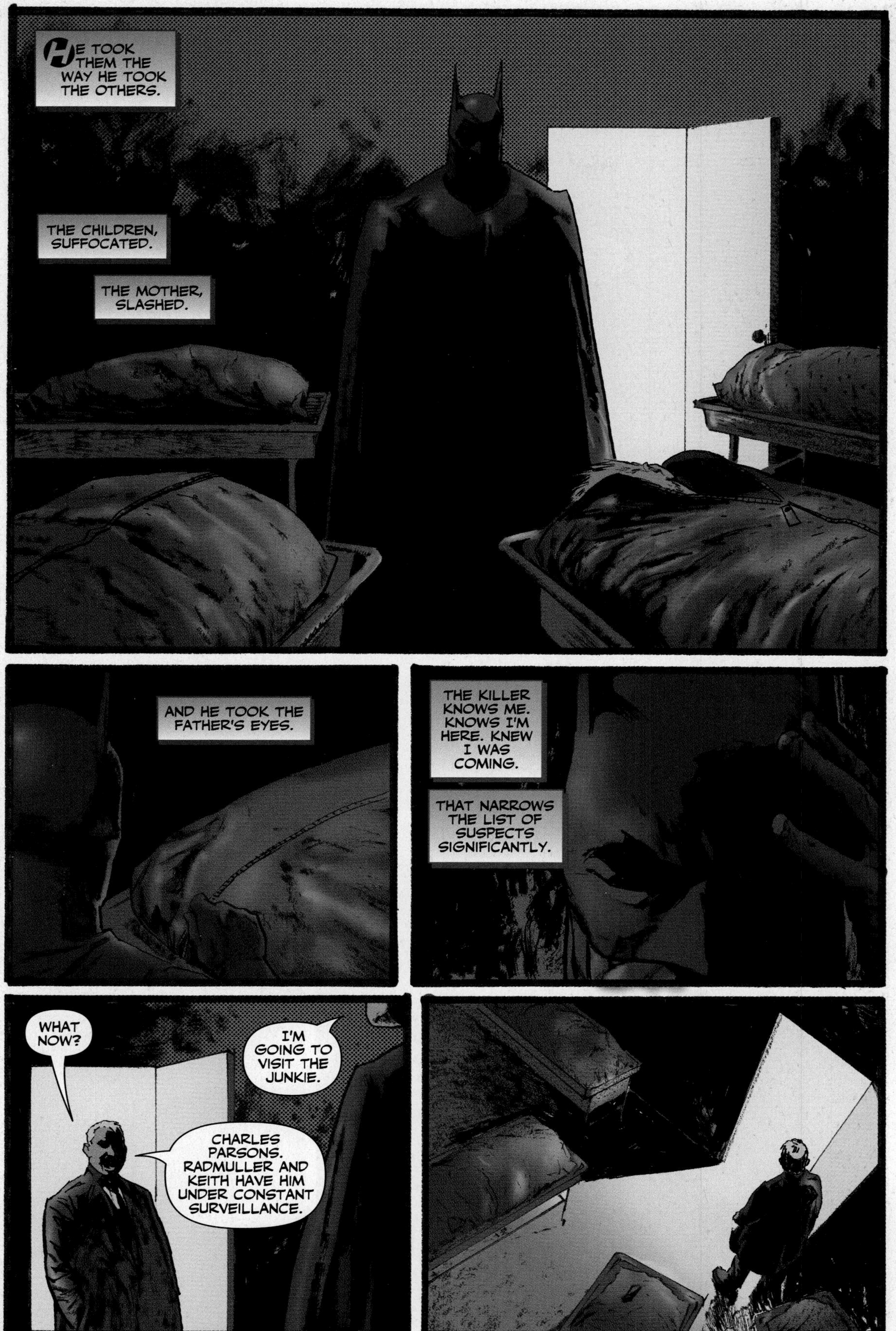
HE TOOK THEM THE WAY HE TOOK THE OTHERS.
THE CHILDREN, SUFFOCATED.
THE MOTHER, SLASHED.
AND HE TOOK THE FATHER'S EYES.
THE KILLER KNOWS ME. KNOWS I'M HERE. KNEW I WAS COMING.
THAT NARROWS THE LIST OF SUSPECTS SIGNIFICANTLY.
WHAT NOW?
I'M GOING TO VISIT THE JUNKIE.
CHARLES PARSONS. RADMULLER AND KEITH HAVE HIM UNDER CONSTANT SURVEILLANCE.

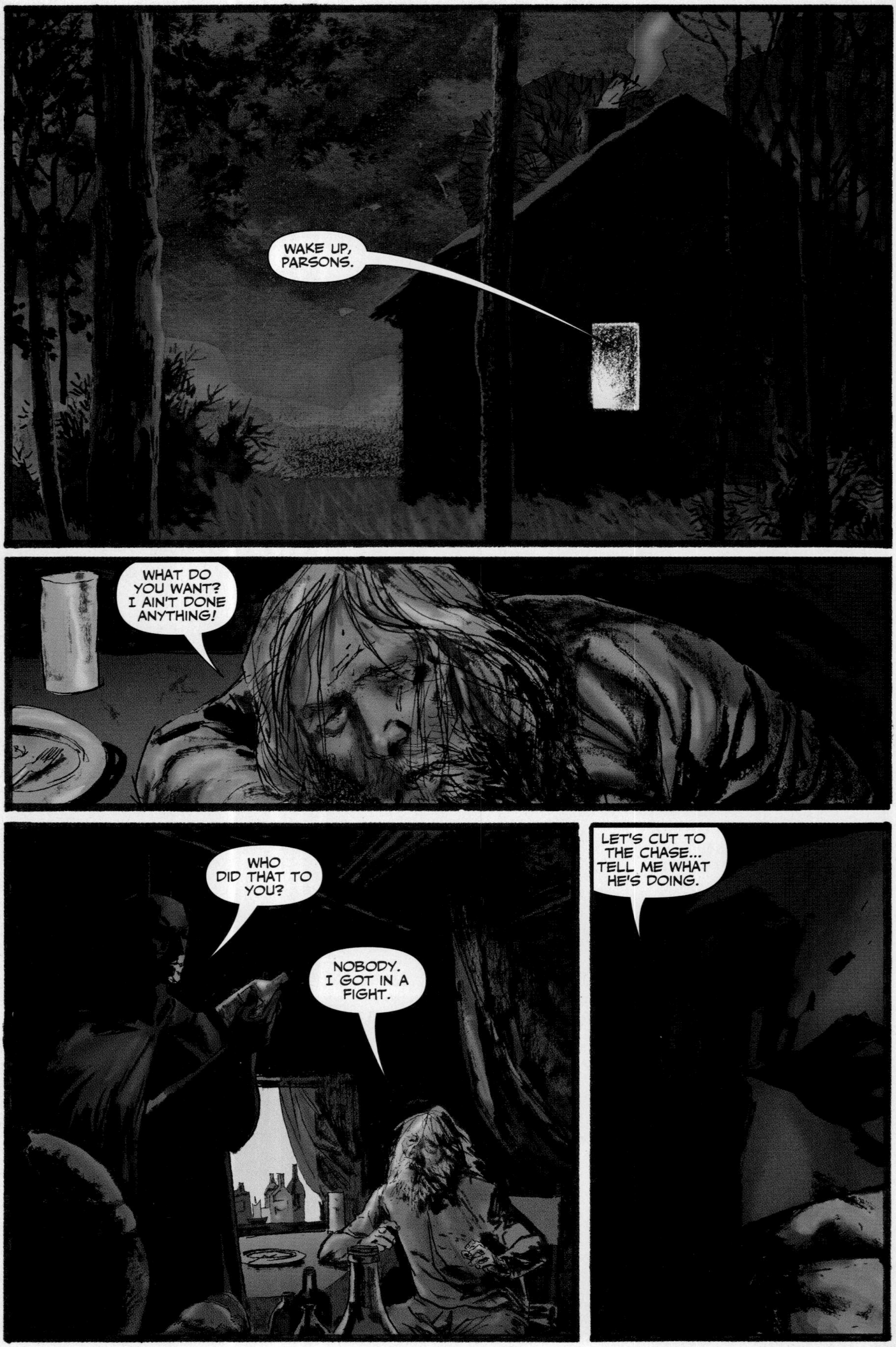
WAKE UP, PARSONS.
WHAT DO YOU WANT? I AIN'T DONE ANYTHING!
WHO DID THAT TO YOU?
NOBODY. I GOT IN A FIGHT.
LET'S CUT TO THE CHASE... TELL ME WHAT HE'S DOING.

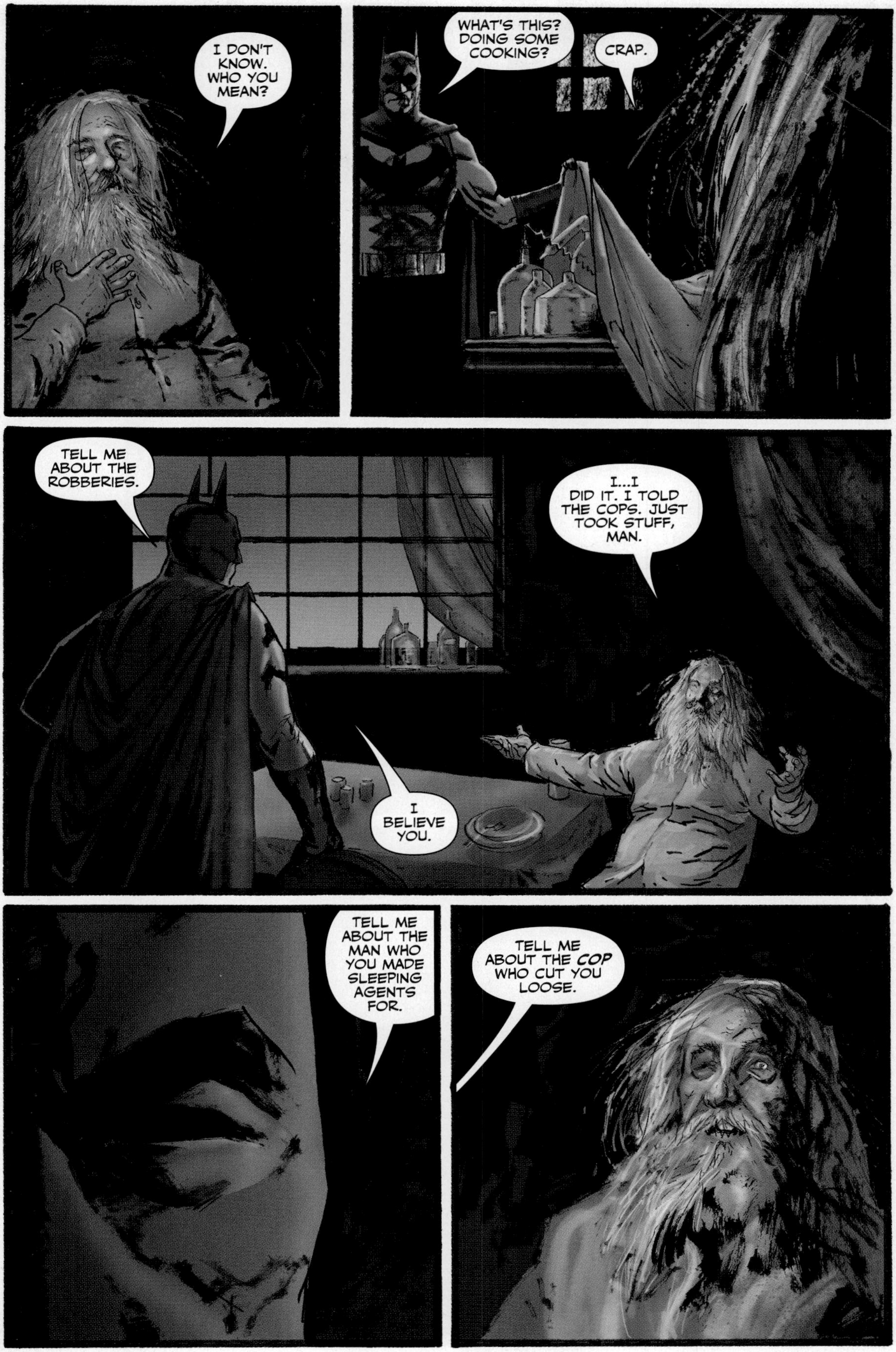
I DON'T KNOW. WHO YOU MEAN?
WHAT'S THIS? DOING SOME COOKING?
CRAP.
TELL ME ABOUT THE ROBBERIES.
I...I DID IT. I TOLD THE COPS. JUST TOOK STUFF, MAN.
I BELIEVE YOU.
TELL ME ABOUT THE MAN WHO YOU MADE SLEEPING AGENTS FOR.
TELL ME ABOUT THE COP WHO CUT YOU LOOSE.

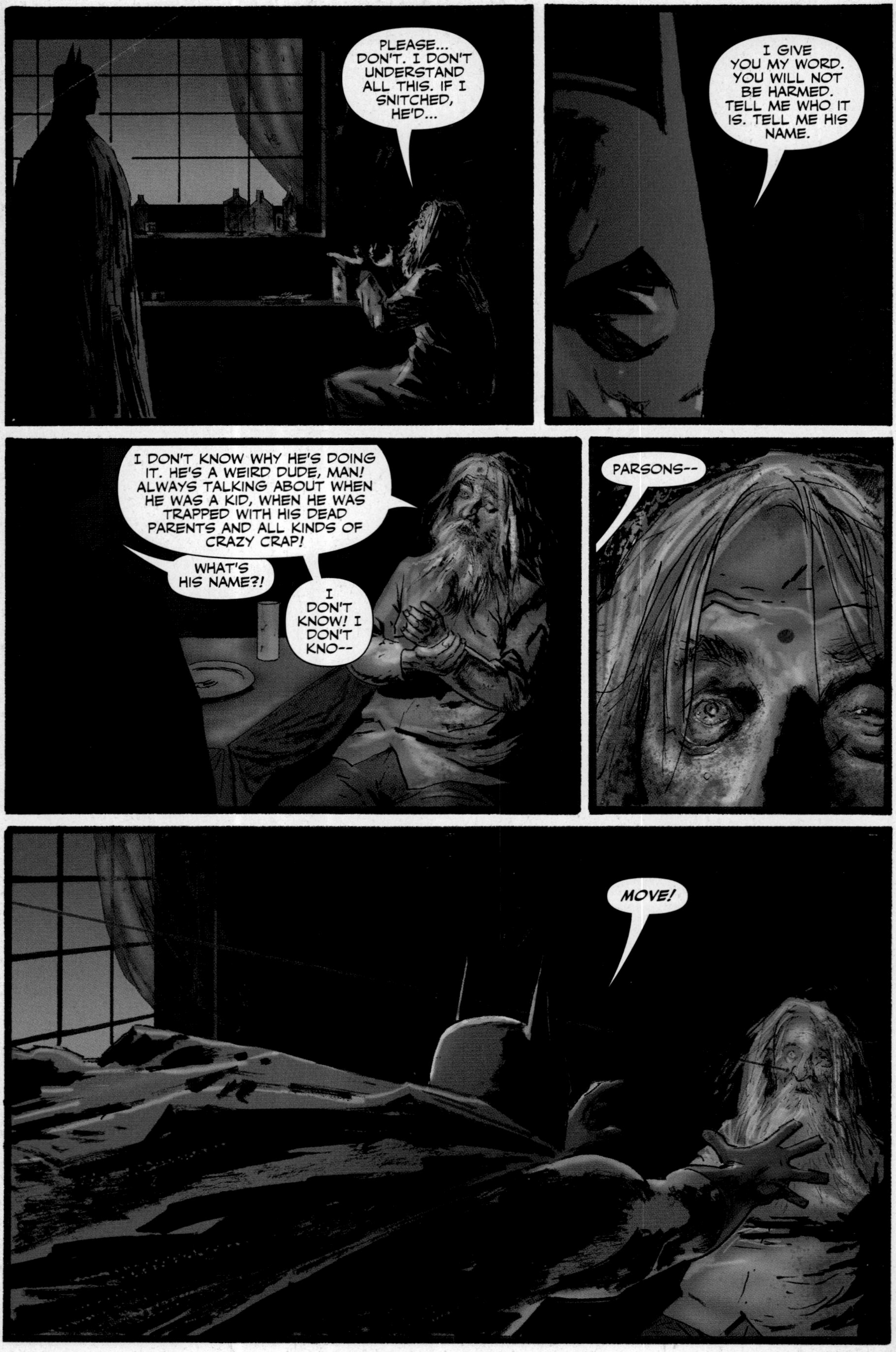
PLEASE... DON'T. I DON'T UNDERSTAND ALL THIS. IF I SNITCHED, HE'D...
I GIVE YOU MY WORD. YOU WILL NOT BE HARMED. TELL ME WHO IT IS. TELL ME HIS NAME.
I DON'T KNOW WHY HE'S DOING IT. HE'S A WEIRD DUDE, MAN! ALWAYS TALKING ABOUT WHEN HE WAS A KID, WHEN HE WAS TRAPPED WITH HIS DEAD PARENTS AND ALL KINDS OF CRAZY CRAP!
WHAT'S HIS NAME?!
I DON'T KNOW! I DON'T KNO--
PARSONS--
MOVE!

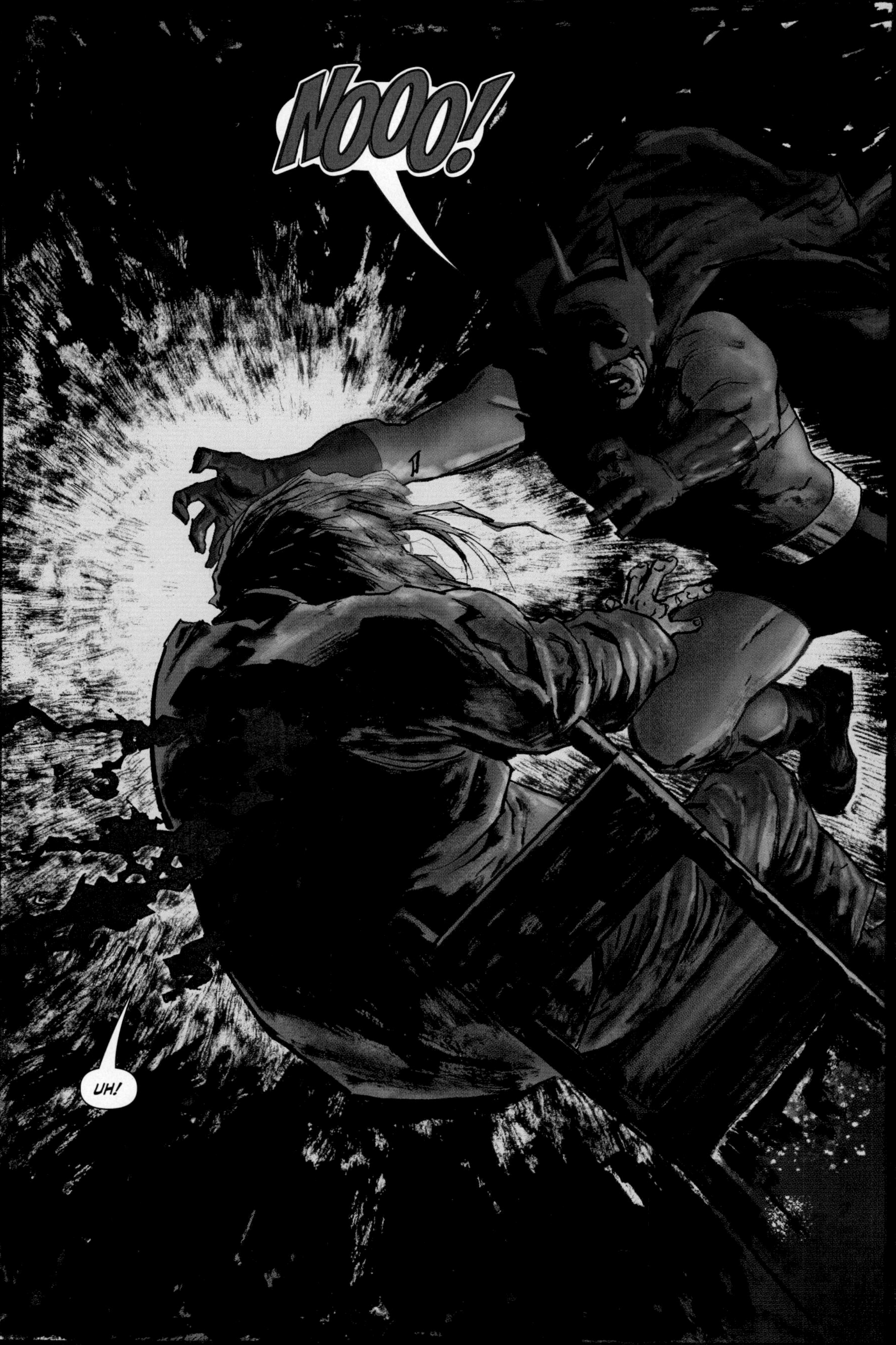
NOOO!
UH!

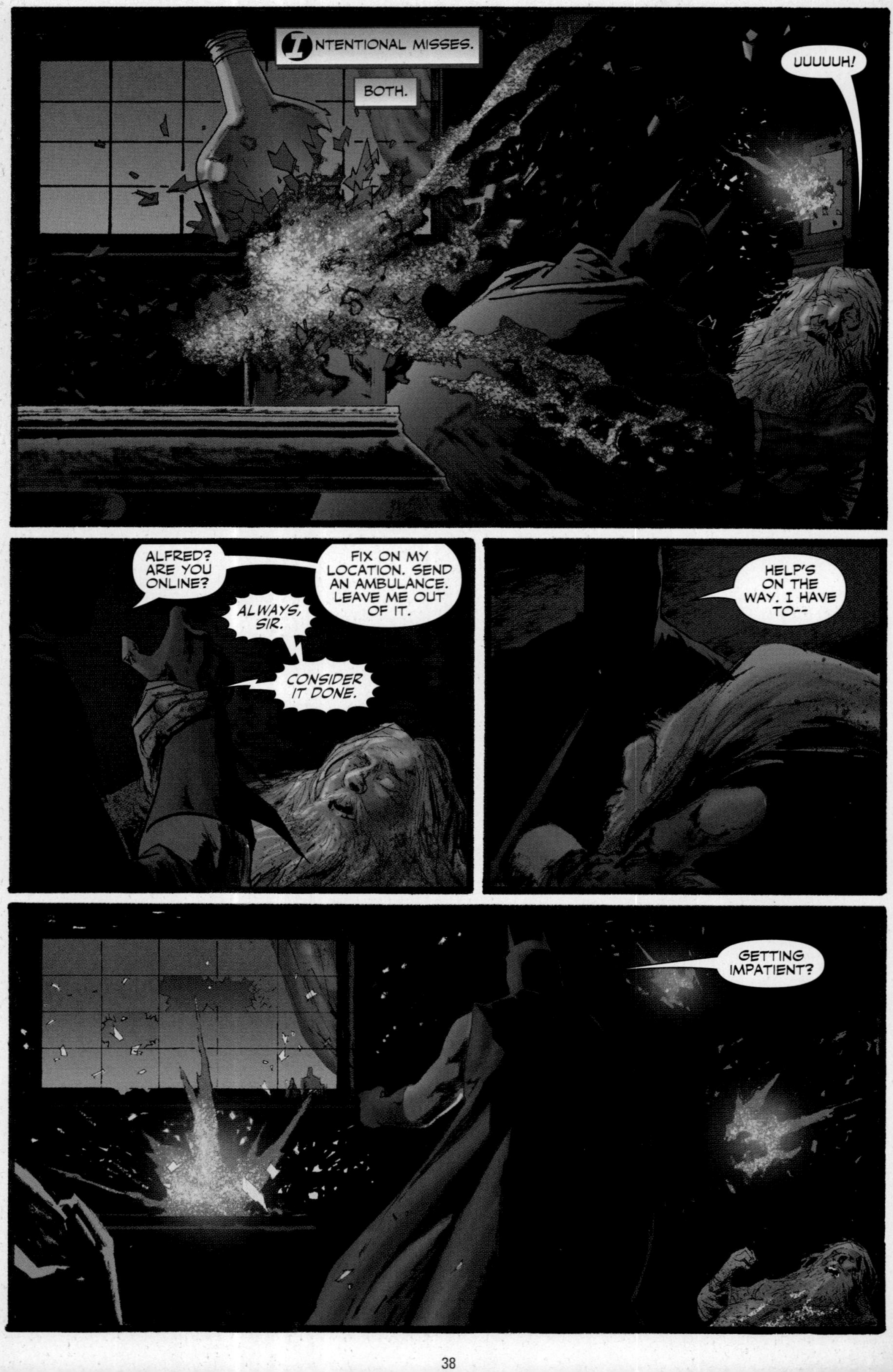
INTENTIONAL MISSES.
BOTH.
UUUUUH!
ALFRED? ARE YOU ONLINE?
FIX ON MY LOCATION. SEND AN AMBULANCE. LEAVE ME OUT OF IT.
ALWAYS, SIR.
CONSIDER IT DONE.
HELP'S ON THE WAY. I HAVE TO--
GETTING IMPATIENT?

Bosco's Gas
BEER · DAIRY · CIGARETTES · GAS · SODAS

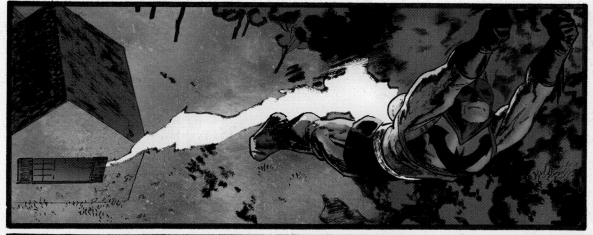

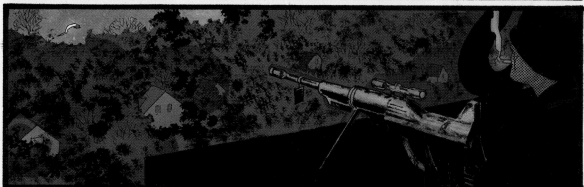

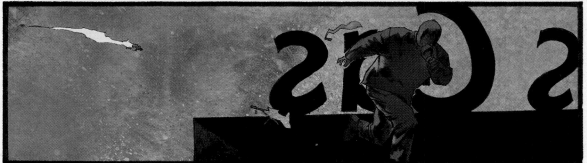

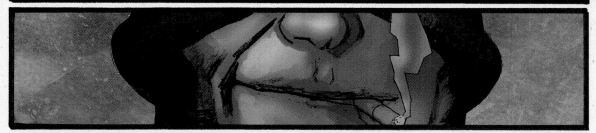

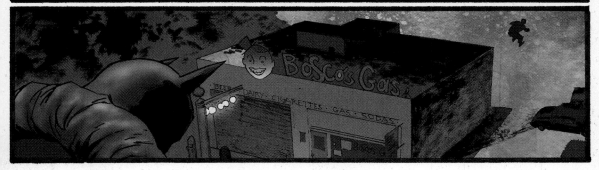

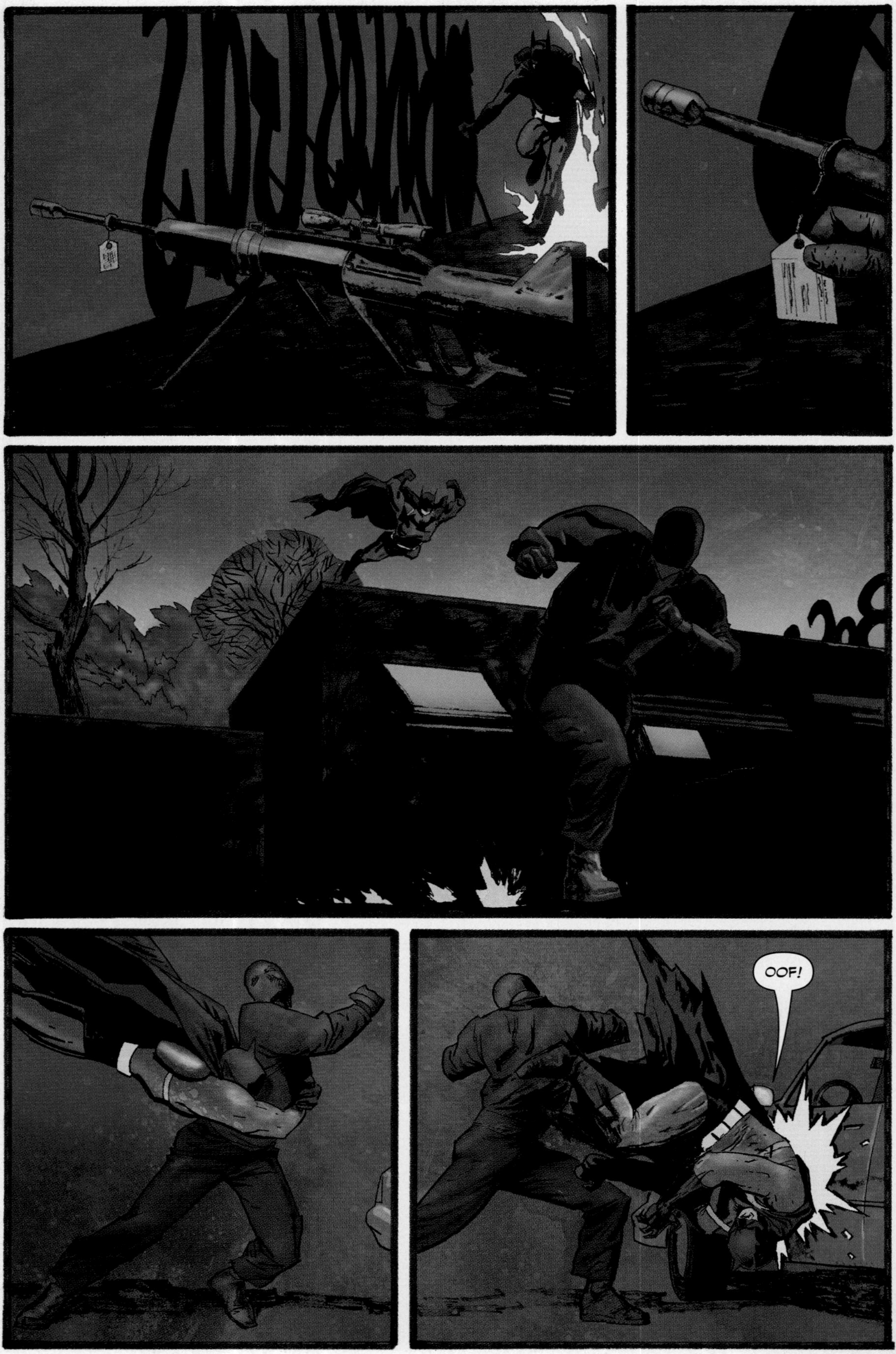
OOF!

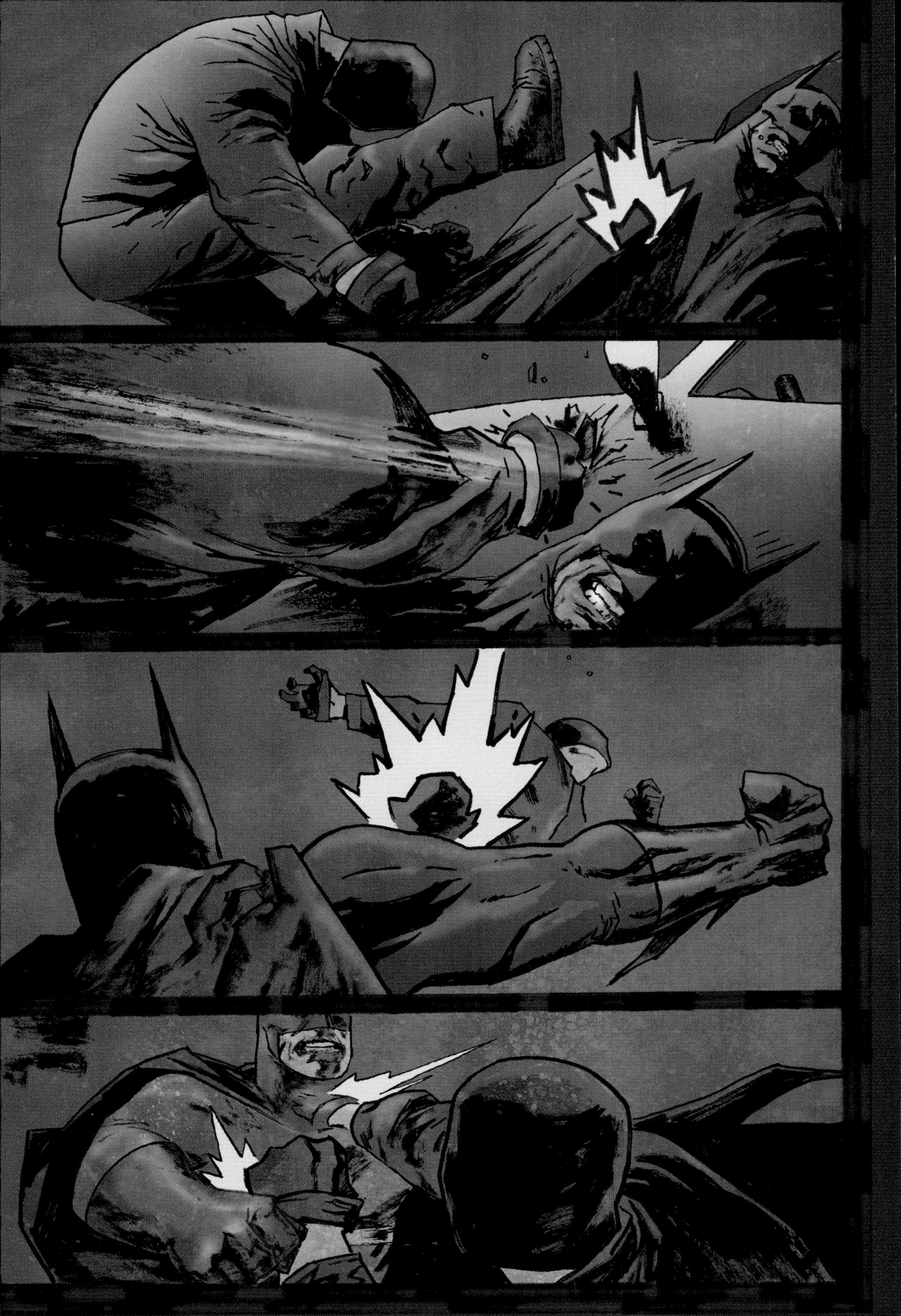

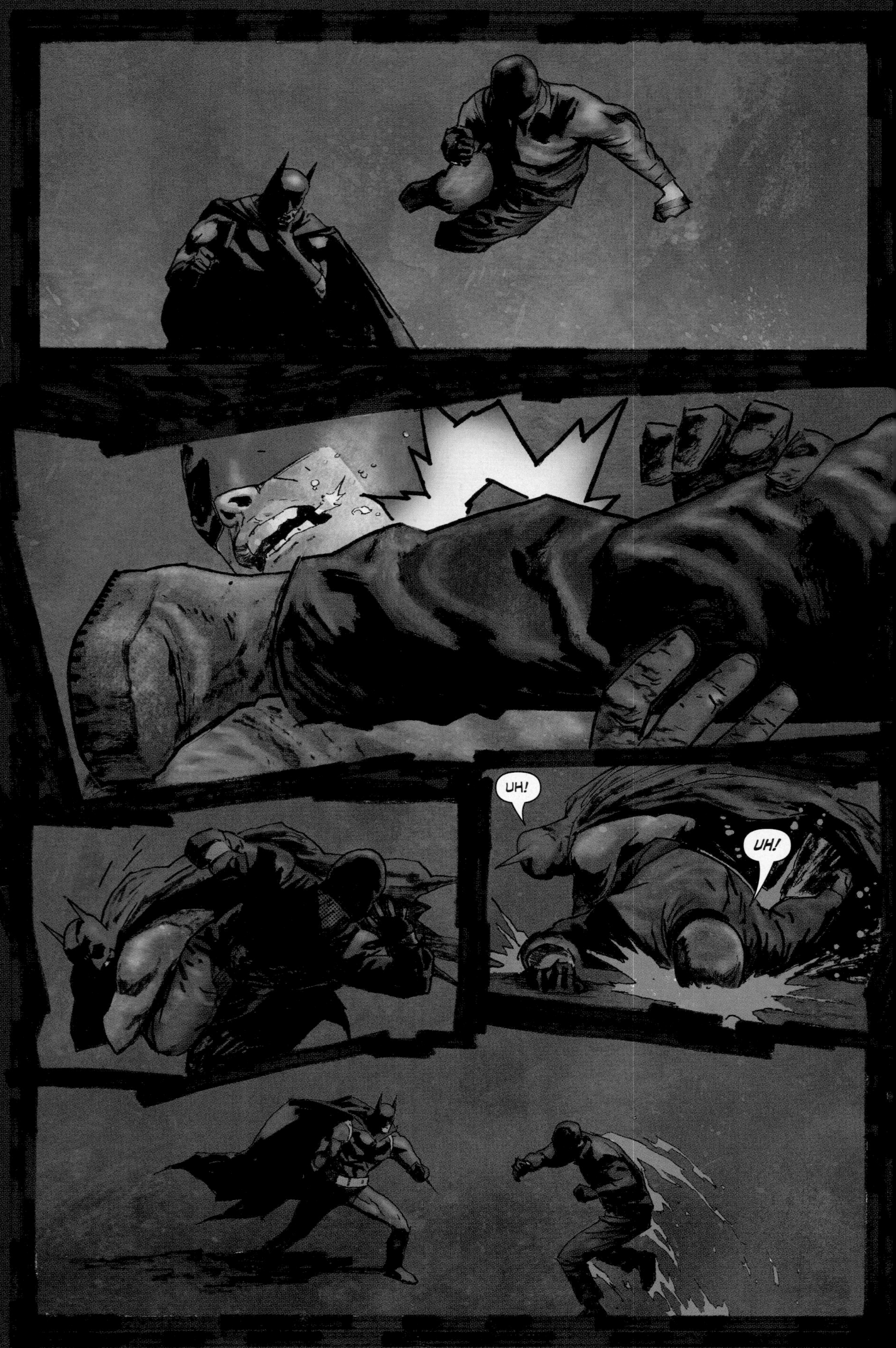
UH!
UH!

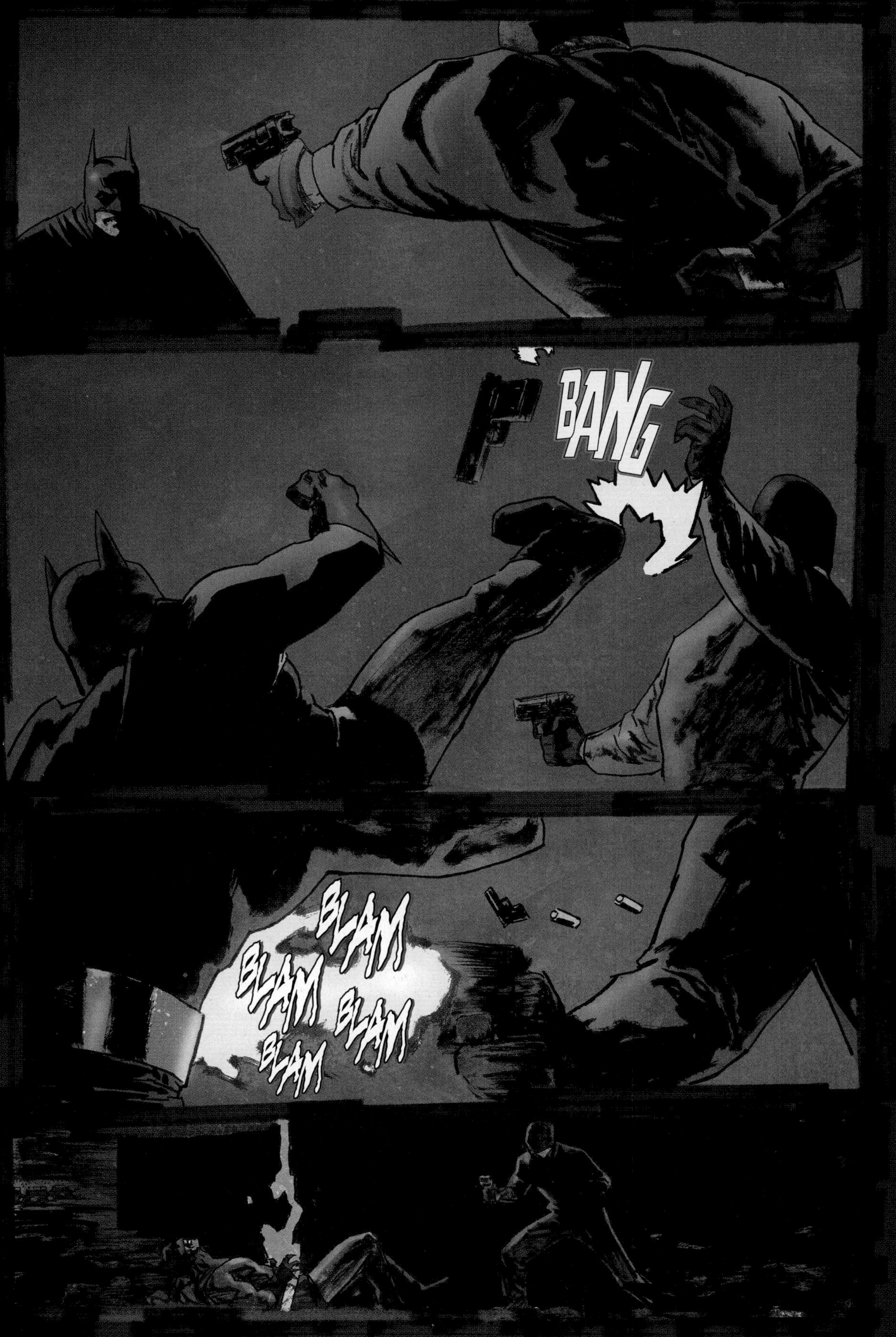
BANG
BLAM
BLAM
BLAM
BLAM
BLAM

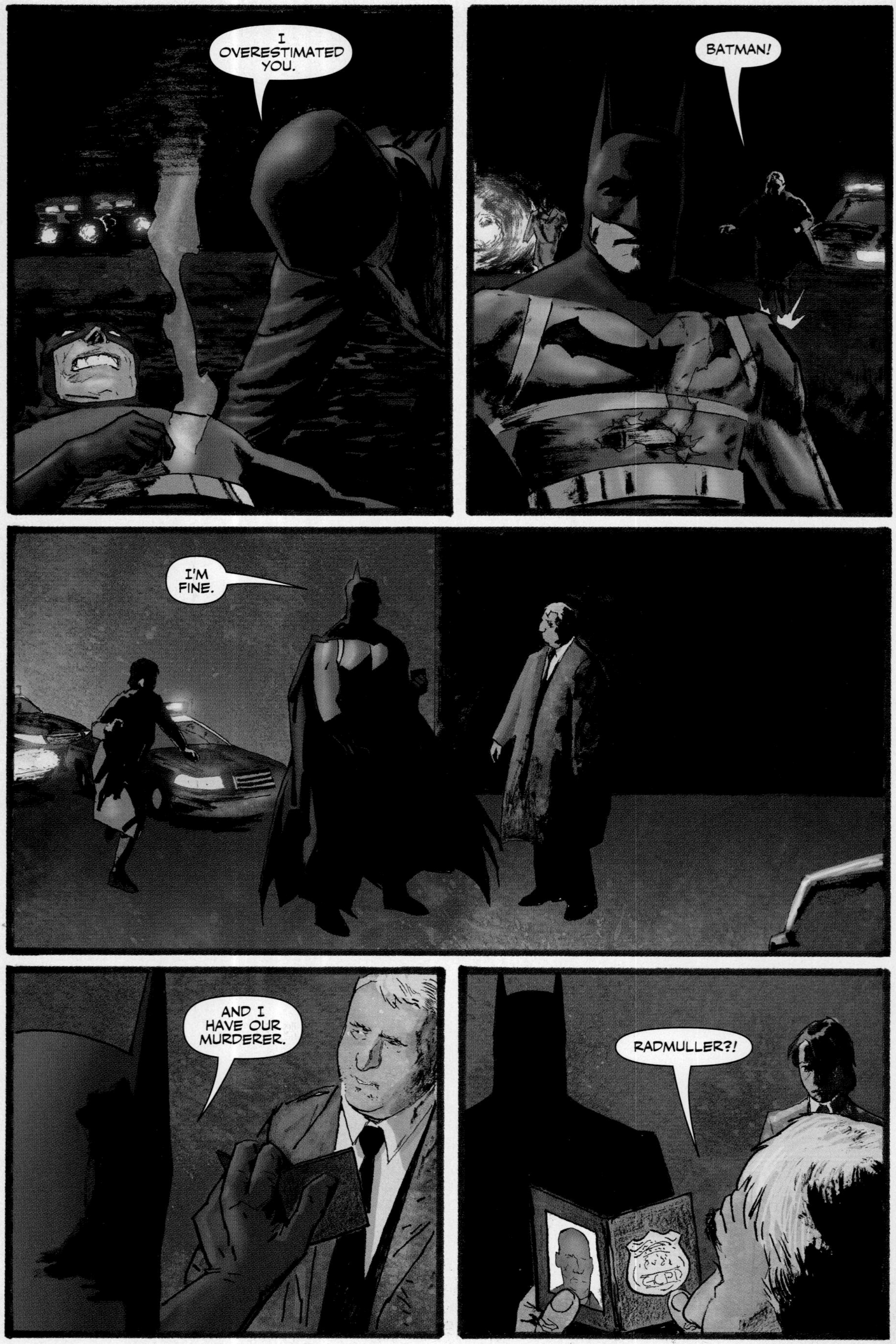
I OVERESTIMATED YOU.
BATMAN!
I'M FINE.
AND I HAVE OUR MURDERER.
RADMULLER?!

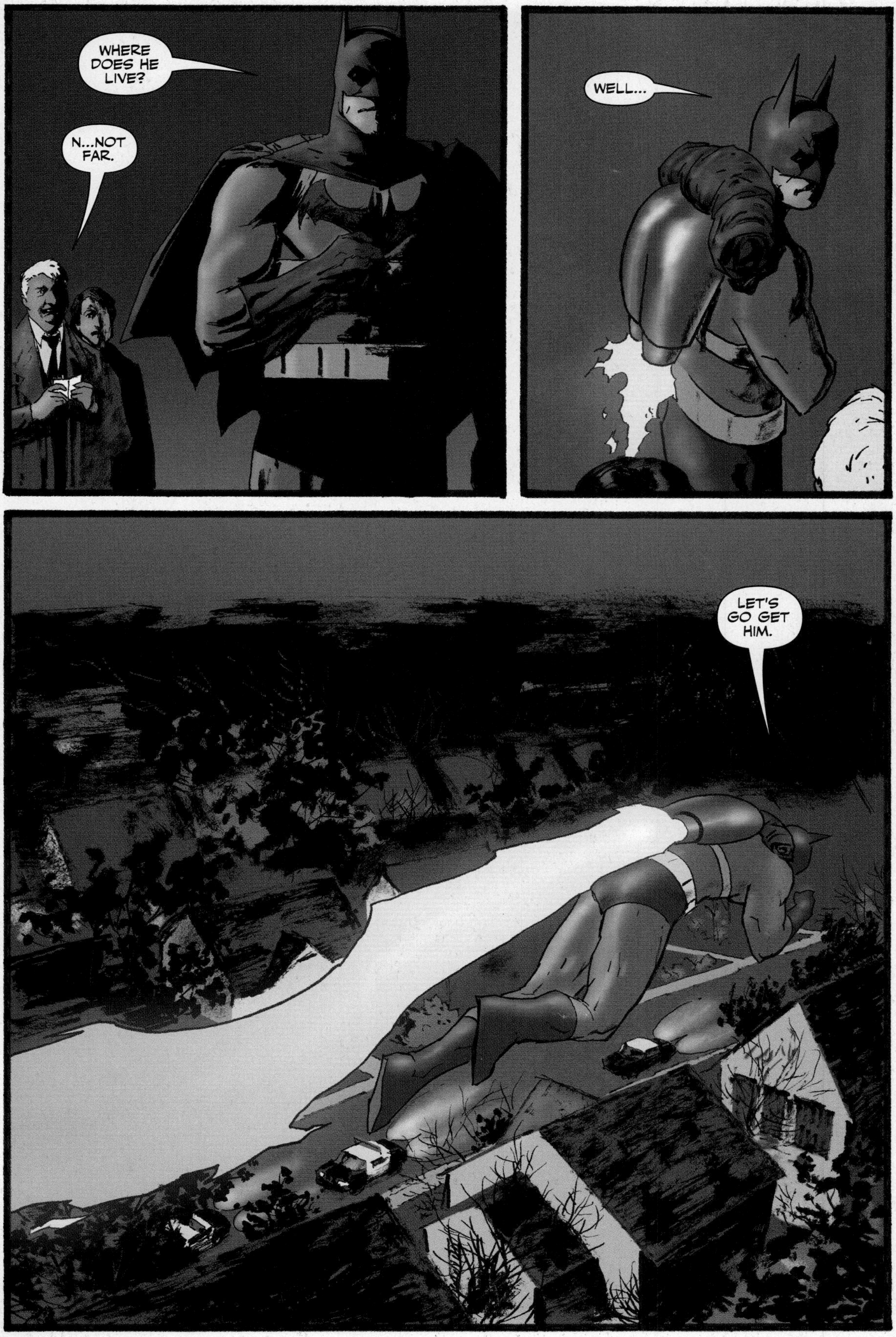

WHERE DOES HE LIVE?
N...NOT FAR.
WELL...
LET'S GO GET HIM.

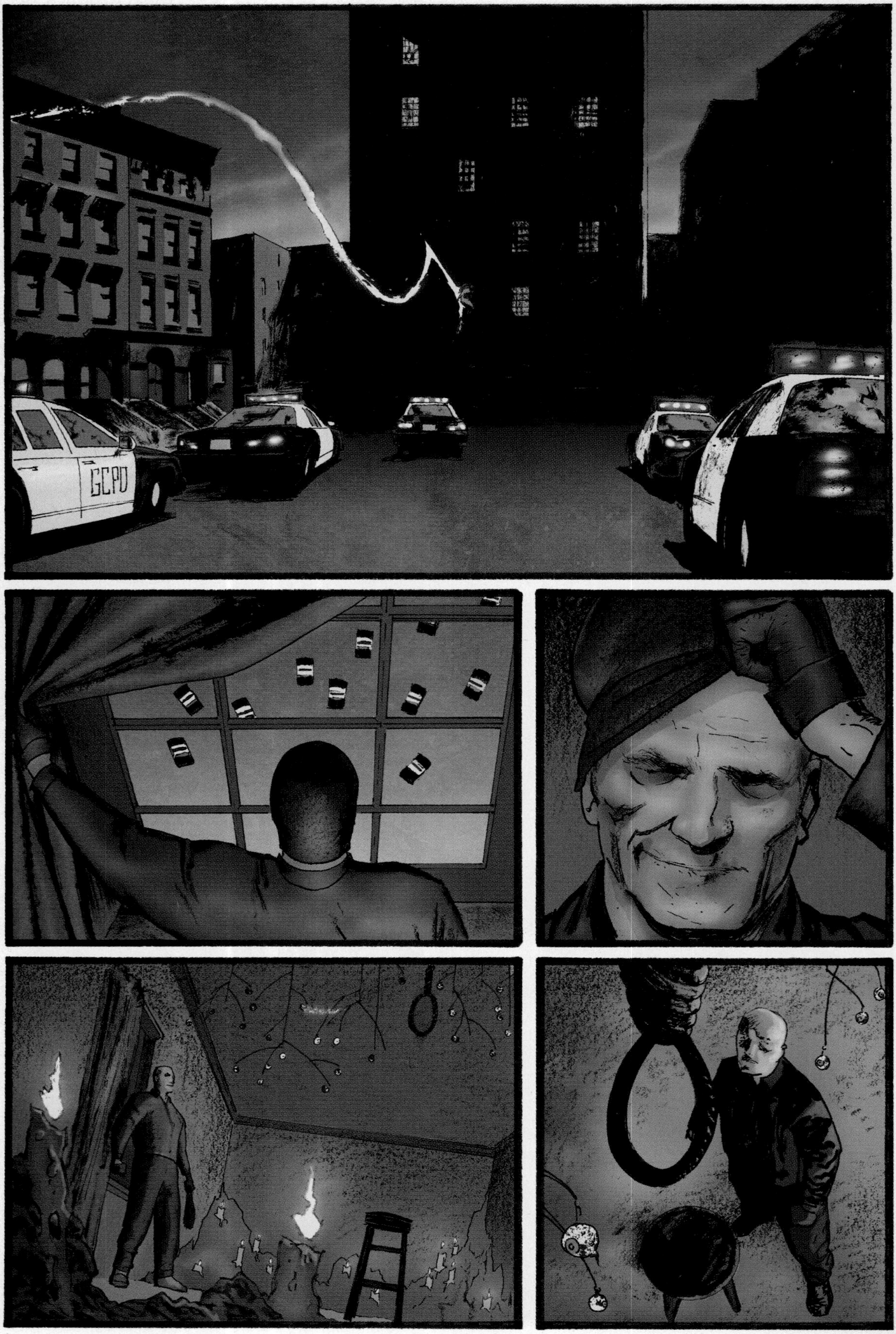
GCPD

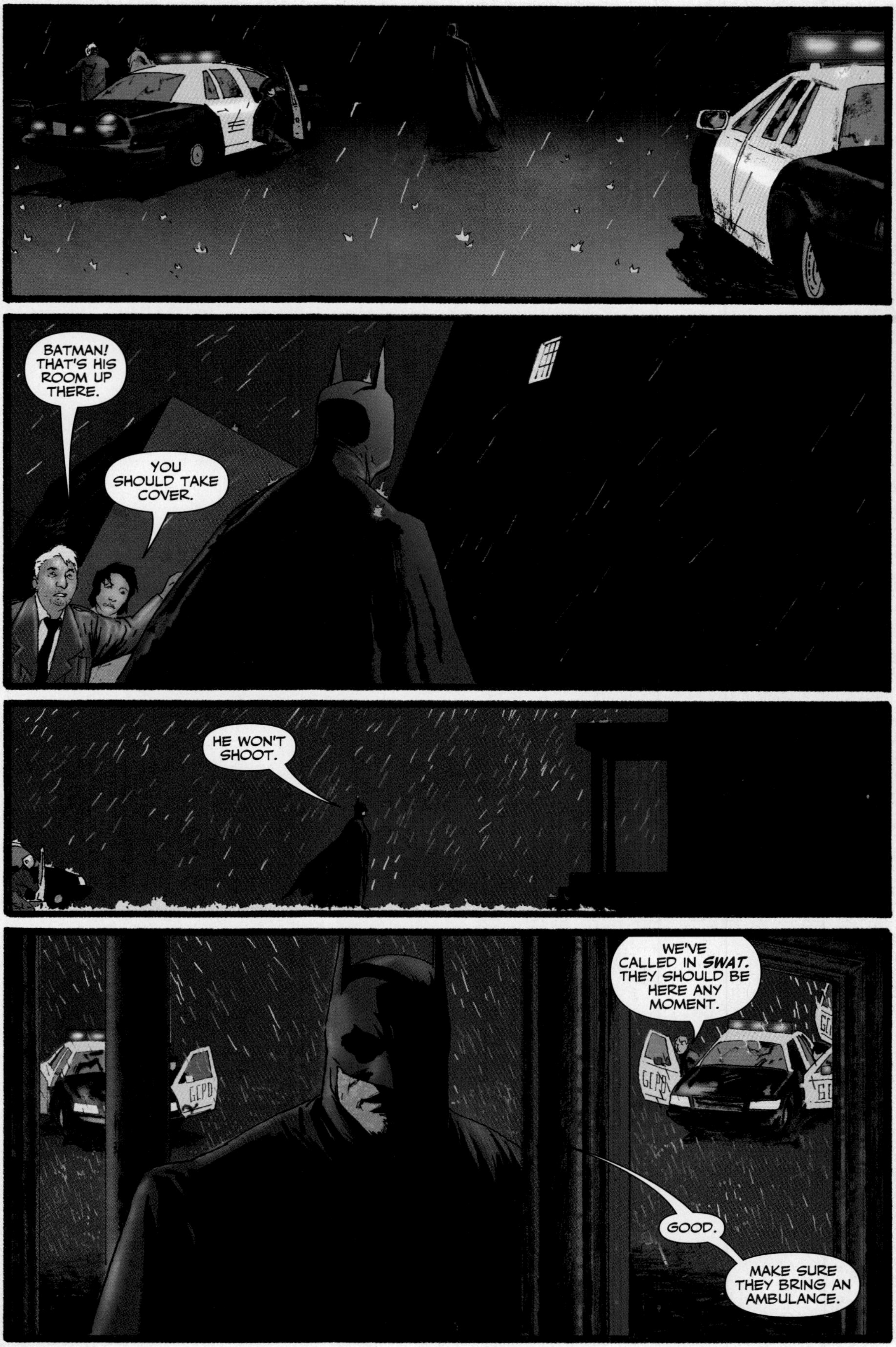
BATMAN! THAT'S HIS ROOM UP THERE.
YOU SHOULD TAKE COVER.
HE WON'T SHOOT.
WE'VE CALLED IN SWAT. THEY SHOULD BE HERE ANY MOMENT.
GOOD.
MAKE SURE THEY BRING AN AMBULANCE.
GCPD
GCPD

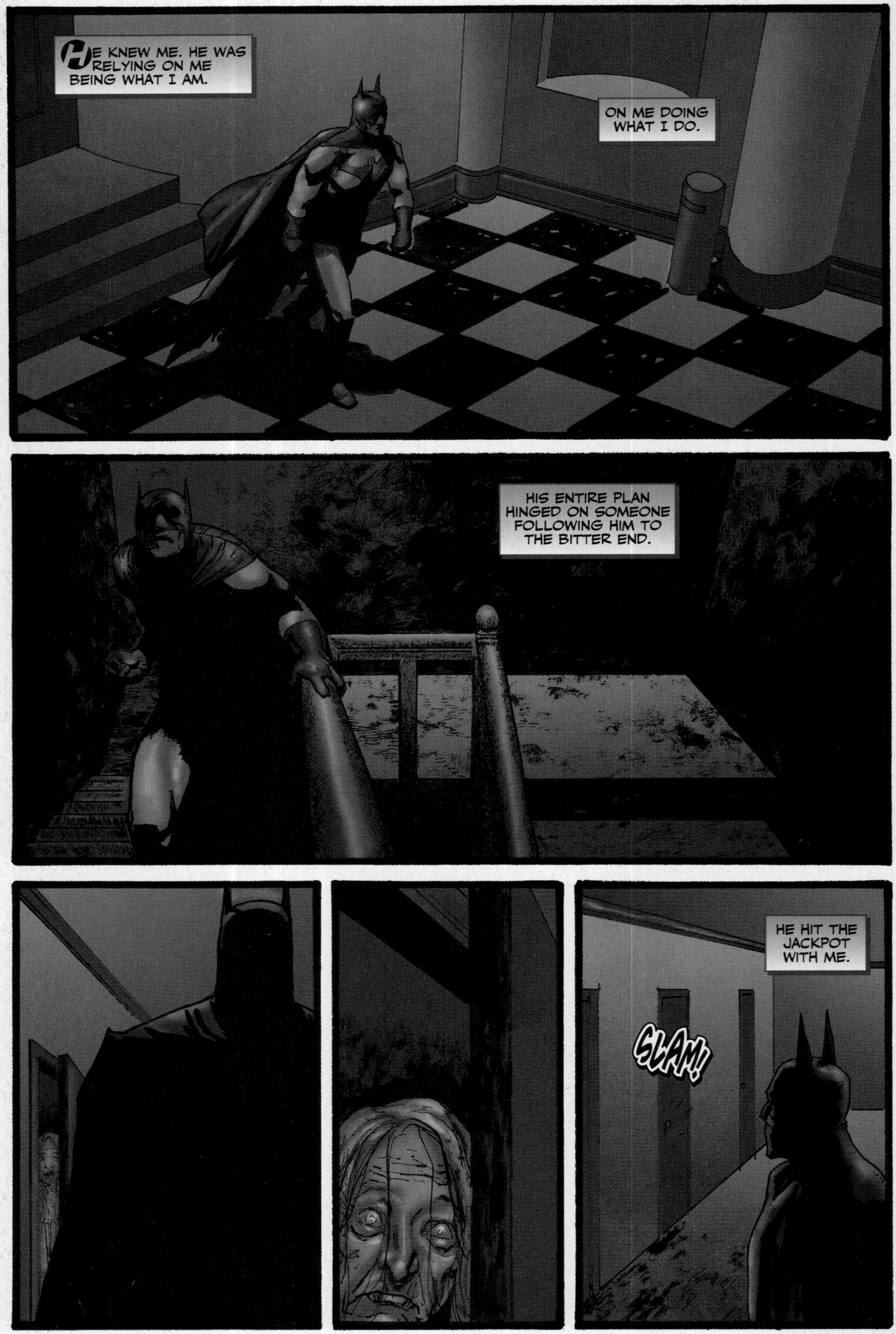
HE KNEW ME. HE WAS RELYING ON ME BEING WHAT I AM.
ON ME DOING WHAT I DO.
HIS ENTIRE PLAN HINGED ON SOMEONE FOLLOWING HIM TO THE BITTER END.
HE HIT THE JACKPOT WITH ME.
SLAM!

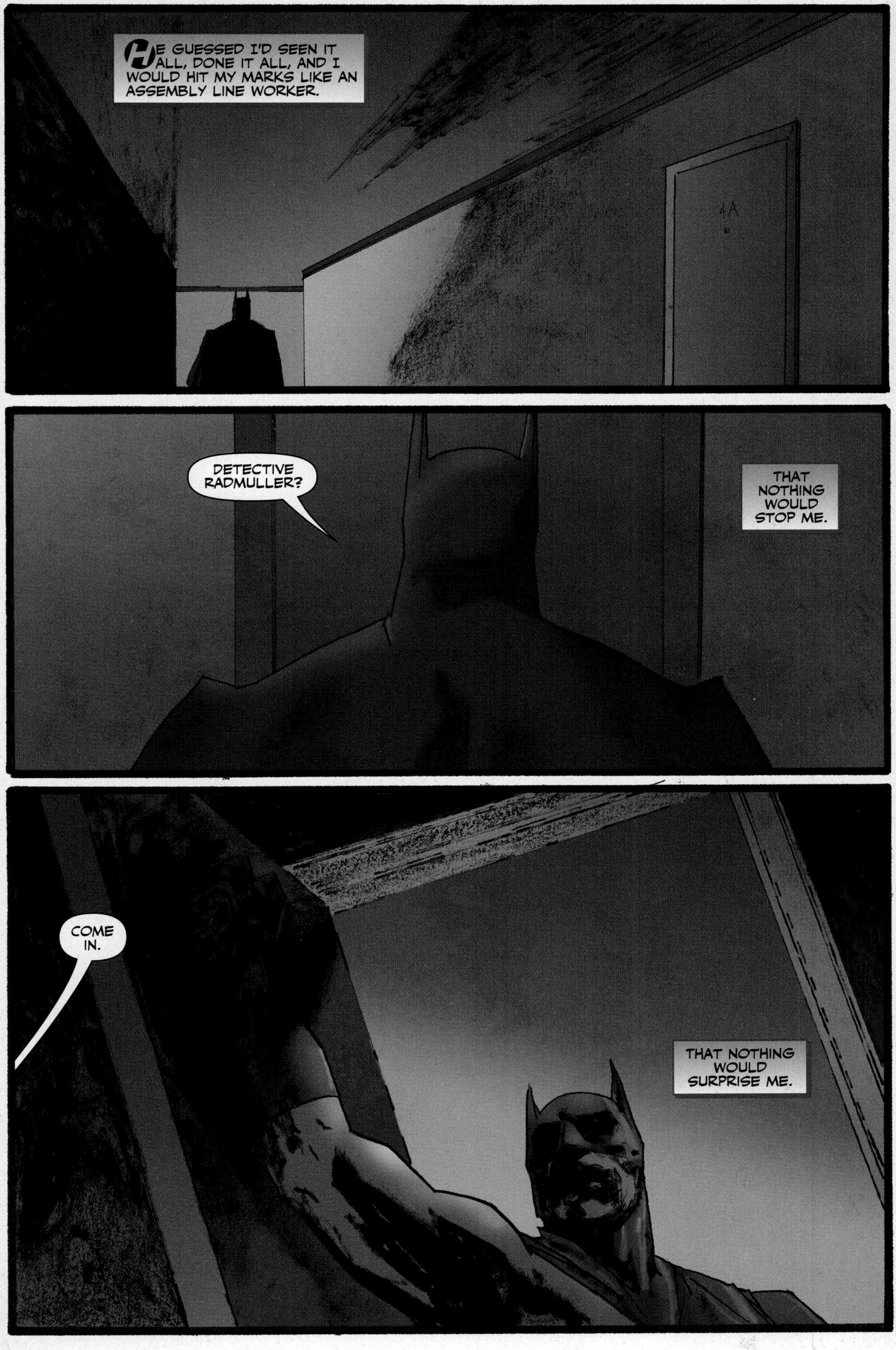
HE GUESSED I'D SEEN IT ALL, DONE IT ALL, AND I WOULD HIT MY MARKS LIKE AN ASSEMBLY LINE WORKER.
4A
DETECTIVE RADMULLER?
THAT NOTHING WOULD STOP ME.
COME IN.
THAT NOTHING WOULD SURPRISE ME.

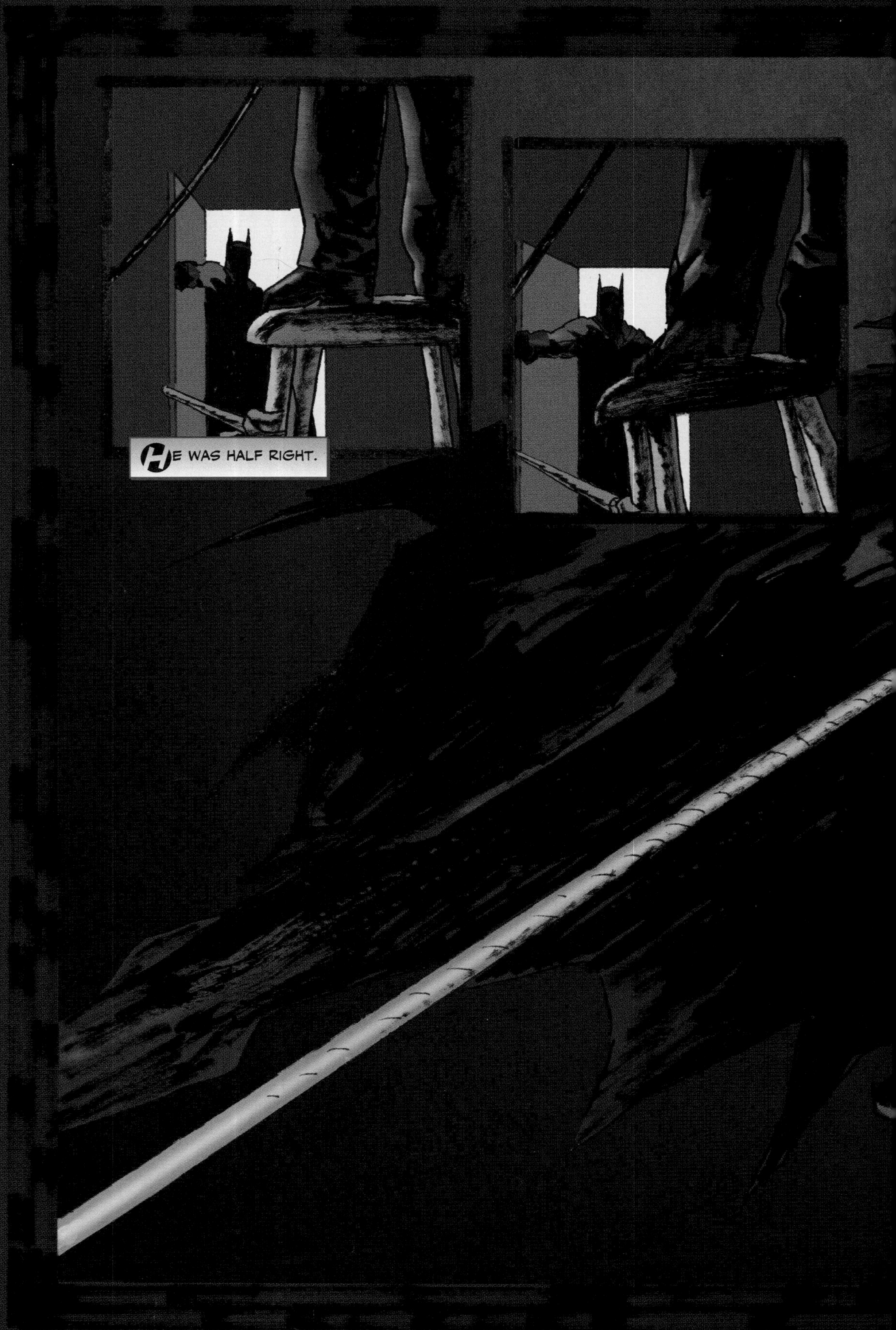
HE WAS HALF RIGHT.

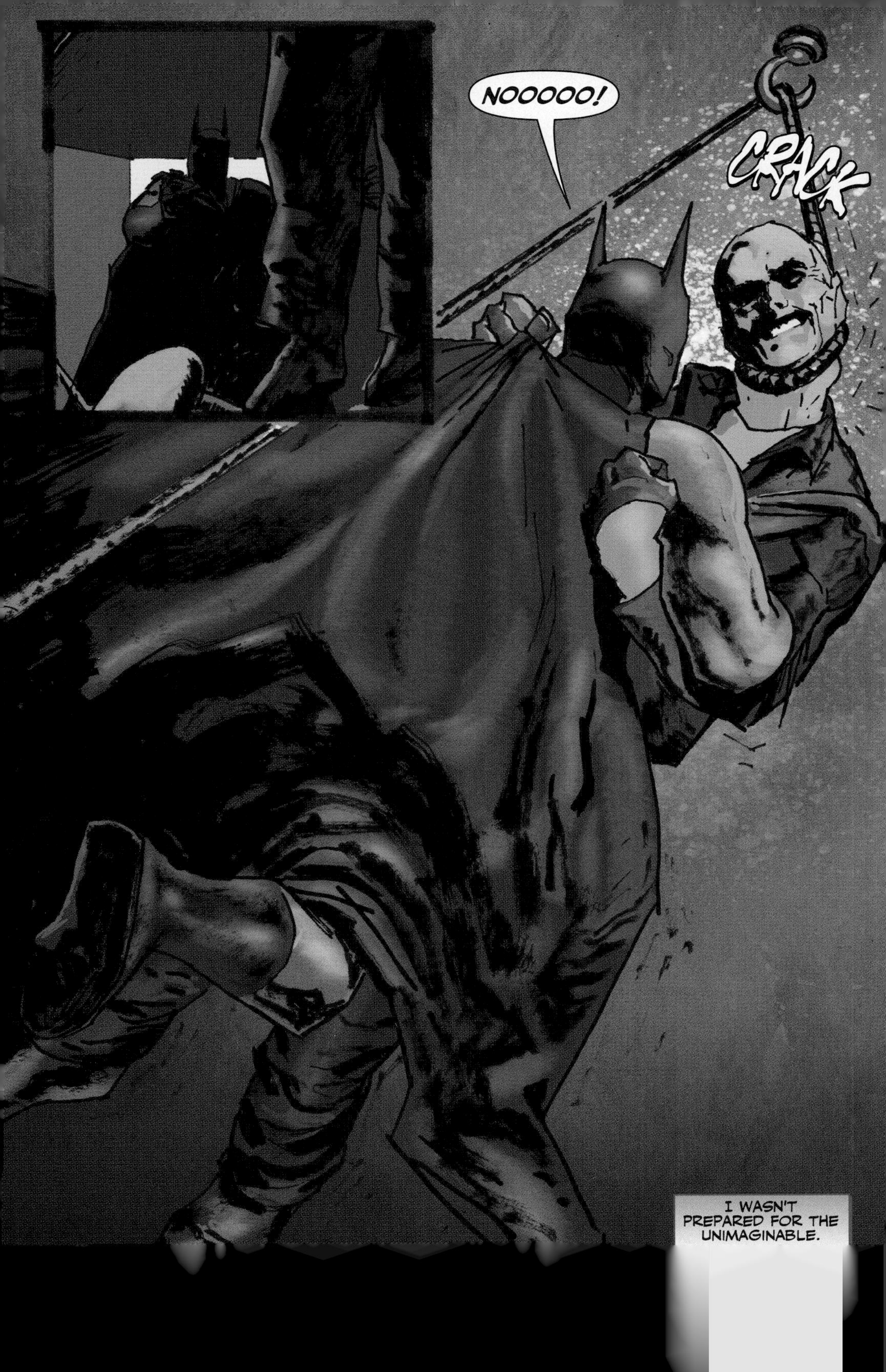
NOOOOO!
CRACK
I WASN'T PREPARED FOR THE UNIMAGINABLE.

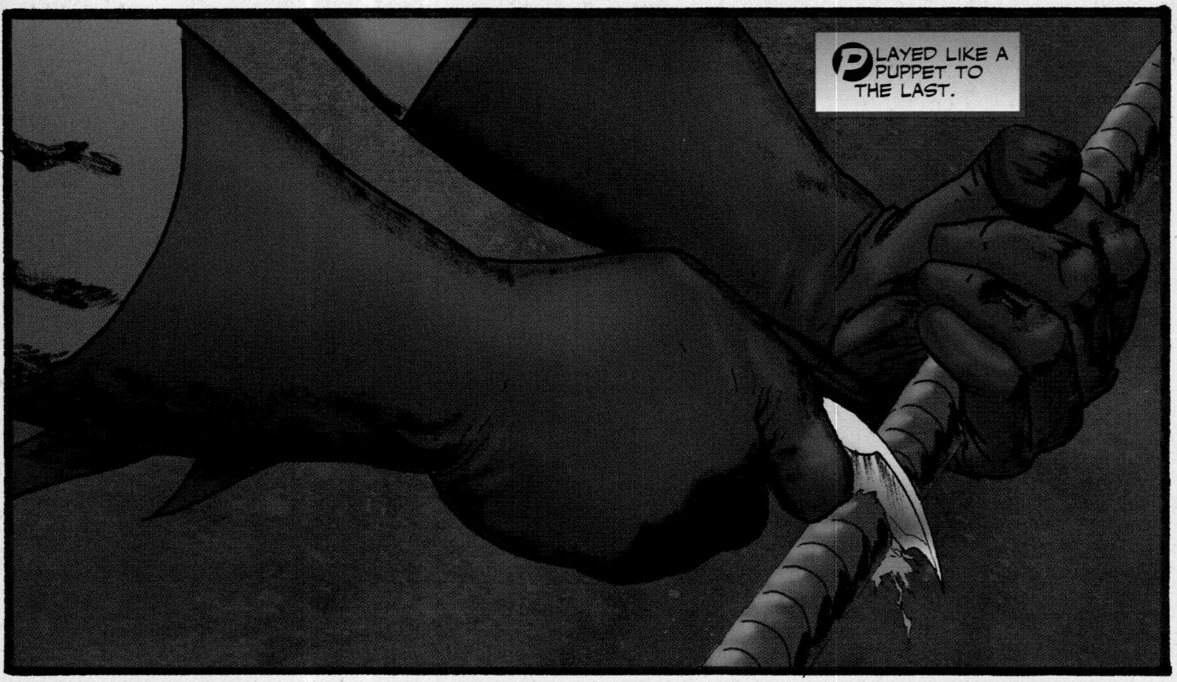
PLAYED LIKE A PUPPET TO THE LAST.

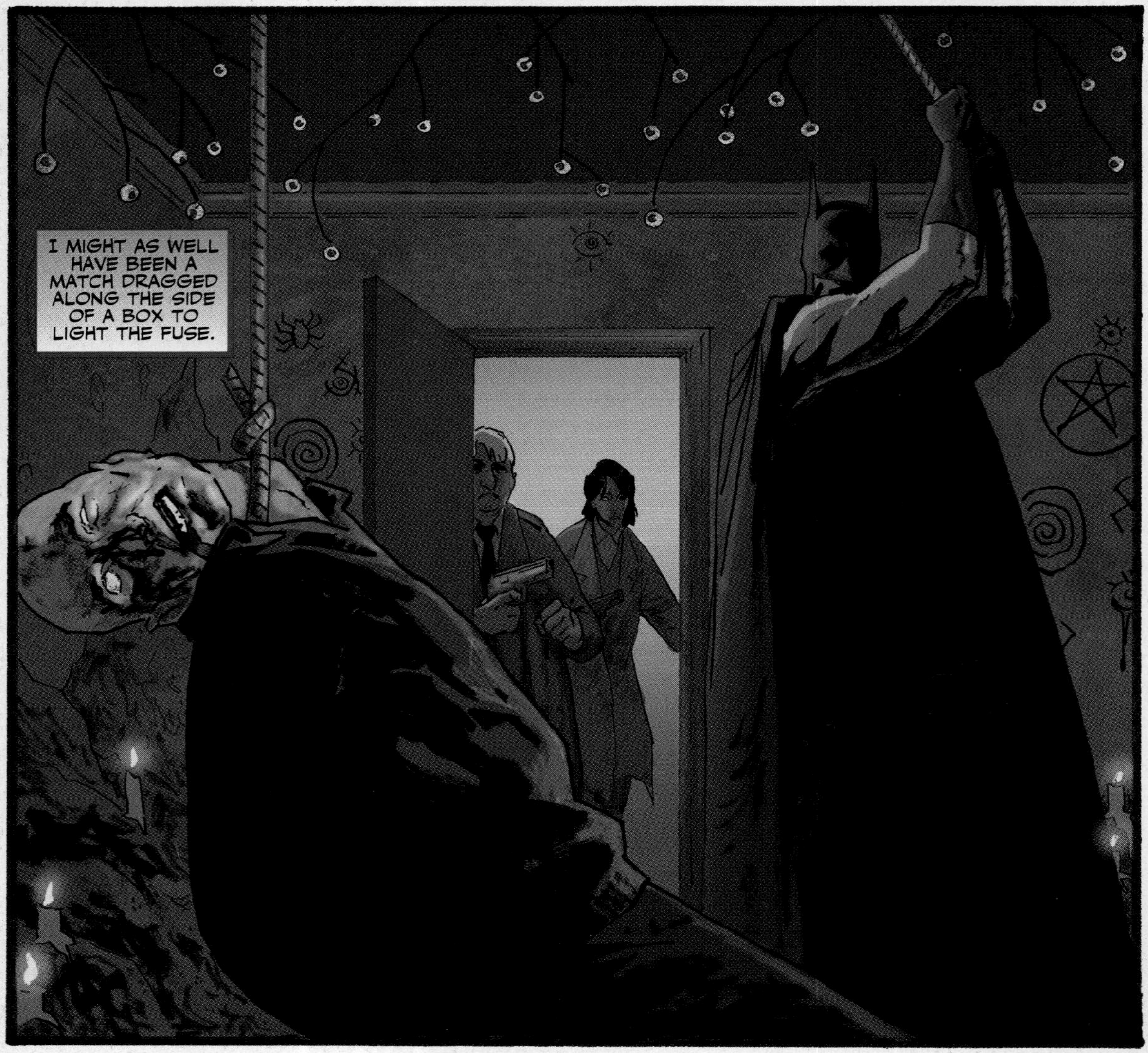
I MIGHT AS WELL HAVE BEEN A MATCH DRAGGED ALONG THE SIDE OF A BOX TO LIGHT THE FUSE.

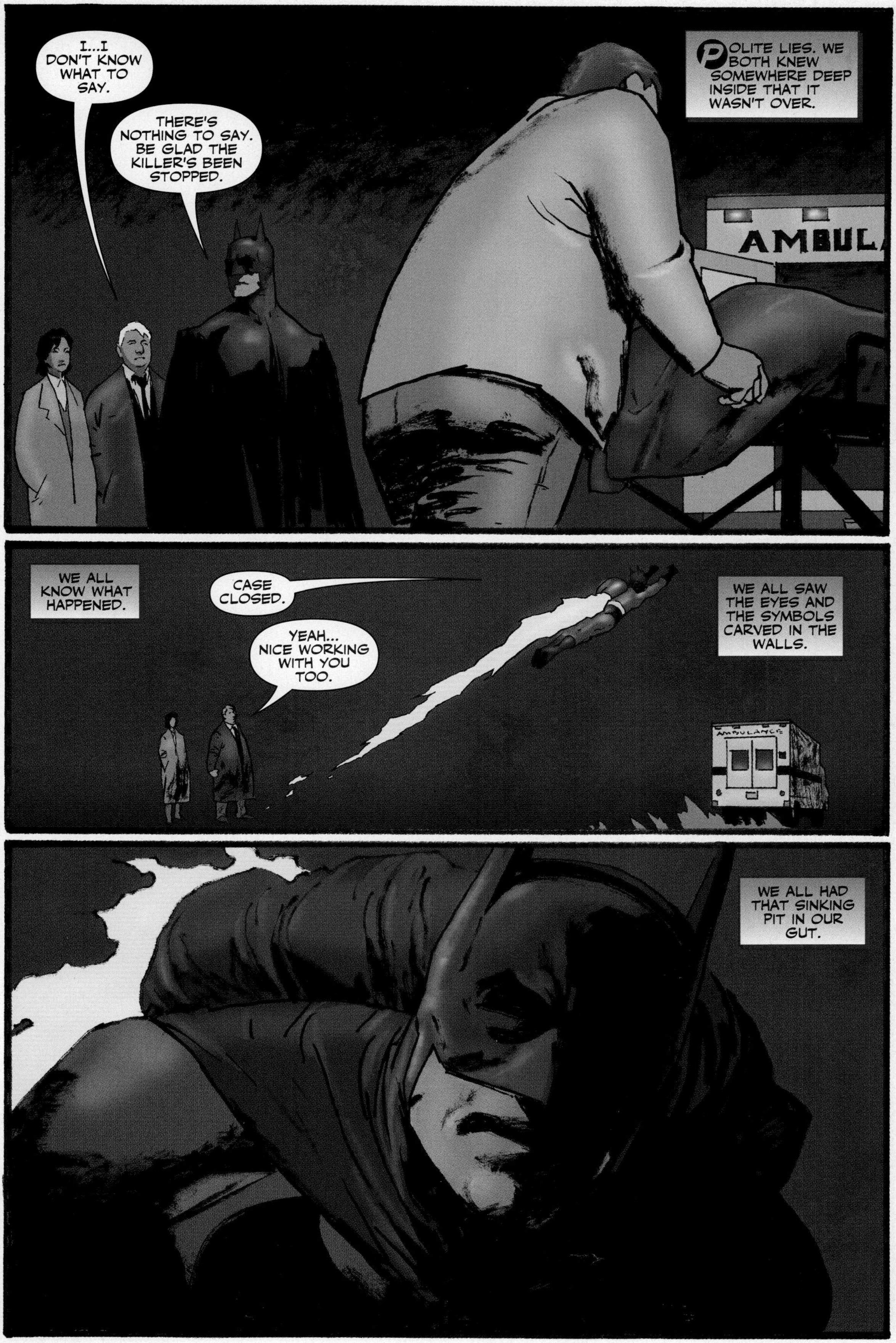
I...I DON'T KNOW WHAT TO SAY.
THERE'S NOTHING TO SAY. BE GLAD THE KILLER'S BEEN STOPPED.
POLITE LIES. WE BOTH KNEW SOMEWHERE DEEP INSIDE THAT IT WASN'T OVER.
AMBULA
WE ALL KNOW WHAT HAPPENED.
CASE CLOSED.
YEAH... NICE WORKING WITH YOU TOO.
WE ALL SAW THE EYES AND THE SYMBOLS CARVED IN THE WALLS.
AMBULANCE
WE ALL HAD THAT SINKING PIT IN OUR GUT.

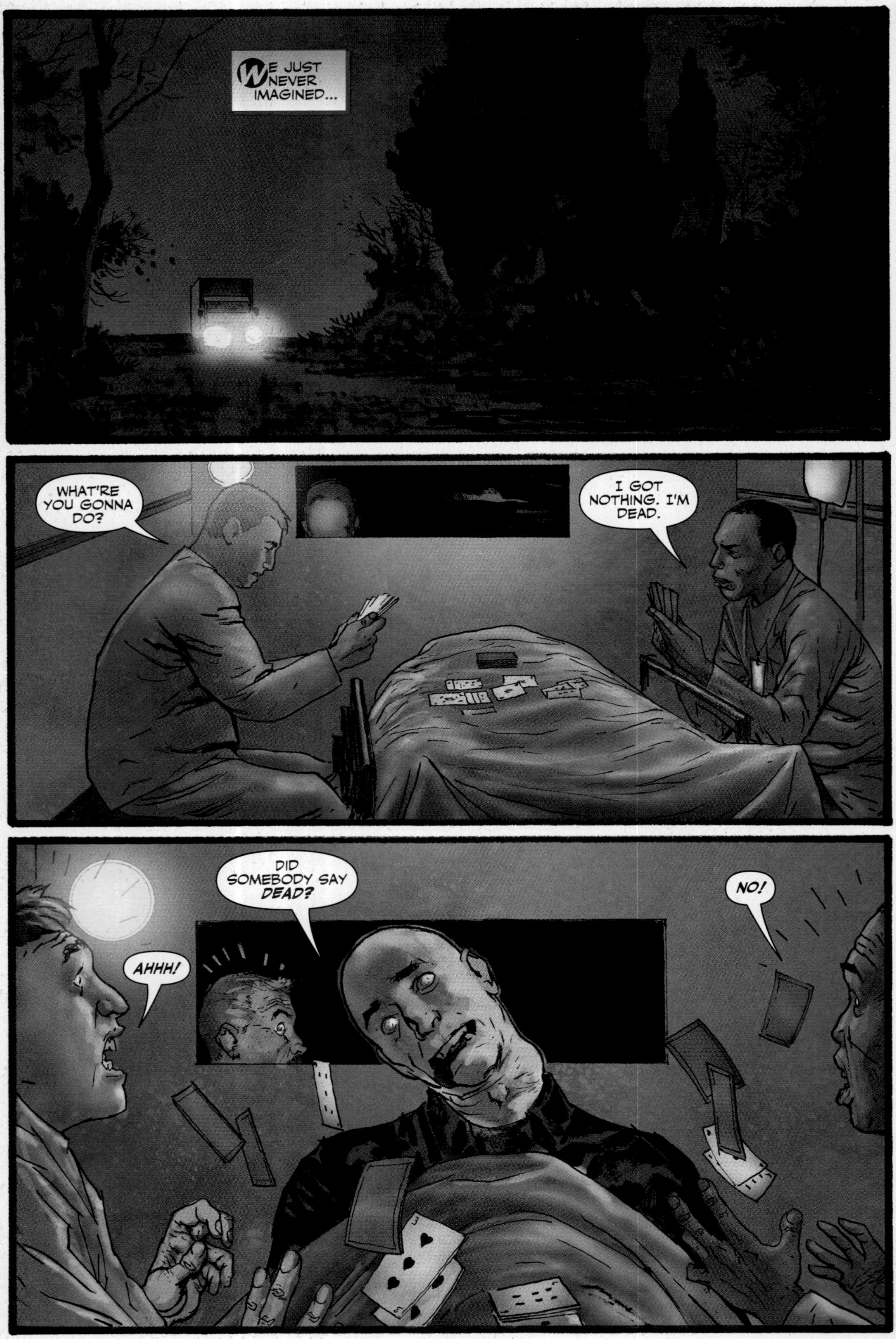
WE JUST NEVER IMAGINED...
WHAT'RE YOU GONNA DO?
I GOT NOTHING. I'M DEAD.
DID SOMEBODY SAY *DEAD?*
AHHH!
NO!

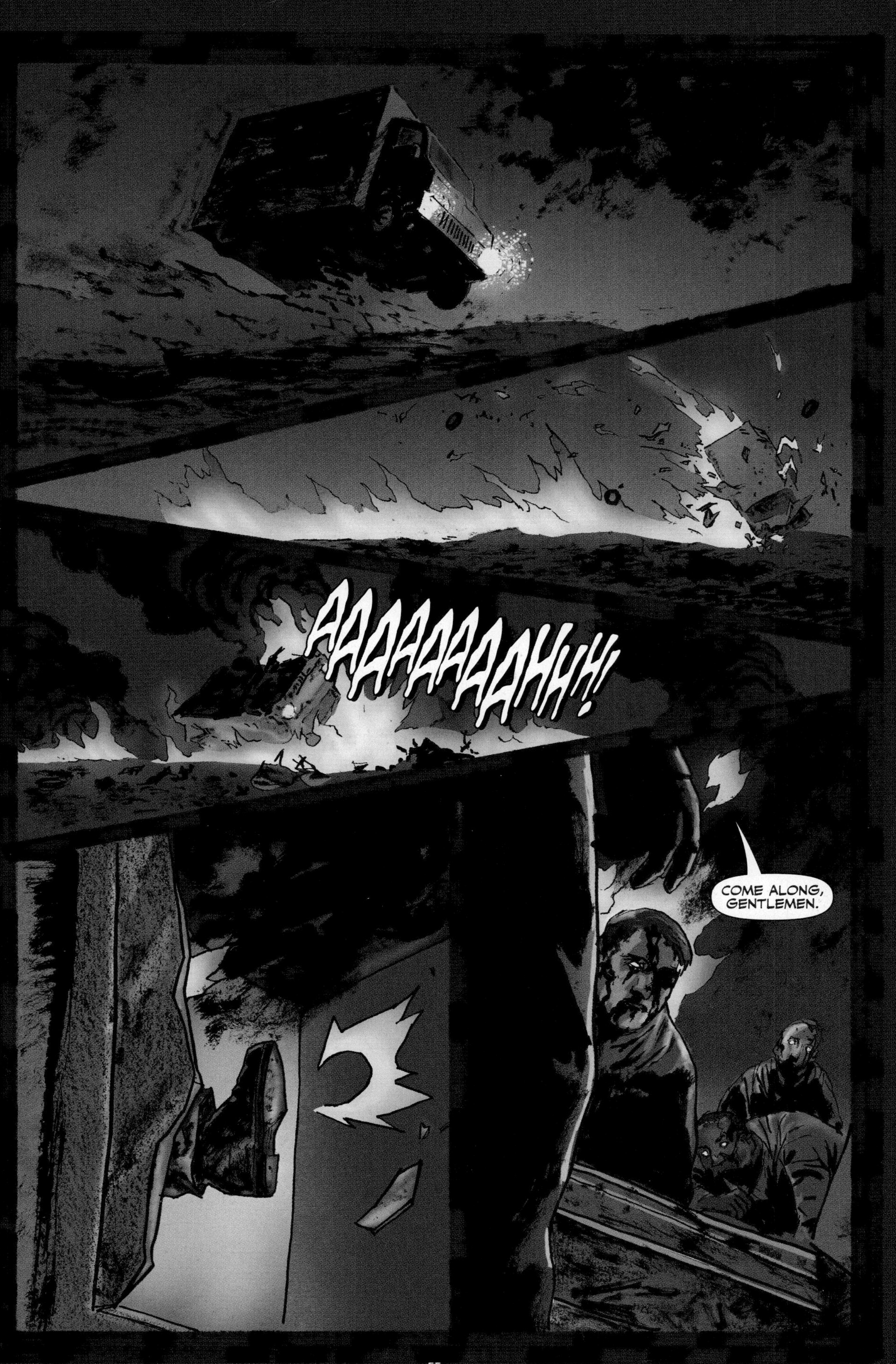
AAAAAAAAAHHH!
COME ALONG, GENTLEMEN.

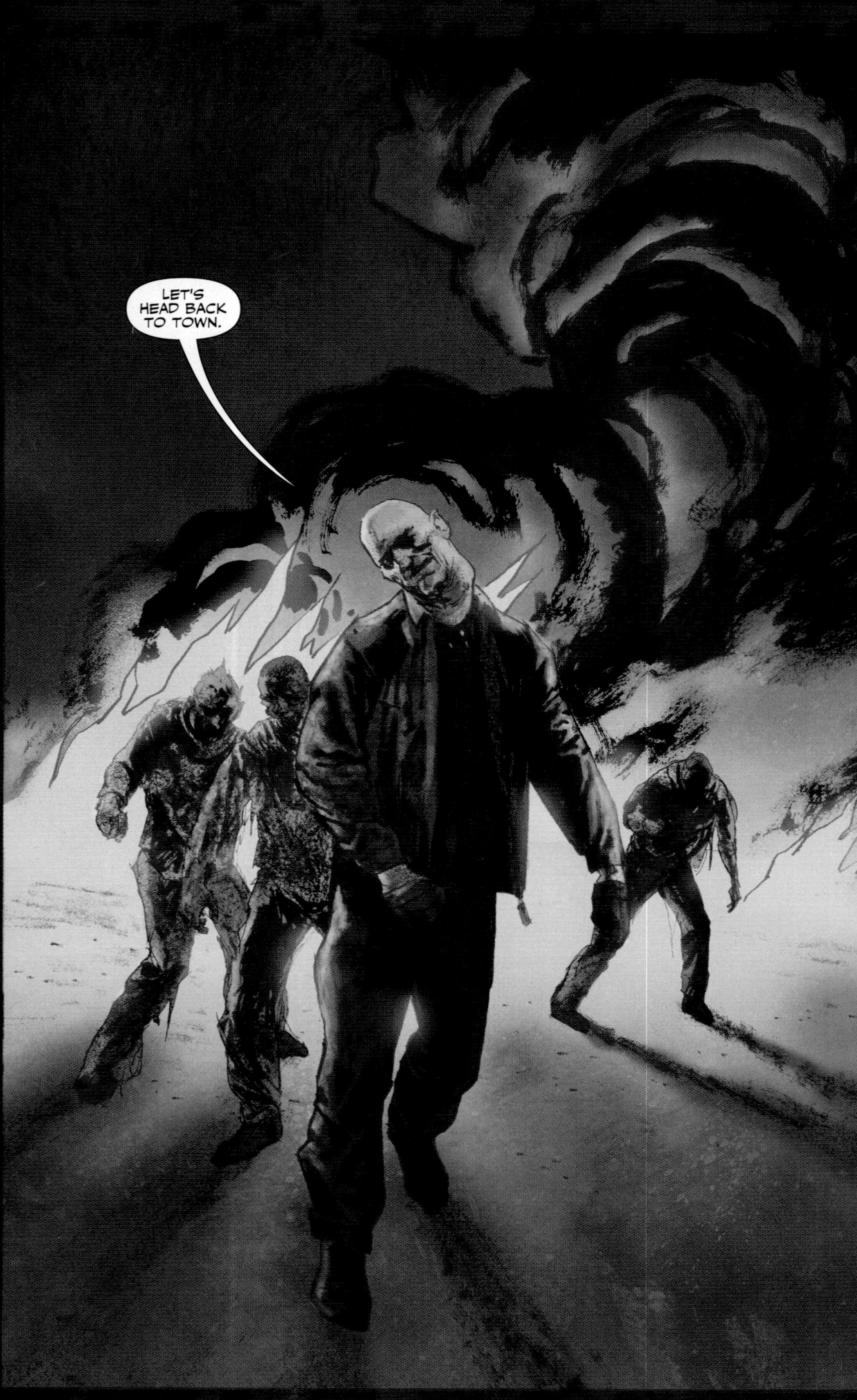
LET'S HEAD BACK TO TOWN.

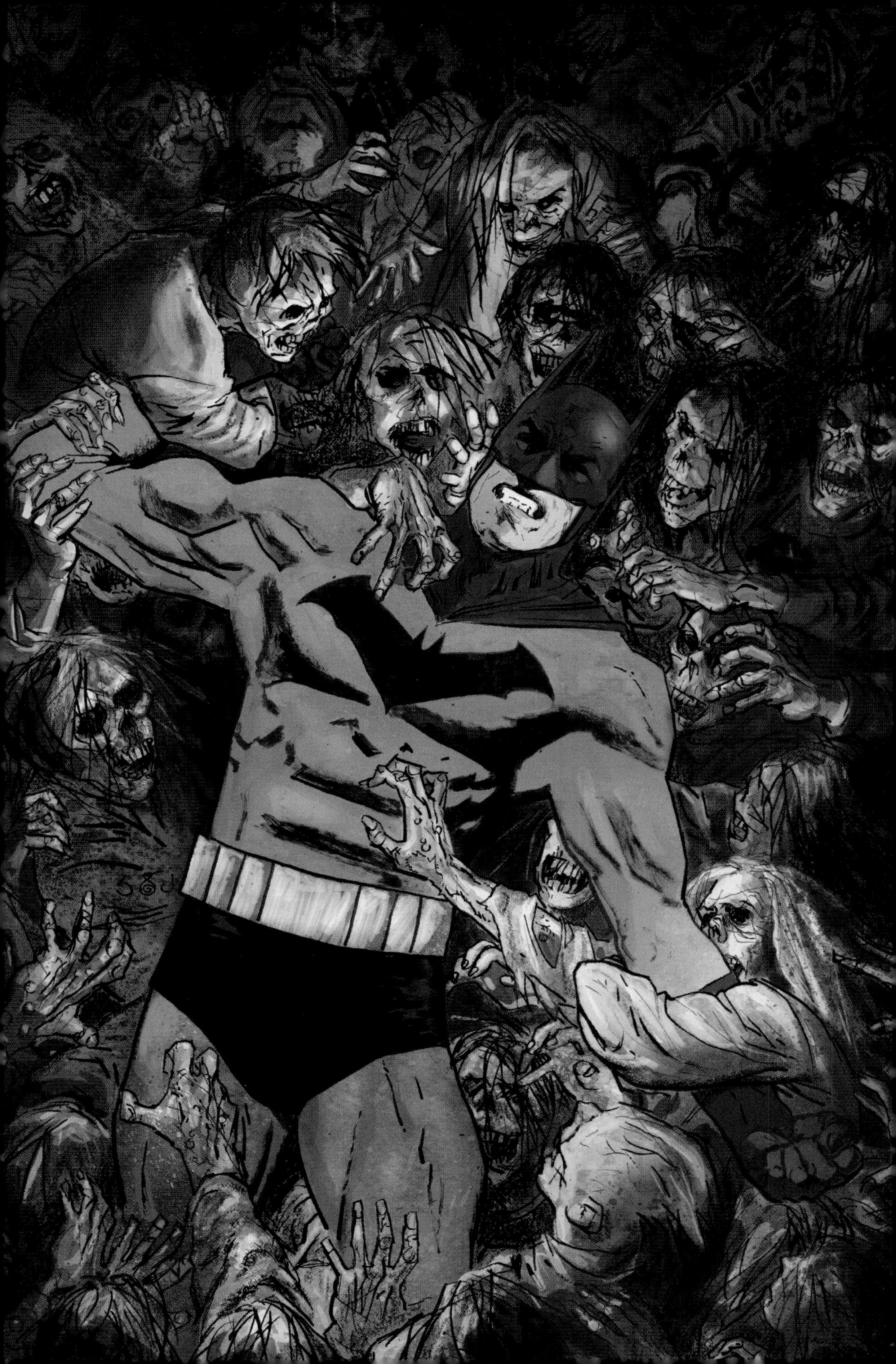

BOOK TWO:
DEATH'S HIGHWAY

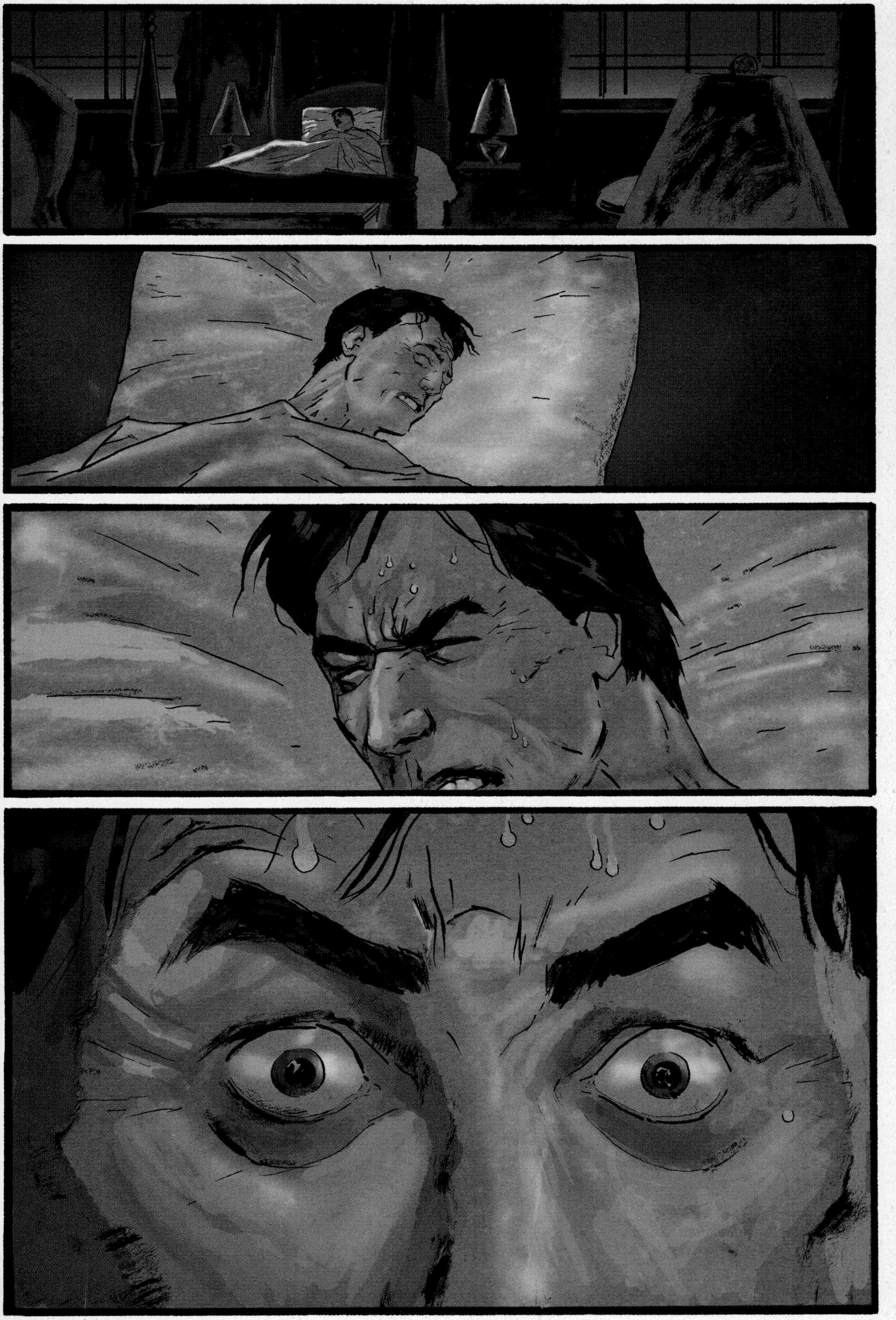

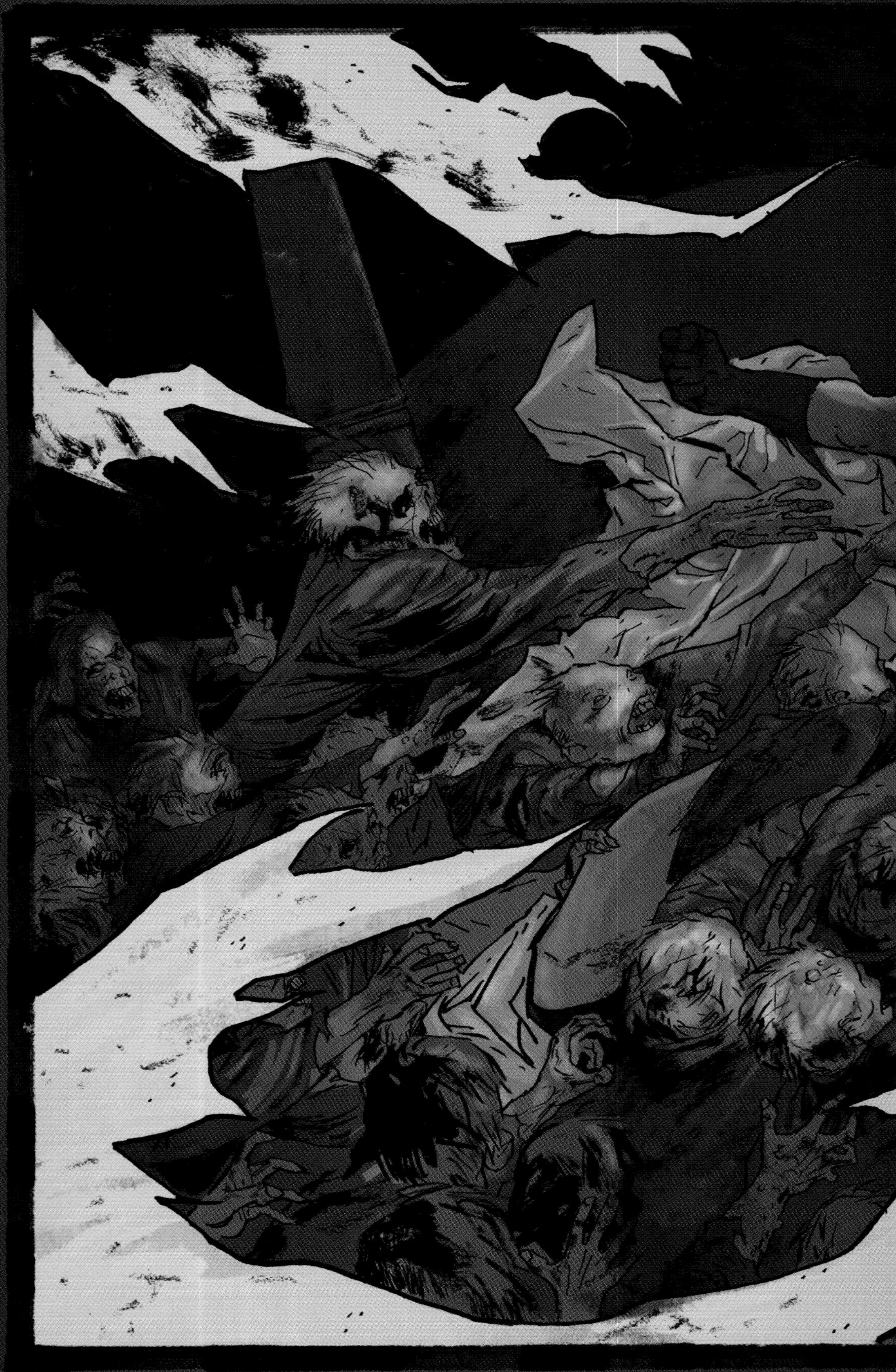

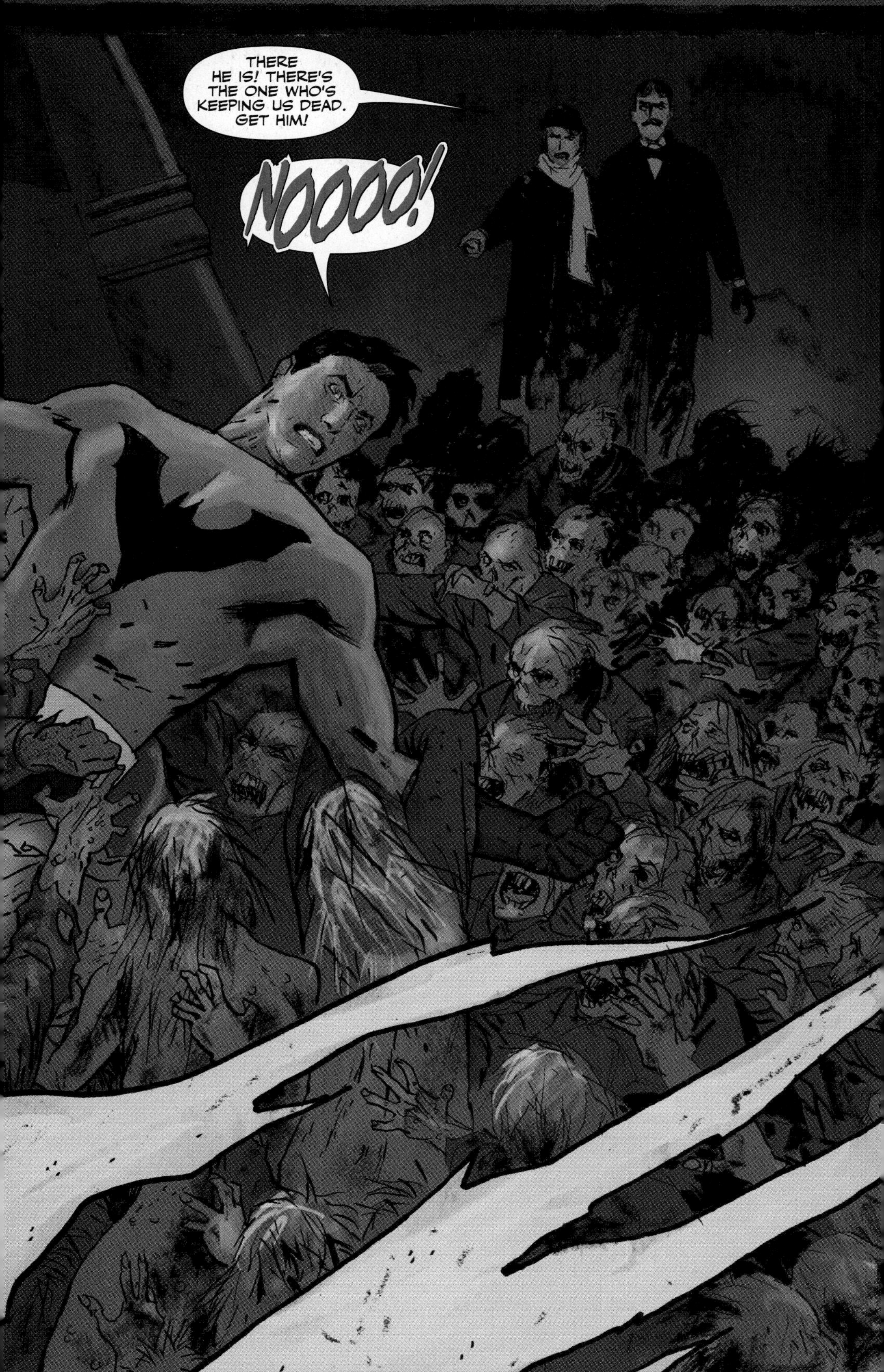
THERE HE IS! THERE'S THE ONE WHO'S KEEPING US DEAD. GET HIM!
NOOOO!

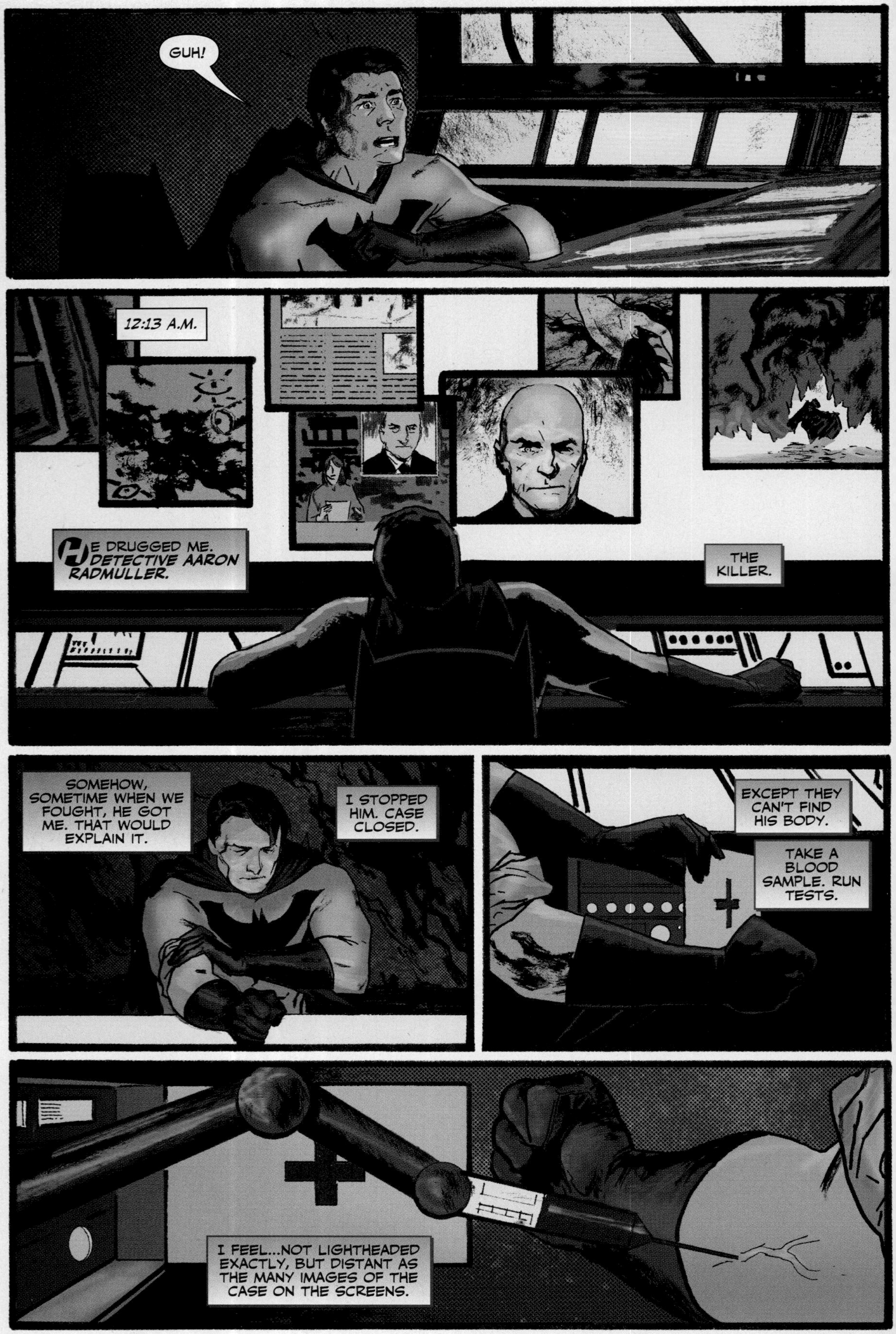
GUH!
12:13 A.M.
HE DRUGGED ME. DETECTIVE AARON RADMULLER.
THE KILLER.
SOMEHOW, SOMETIME WHEN WE FOUGHT, HE GOT ME. THAT WOULD EXPLAIN IT.
I STOPPED HIM. CASE CLOSED.
EXCEPT THEY CAN'T FIND HIS BODY.
TAKE A BLOOD SAMPLE. RUN TESTS.
I FEEL...NOT LIGHTHEADED EXACTLY, BUT DISTANT AS THE MANY IMAGES OF THE CASE ON THE SCREENS.

THERE'S NO OTHER WAY TO EXPLAIN IT.

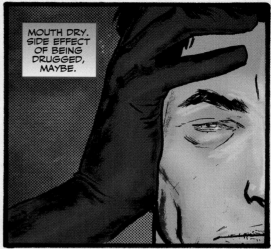

MOUTH DRY. SIDE EFFECT OF BEING DRUGGED, MAYBE.

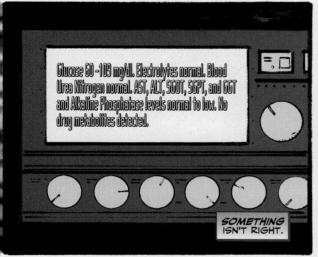

Glucose 60 -109 mg/dl. Electrolytes normal. Blood Urea Nitrogen normal. AST, ALT, SGOT, SGPT, and GGT and Alkaline Phosphatase levels normal to low. No drug metabolites detected.

SOMETHING ISN'T RIGHT.

OR SOMEONE.

YOU HAVEN'T SLEPT ONCE AGAIN. A RESTED MIND SEES THINGS THE EXHAUSTED MIND OVERLOOKS.

I JUST CAUGHT A NAP. IT WASN'T VERY RESTFUL.

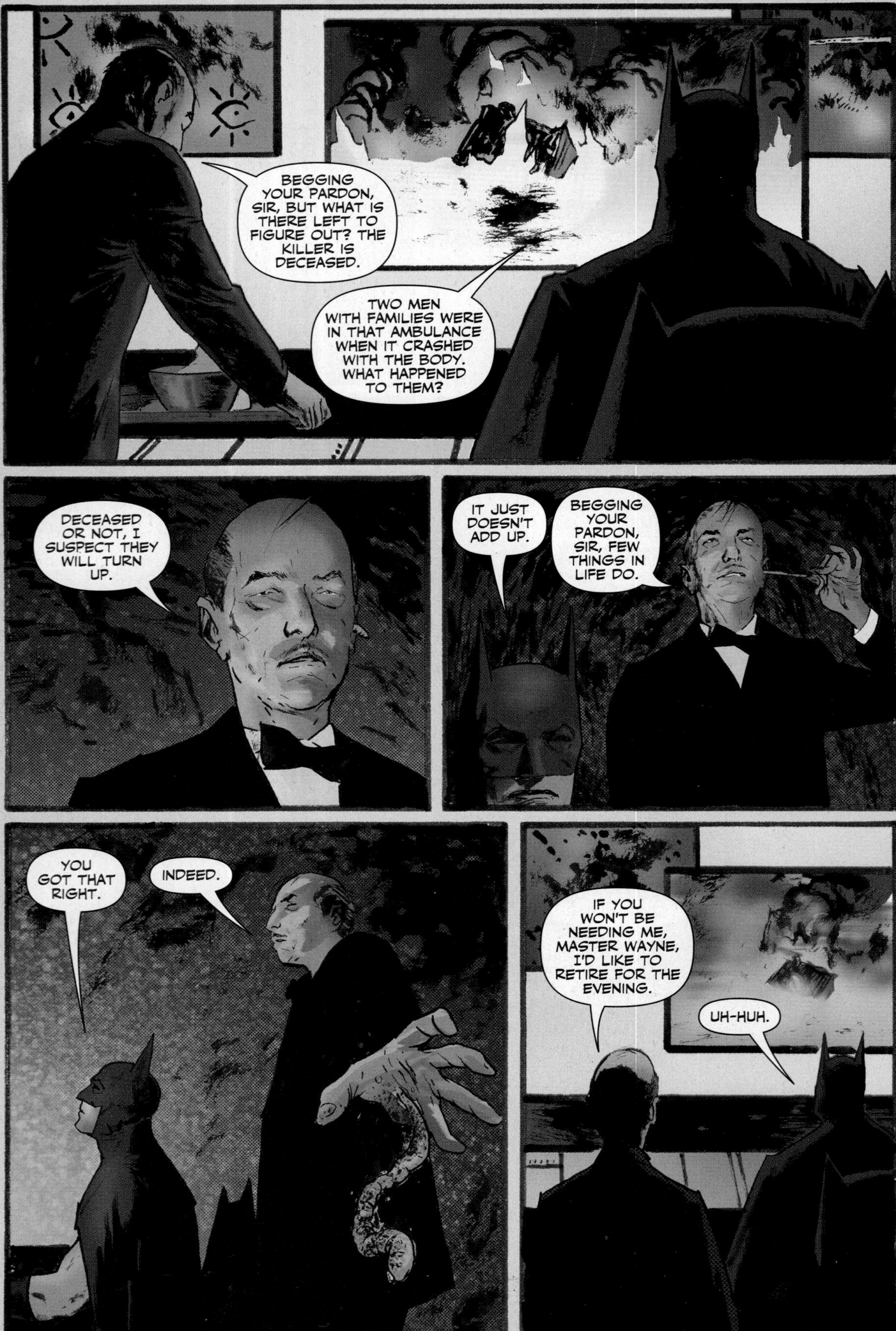
BEGGING YOUR PARDON, SIR, BUT WHAT IS THERE LEFT TO FIGURE OUT? THE KILLER IS DECEASED.
TWO MEN WITH FAMILIES WERE IN THAT AMBULANCE WHEN IT CRASHED WITH THE BODY. WHAT HAPPENED TO THEM?
DECEASED OR NOT, I SUSPECT THEY WILL TURN UP.
IT JUST DOESN'T ADD UP.
BEGGING YOUR PARDON, SIR, FEW THINGS IN LIFE DO.
YOU GOT THAT RIGHT.
INDEED.
IF YOU WON'T BE NEEDING ME, MASTER WAYNE, I'D LIKE TO RETIRE FOR THE EVENING.
UH-HUH.

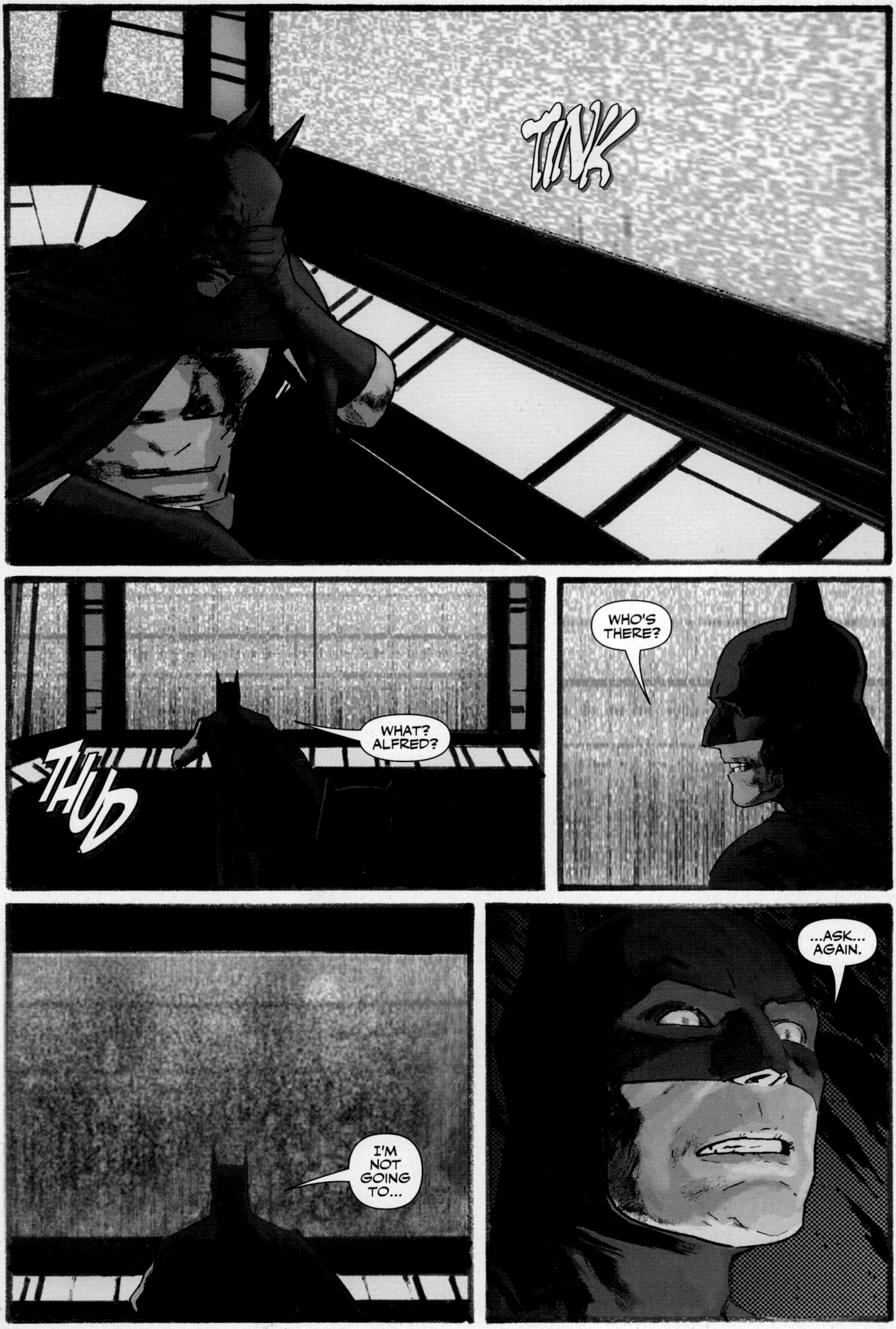
TINK
THUD
WHAT? ALFRED?
WHO'S THERE?
I'M NOT GOING TO...
...ASK... AGAIN.

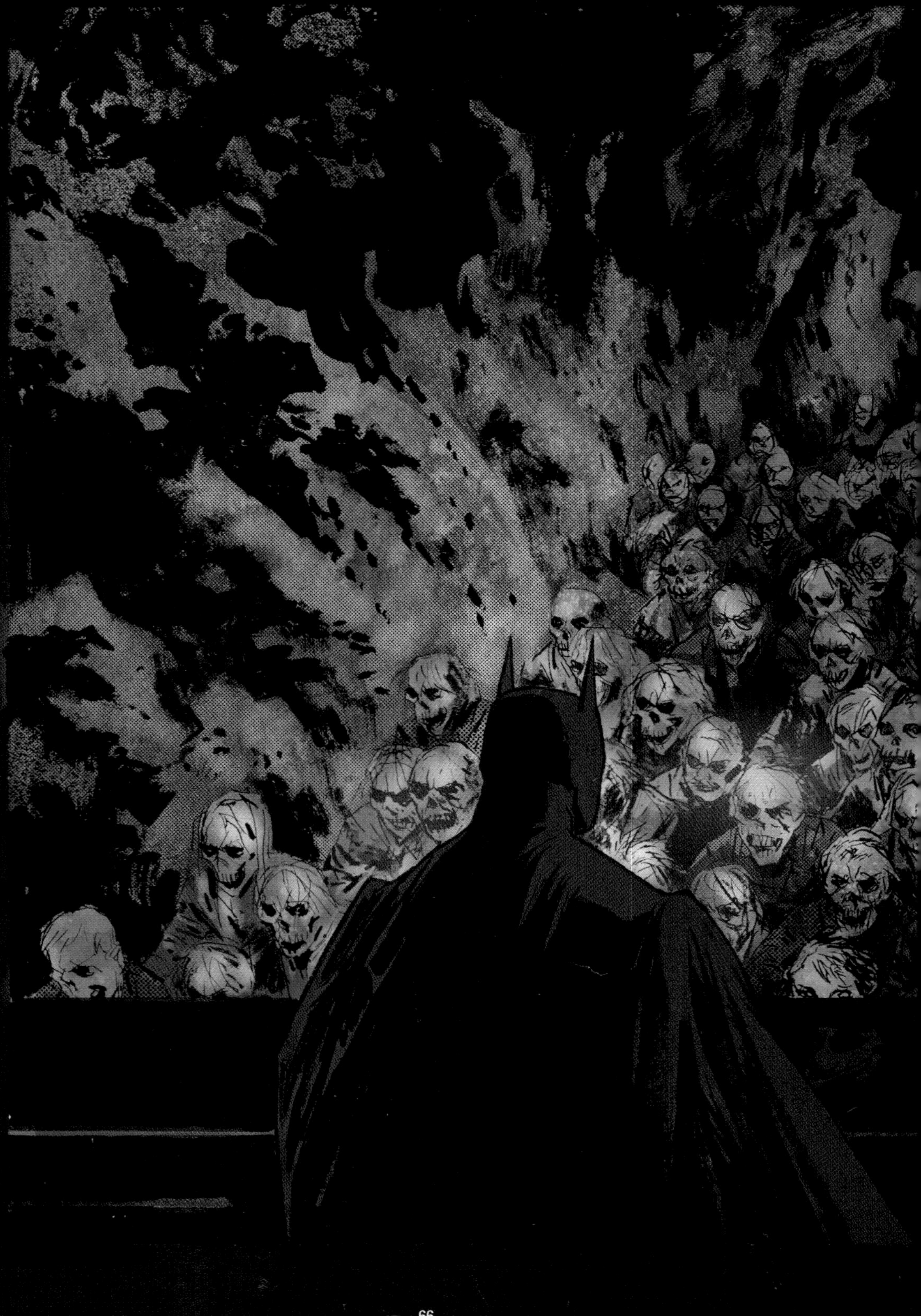

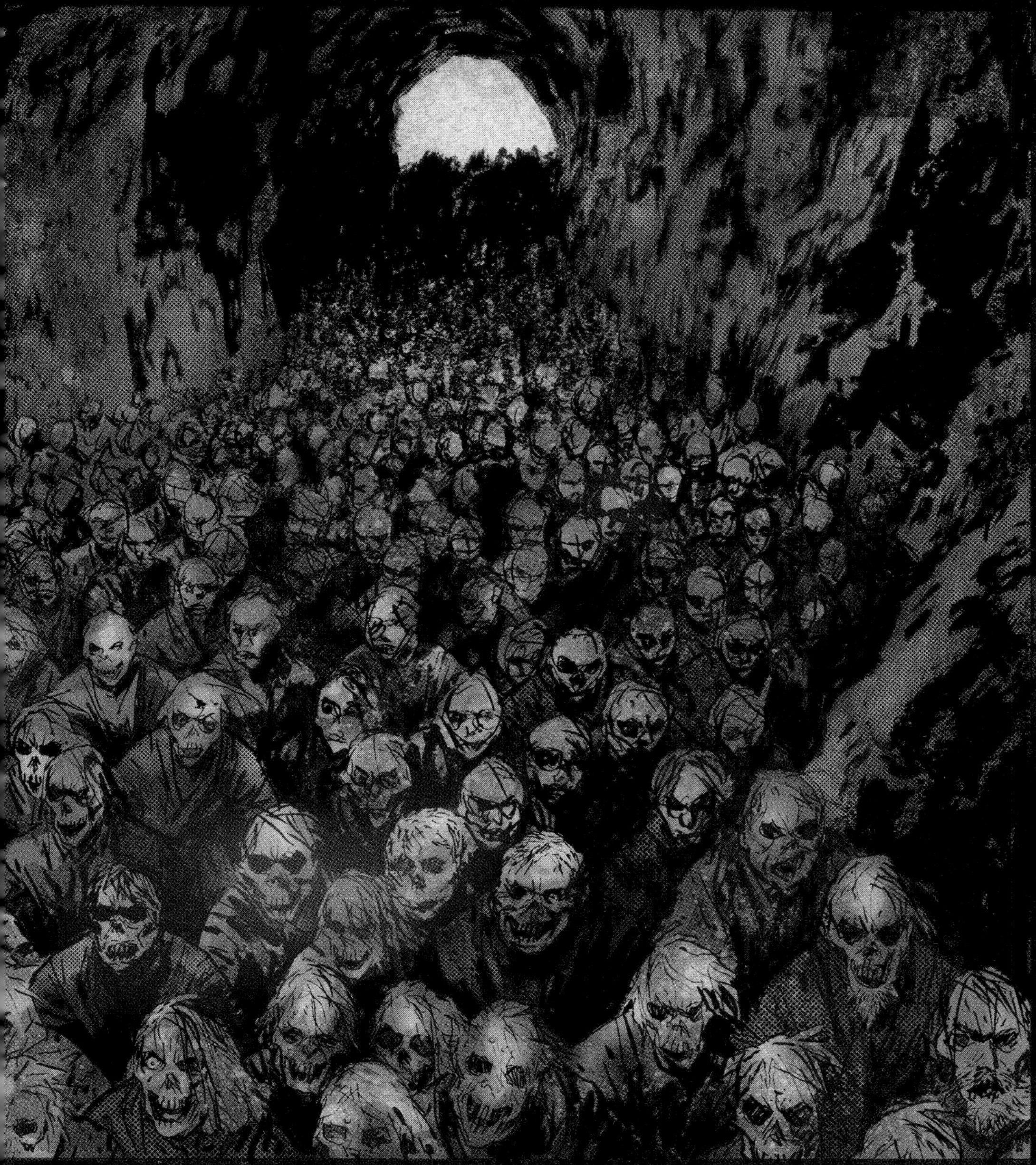

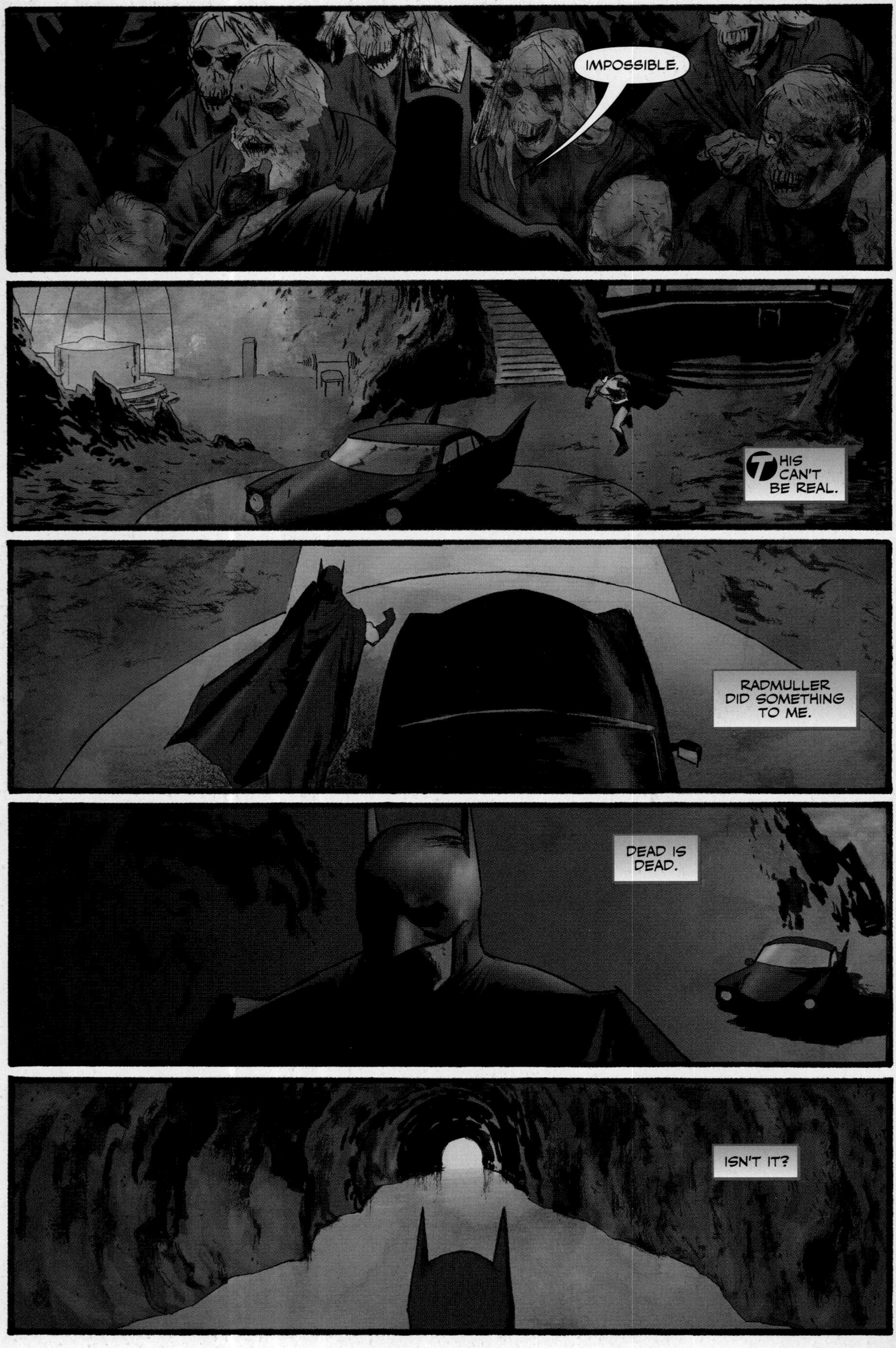
IMPOSSIBLE.
THIS CAN'T BE REAL.
RADMULLER DID SOMETHING TO ME.
DEAD IS DEAD.
ISN'T IT?

EITHER I'M LOSING MY MIND OR...

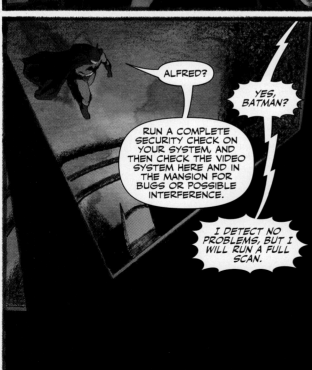

ALFRED?

YES, BATMAN?

RUN A COMPLETE SECURITY CHECK ON YOUR SYSTEM, AND THEN CHECK THE VIDEO SYSTEM HERE AND IN THE MANSION FOR BUGS OR POSSIBLE INTERFERENCE.

I DETECT NO PROBLEMS, BUT I WILL RUN A FULL SCAN.

RADMULLER.

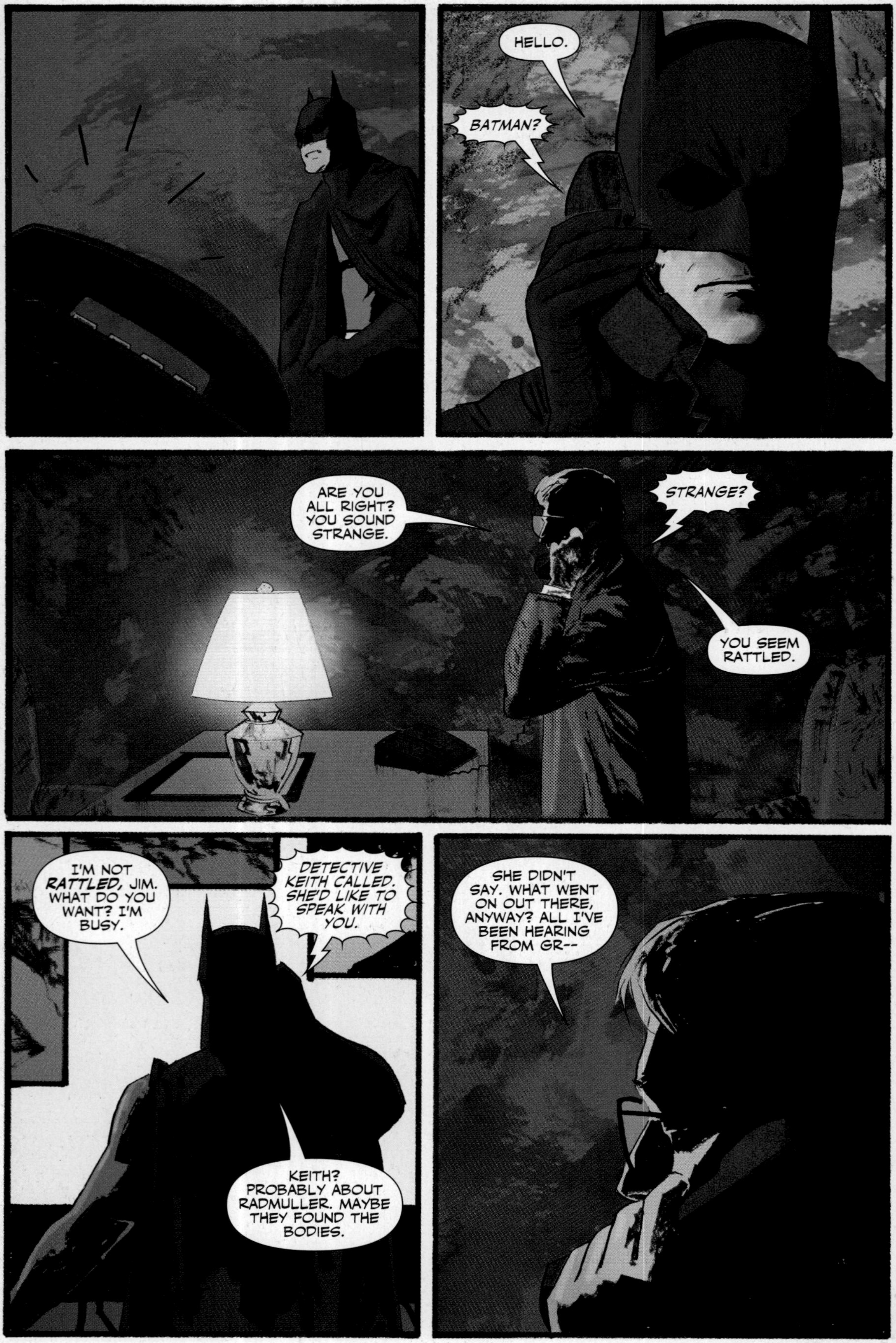
HELLO.
BATMAN?
ARE YOU ALL RIGHT? YOU SOUND STRANGE.
STRANGE?
YOU SEEM RATTLED.
I'M NOT *RATTLED,* JIM. WHAT DO YOU WANT? I'M BUSY.
DETECTIVE KEITH CALLED. SHE'D LIKE TO SPEAK WITH YOU.
KEITH? PROBABLY ABOUT RADMULLER. MAYBE THEY FOUND THE BODIES.
SHE DIDN'T SAY. WHAT WENT ON OUT THERE, ANYWAY? ALL I'VE BEEN HEARING FROM GR--

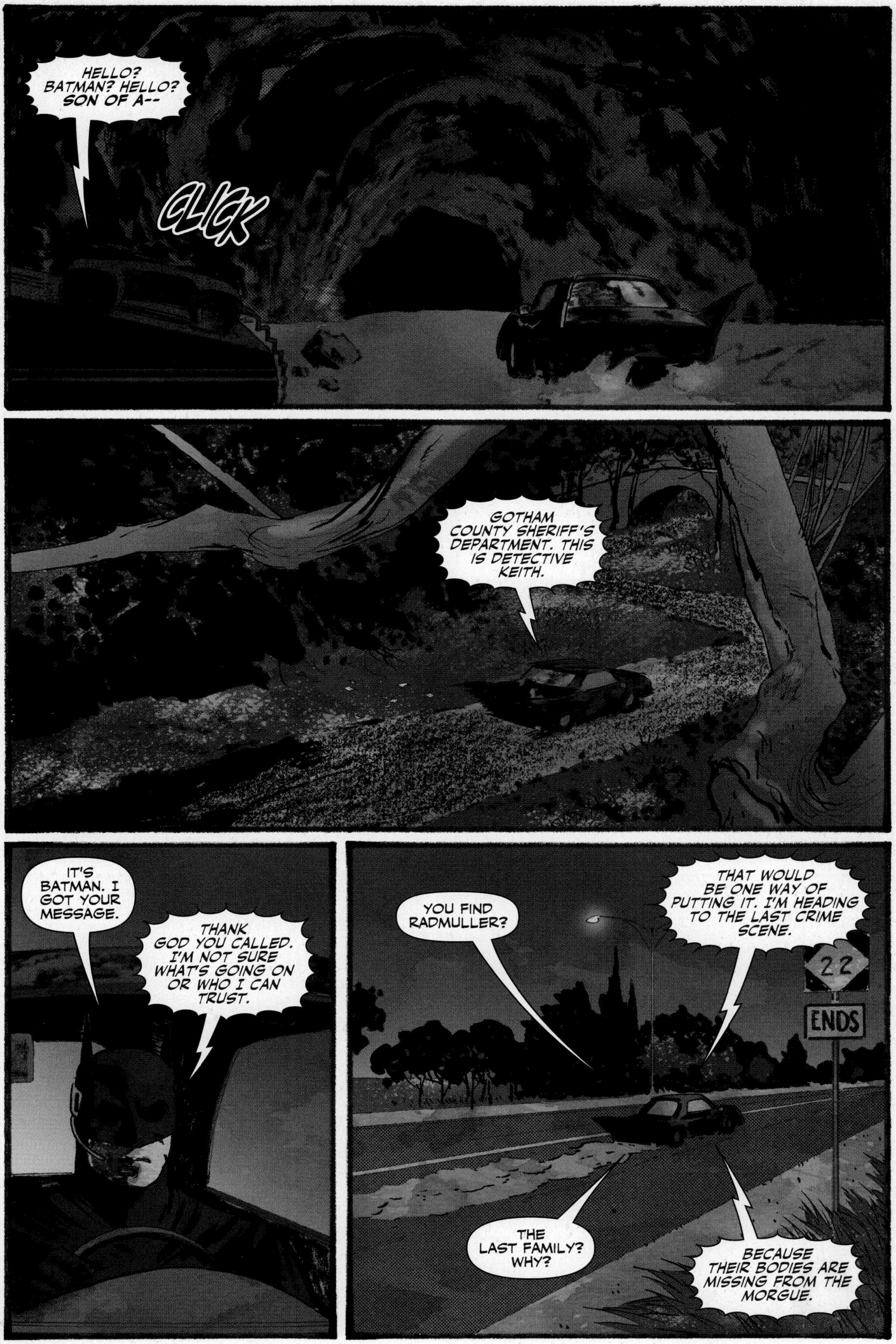

HELLO? BATMAN? HELLO? SON OF A--
CLICK
GOTHAM COUNTY SHERIFF'S DEPARTMENT. THIS IS DETECTIVE KEITH.
IT'S BATMAN. I GOT YOUR MESSAGE.
THANK GOD YOU CALLED. I'M NOT SURE WHAT'S GOING ON OR WHO I CAN TRUST.
YOU FIND RADMULLER?
THAT WOULD BE ONE WAY OF PUTTING IT. I'M HEADING TO THE LAST CRIME SCENE.
22
ENDS
THE LAST FAMILY? WHY?
BECAUSE THEIR BODIES ARE MISSING FROM THE MORGUE.

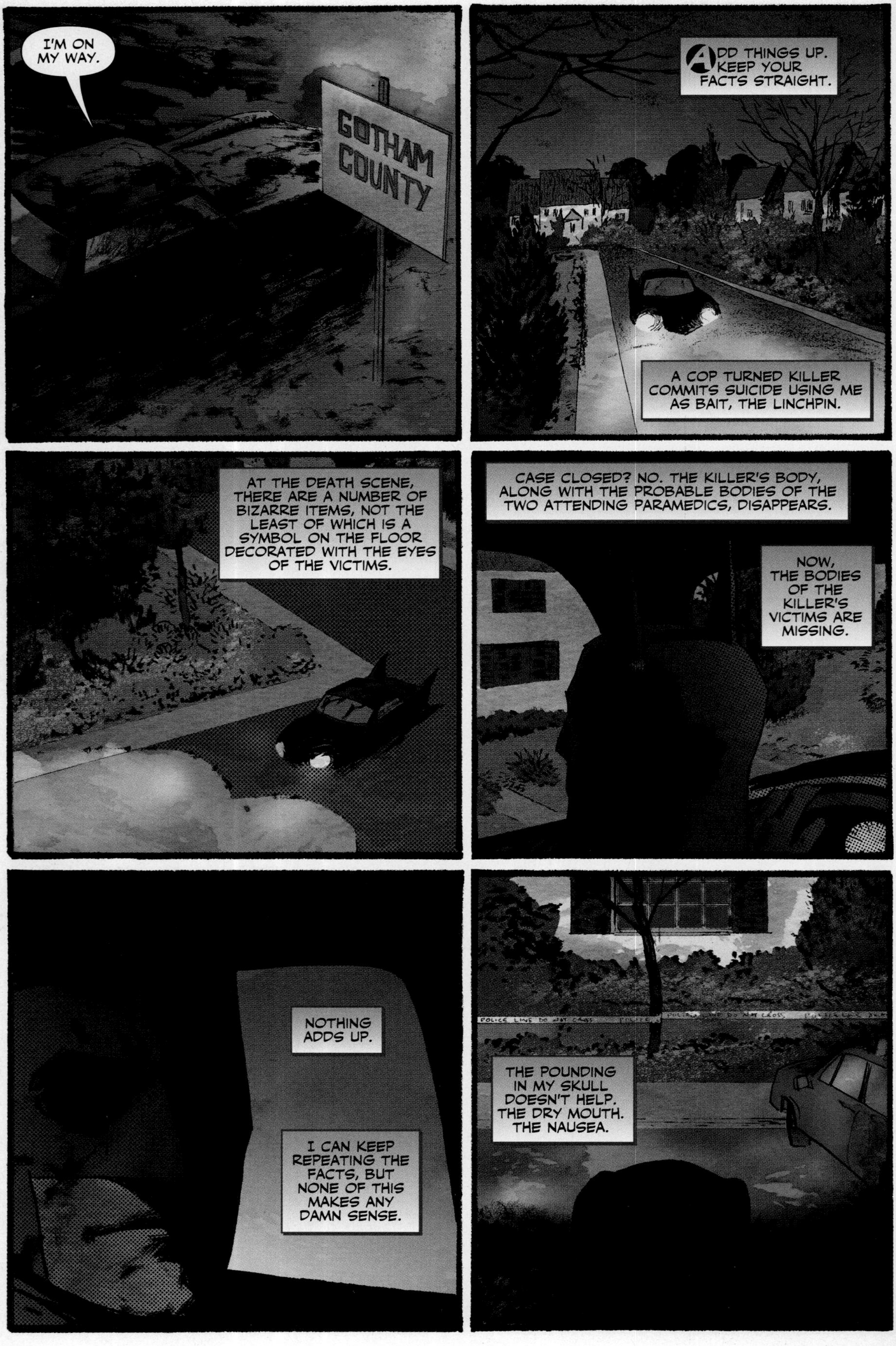
I'M ON MY WAY.
GOTHAM COUNTY
ADD THINGS UP. KEEP YOUR FACTS STRAIGHT.
A COP TURNED KILLER COMMITS SUICIDE USING ME AS BAIT, THE LINCHPIN.
AT THE DEATH SCENE, THERE ARE A NUMBER OF BIZARRE ITEMS, NOT THE LEAST OF WHICH IS A SYMBOL ON THE FLOOR DECORATED WITH THE EYES OF THE VICTIMS.
CASE CLOSED? NO. THE KILLER'S BODY, ALONG WITH THE PROBABLE BODIES OF THE TWO ATTENDING PARAMEDICS, DISAPPEARS.
NOW, THE BODIES OF THE KILLER'S VICTIMS ARE MISSING.
NOTHING ADDS UP.
I CAN KEEP REPEATING THE FACTS, BUT NONE OF THIS MAKES ANY DAMN SENSE.
THE POUNDING IN MY SKULL DOESN'T HELP. THE DRY MOUTH. THE NAUSEA.

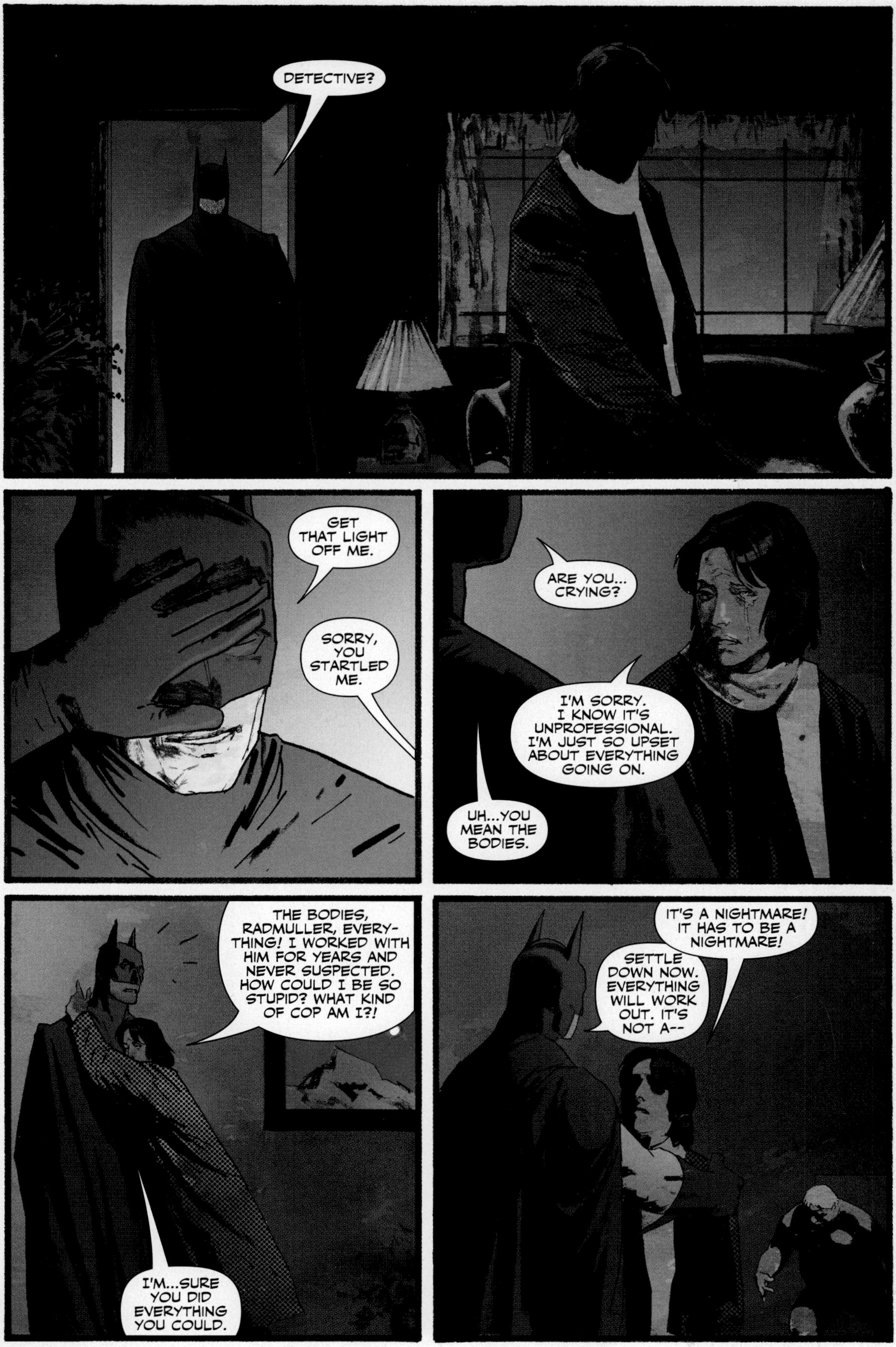
DETECTIVE?
GET THAT LIGHT OFF ME.
SORRY, YOU STARTLED ME.
ARE YOU... CRYING?
I'M SORRY. I KNOW IT'S UNPROFESSIONAL. I'M JUST SO UPSET ABOUT EVERYTHING GOING ON.
UH...YOU MEAN THE BODIES.
THE BODIES, RADMULLER, EVERY-THING! I WORKED WITH HIM FOR YEARS AND NEVER SUSPECTED. HOW COULD I BE SO STUPID? WHAT KIND OF COP AM I?!
I'M...SURE YOU DID EVERYTHING YOU COULD.
IT'S A NIGHTMARE! IT HAS TO BE A NIGHTMARE!
SETTLE DOWN NOW. EVERYTHING WILL WORK OUT. IT'S NOT A--

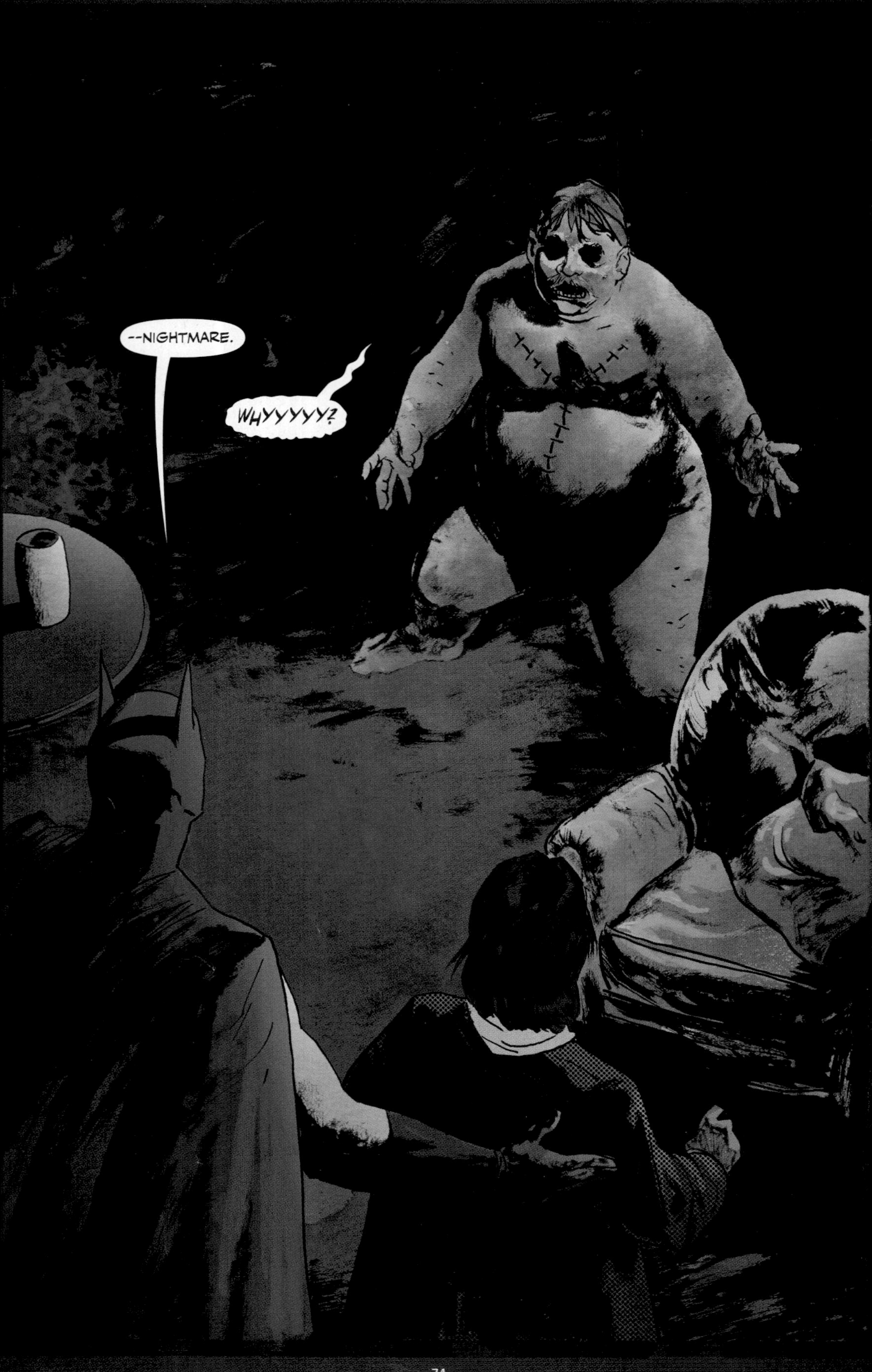
--NIGHTMARE.
WHYYYYY?

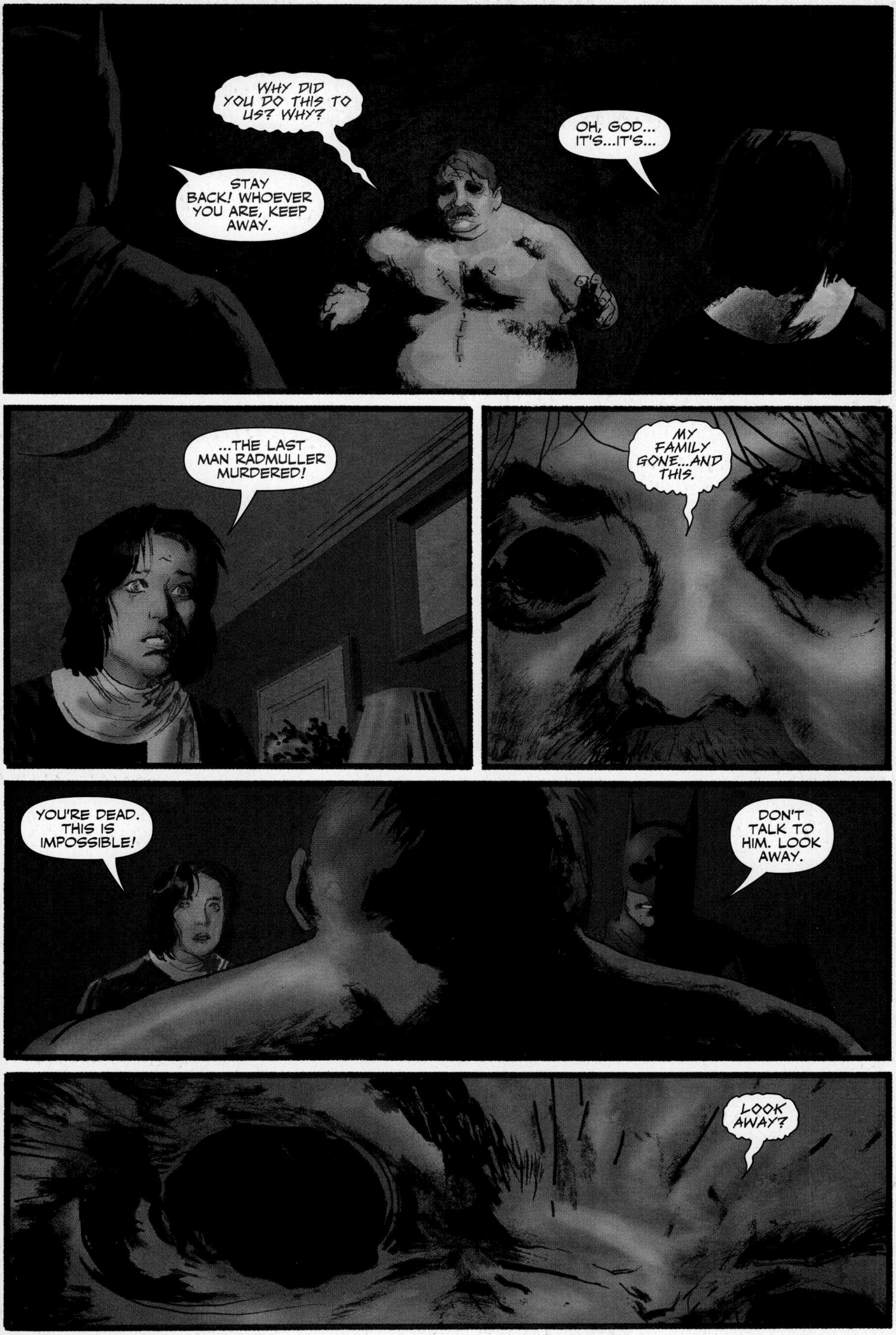
WHY DID YOU DO THIS TO US? WHY?
STAY BACK! WHOEVER YOU ARE, KEEP AWAY.
OH, GOD... IT'S...IT'S...
...THE LAST MAN RADMULLER MURDERED!
MY FAMILY GONE...AND THIS.
YOU'RE DEAD. THIS IS IMPOSSIBLE!
DON'T TALK TO HIM. LOOK AWAY.
LOOK AWAY?

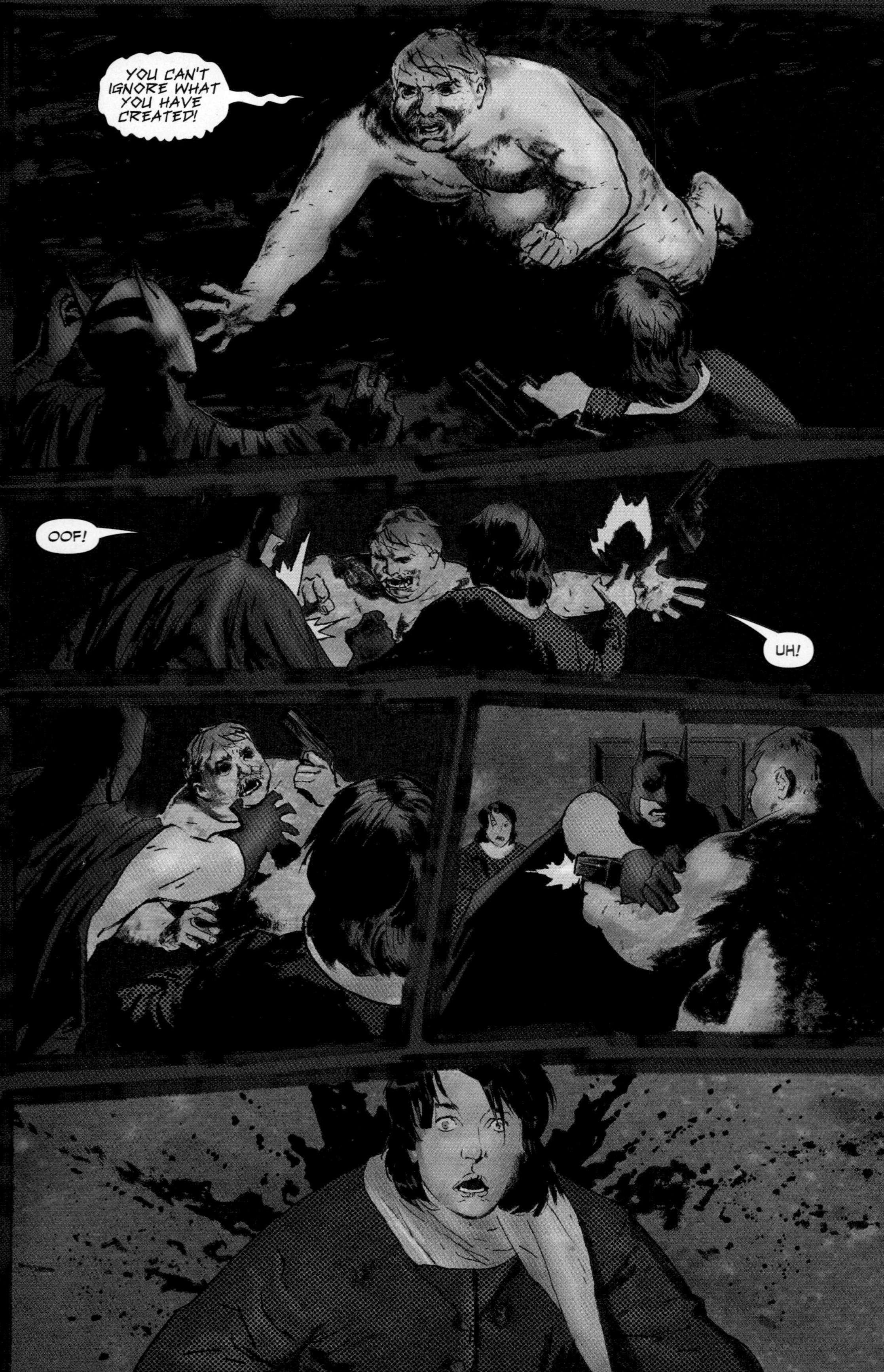
YOU CAN'T IGNORE WHAT YOU HAVE CREATED!
OOF!
UH!

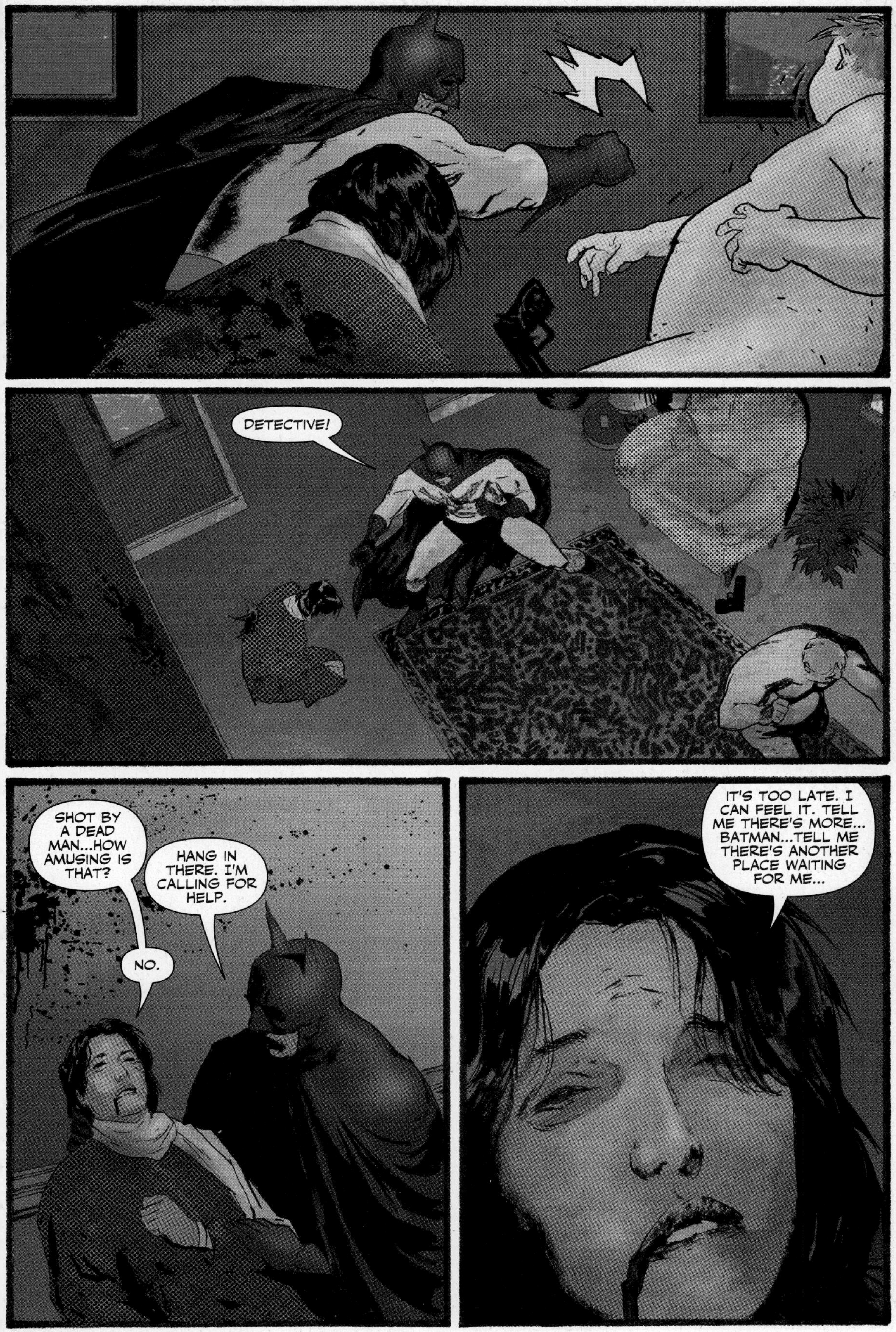
DETECTIVE!
SHOT BY A DEAD MAN...HOW AMUSING IS THAT?
HANG IN THERE. I'M CALLING FOR HELP.
NO.
IT'S TOO LATE. I CAN FEEL IT. TELL ME THERE'S MORE... BATMAN...TELL ME THERE'S ANOTHER PLACE WAITING FOR ME...

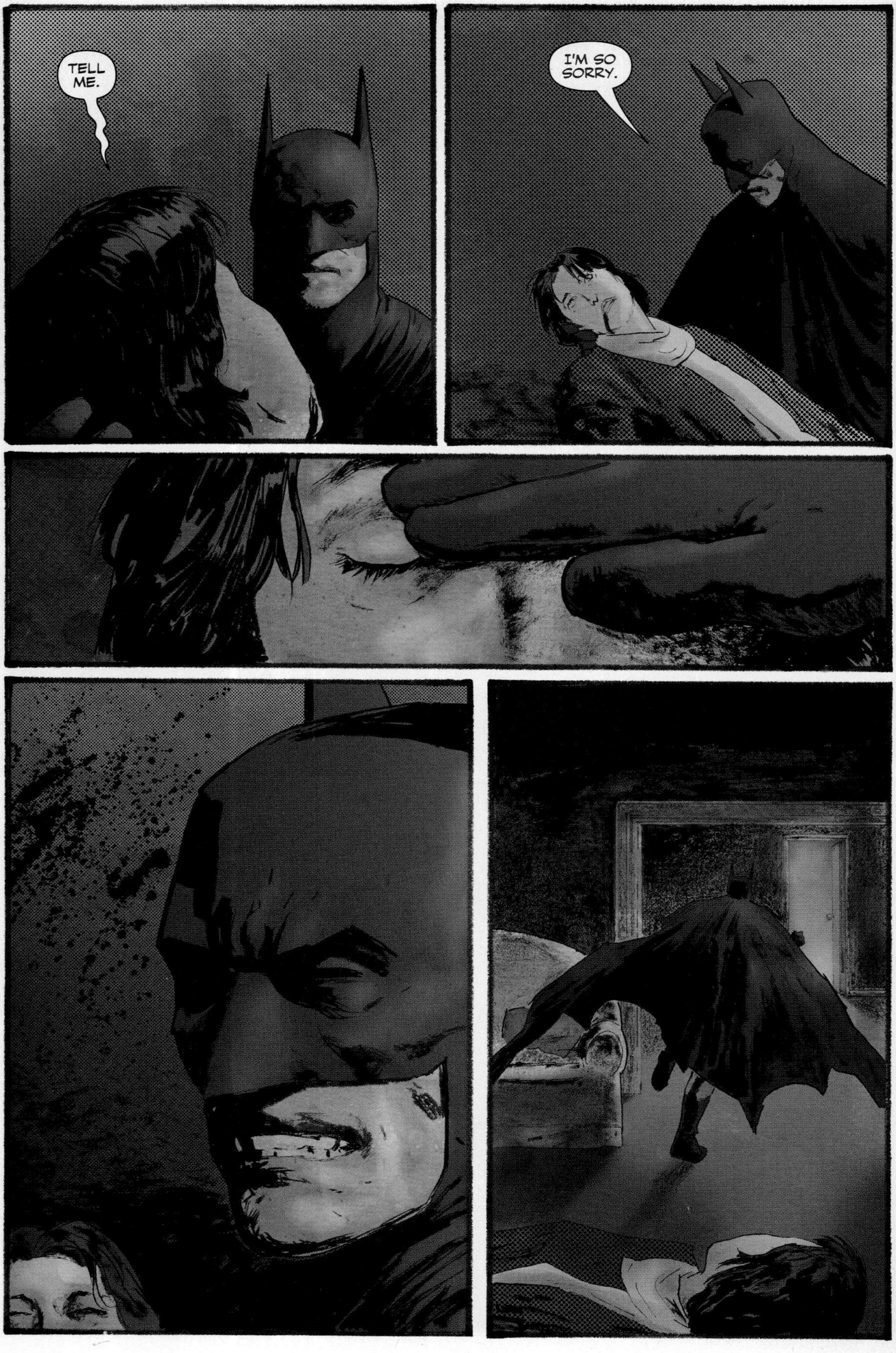
TELL ME.
I'M SO SORRY.

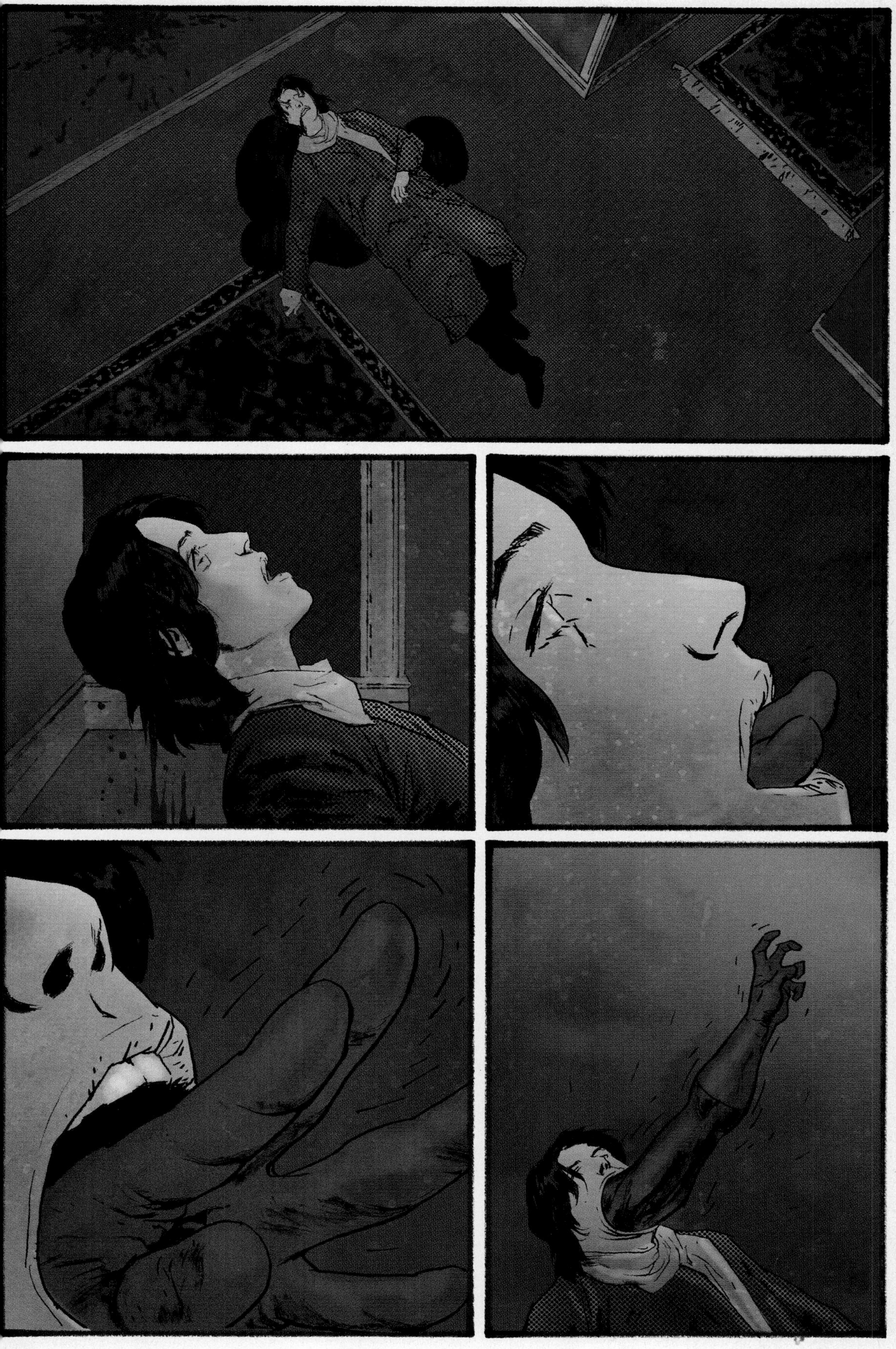

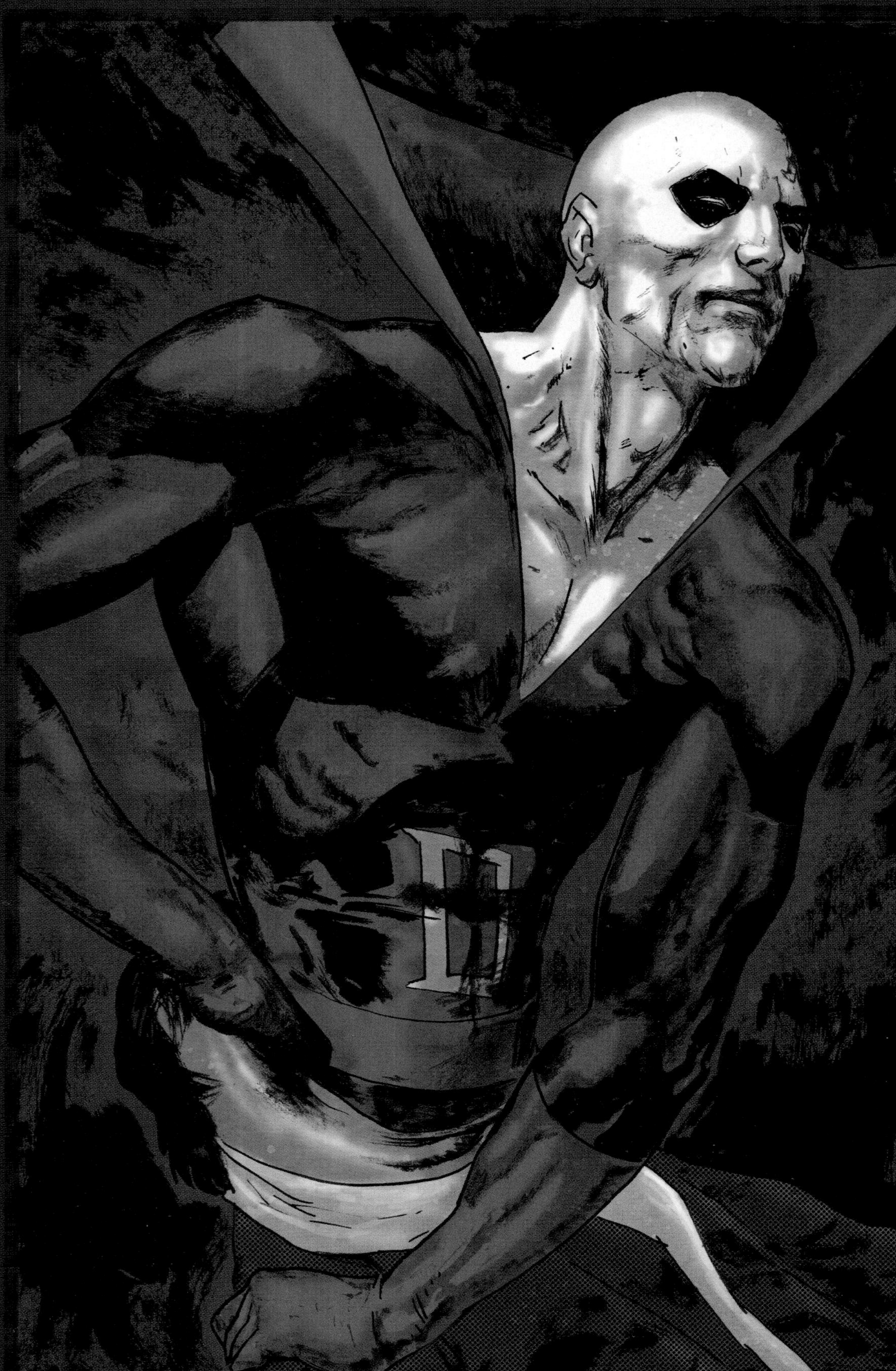

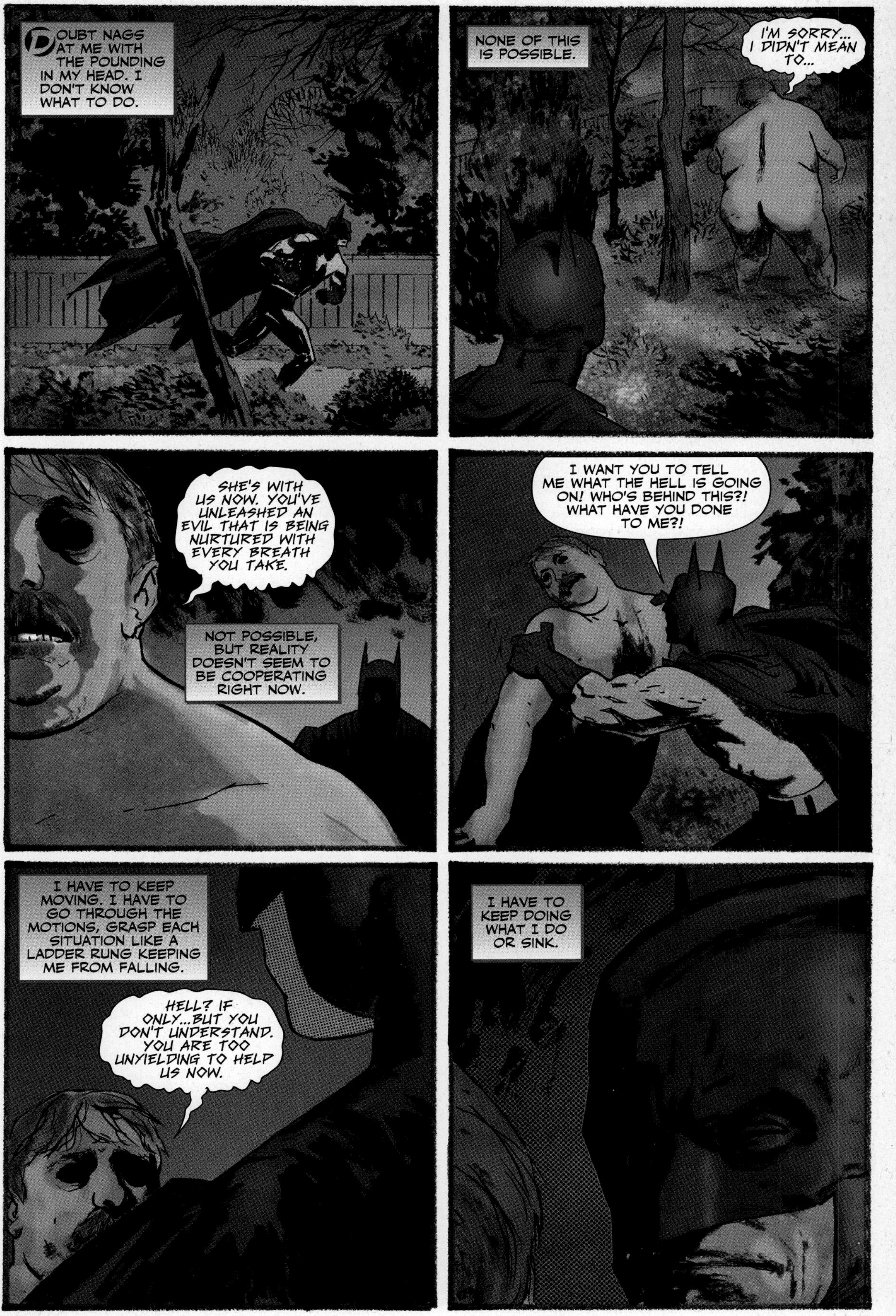
DOUBT NAGS AT ME WITH THE POUNDING IN MY HEAD. I DON'T KNOW WHAT TO DO.
NONE OF THIS IS POSSIBLE.
I'M SORRY... I DIDN'T MEAN TO...
SHE'S WITH US NOW. YOU'VE UNLEASHED AN EVIL THAT IS BEING NURTURED WITH EVERY BREATH YOU TAKE.
NOT POSSIBLE, BUT REALITY DOESN'T SEEM TO BE COOPERATING RIGHT NOW.
I WANT YOU TO TELL ME WHAT THE HELL IS GOING ON! WHO'S BEHIND THIS?! WHAT HAVE YOU DONE TO ME?!
I HAVE TO KEEP MOVING. I HAVE TO GO THROUGH THE MOTIONS, GRASP EACH SITUATION LIKE A LADDER RUNG KEEPING ME FROM FALLING.
HELL? IF ONLY...BUT YOU DON'T UNDERSTAND. YOU ARE TOO UNYIELDING TO HELP US NOW.
I HAVE TO KEEP DOING WHAT I DO OR SINK.

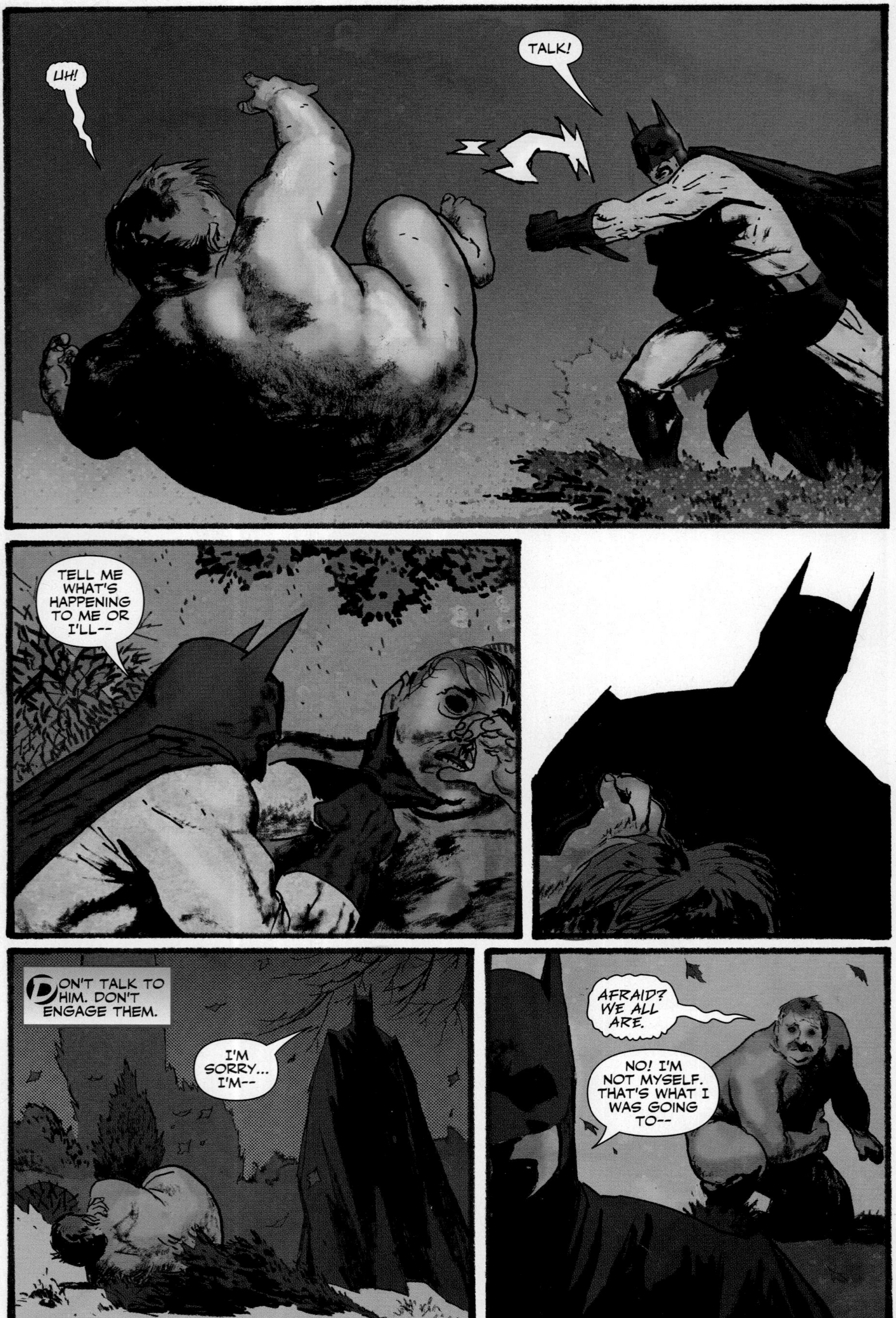
UH!
TALK!
TELL ME WHAT'S HAPPENING TO ME OR I'LL--
DON'T TALK TO HIM. DON'T ENGAGE THEM.
I'M SORRY... I'M--
AFRAID? WE ALL ARE.
NO! I'M NOT MYSELF. THAT'S WHAT I WAS GOING TO--

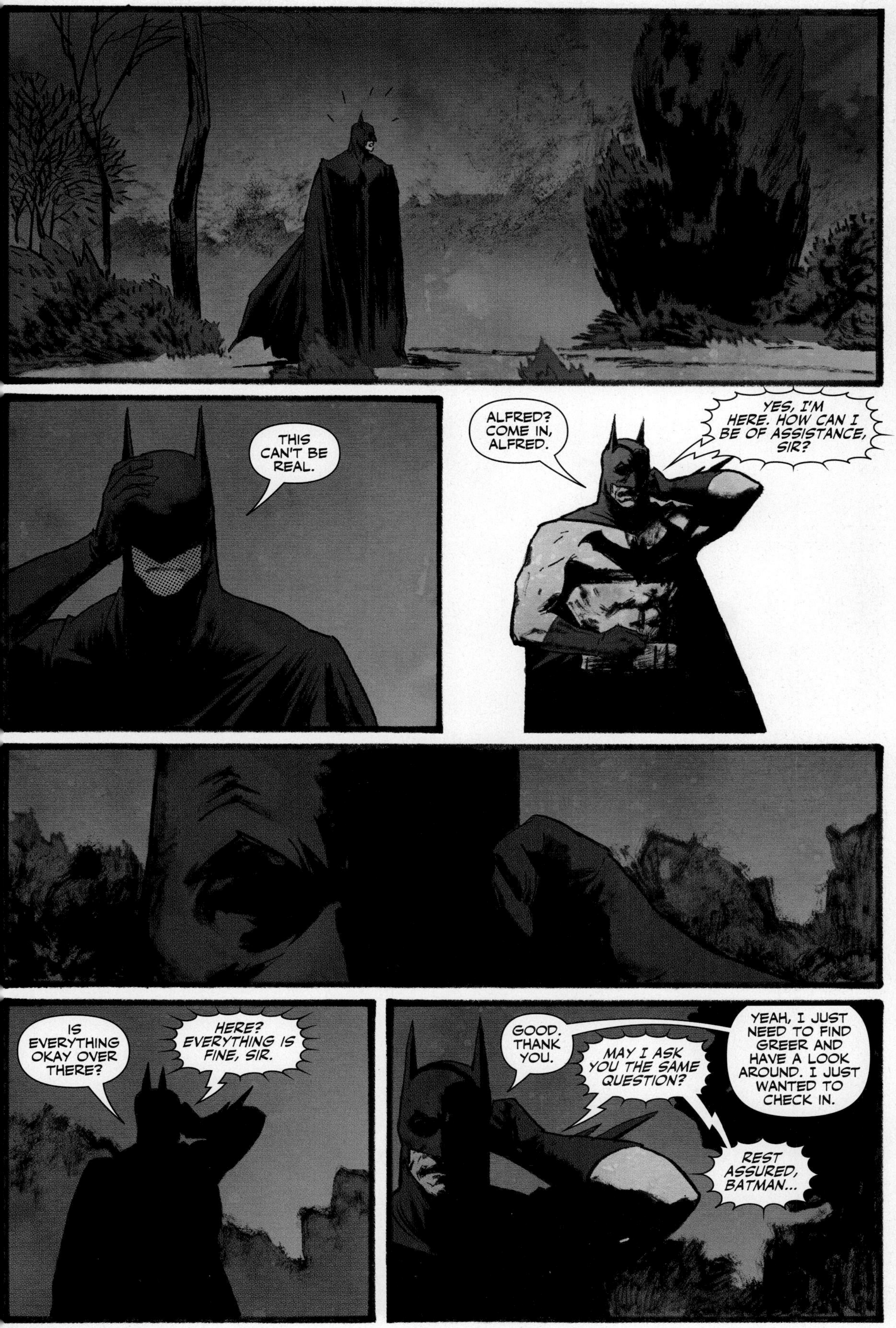
THIS CAN'T BE REAL.
ALFRED? COME IN, ALFRED.
YES, I'M HERE. HOW CAN I BE OF ASSISTANCE, SIR?
IS EVERYTHING OKAY OVER THERE?
HERE? EVERYTHING IS FINE, SIR.
GOOD. THANK YOU.
MAY I ASK YOU THE SAME QUESTION?
YEAH, I JUST NEED TO FIND GREER AND HAVE A LOOK AROUND. I JUST WANTED TO CHECK IN.
REST ASSURED, BATMAN...

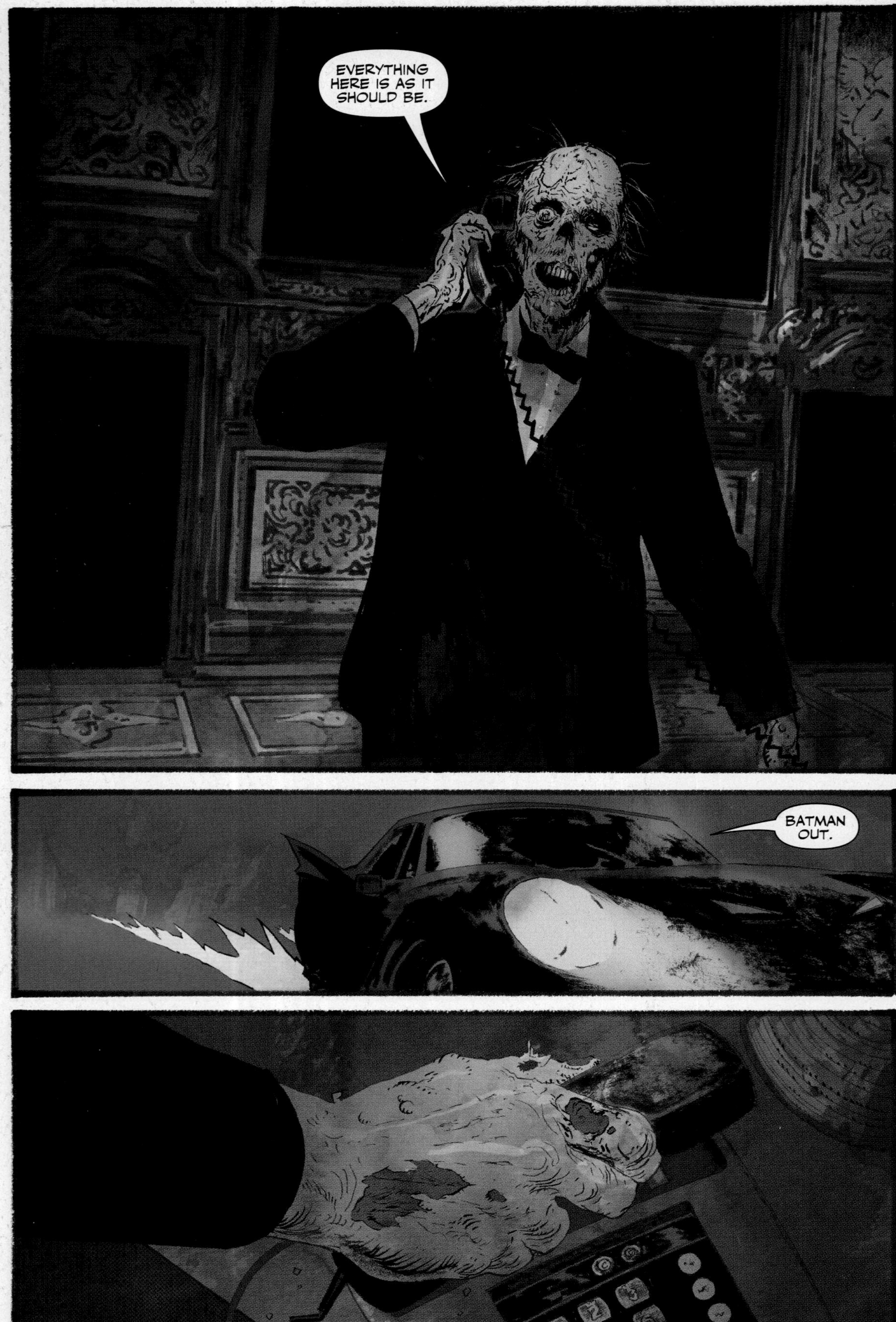
EVERYTHING HERE IS AS IT SHOULD BE.
BATMAN OUT.

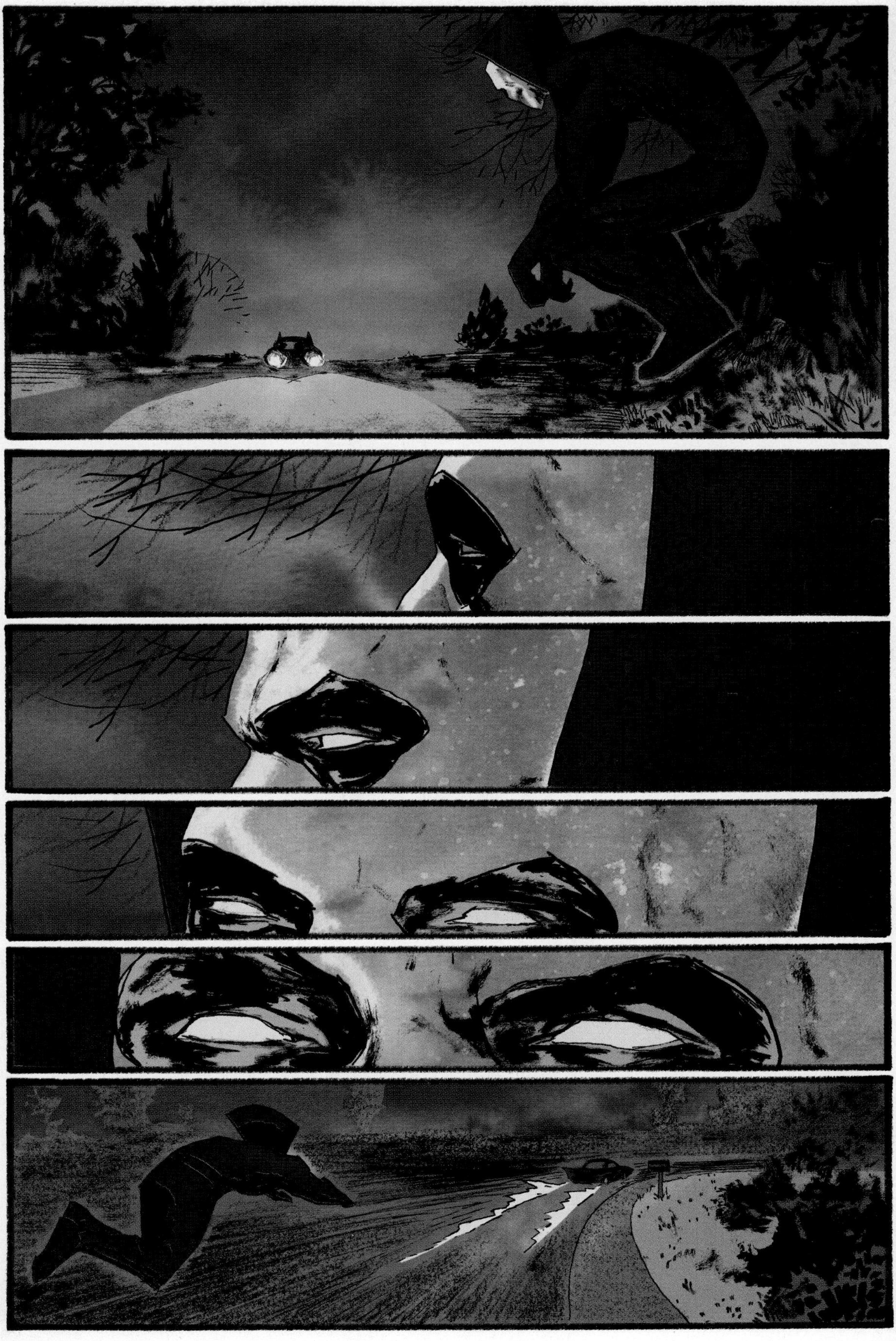

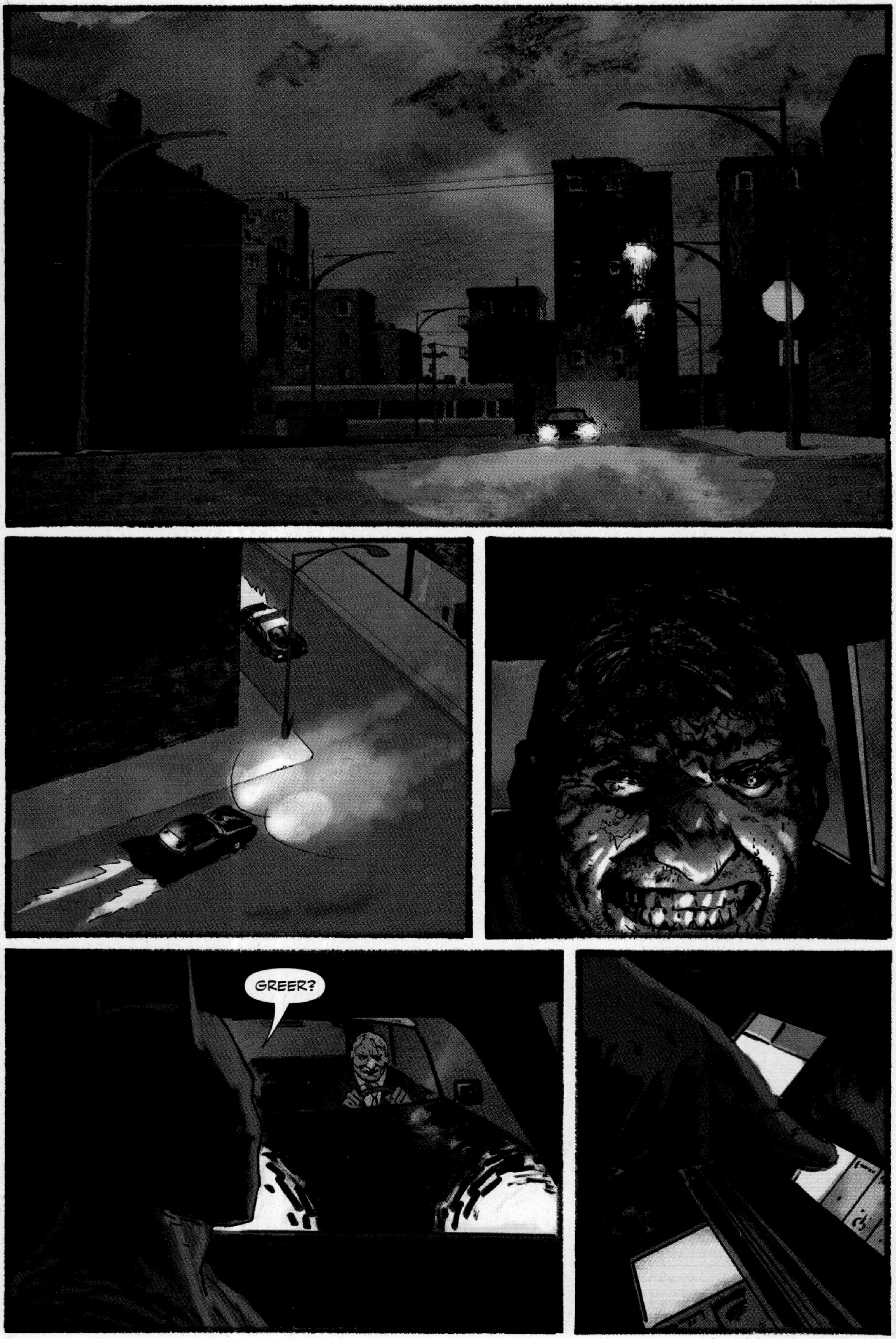
GREER?

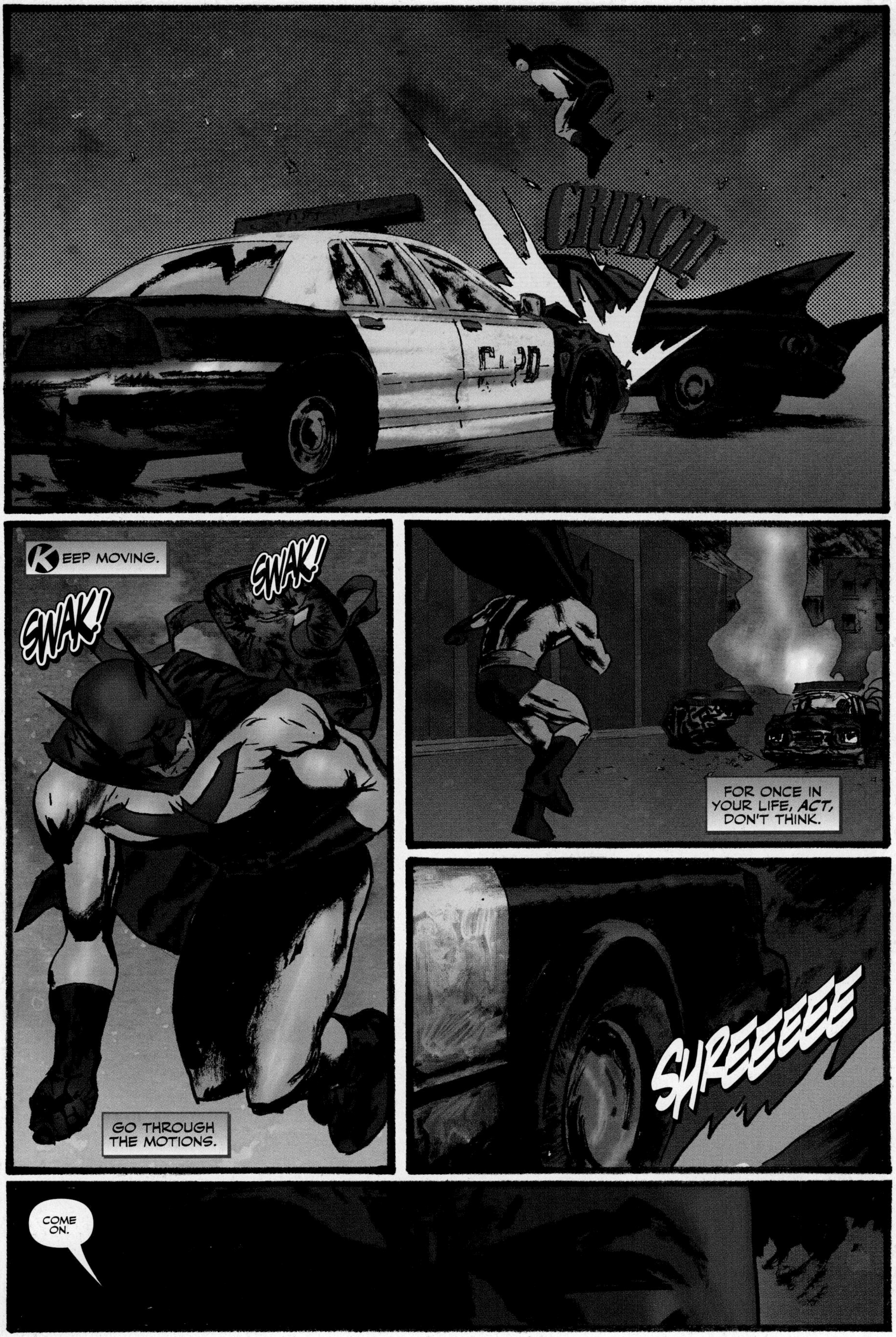
CRUNCH!
KEEP MOVING.
SWAK!
SWAK!
GO THROUGH THE MOTIONS.
FOR ONCE IN YOUR LIFE, ACT, DON'T THINK.
SHREEEEE
COME ON.

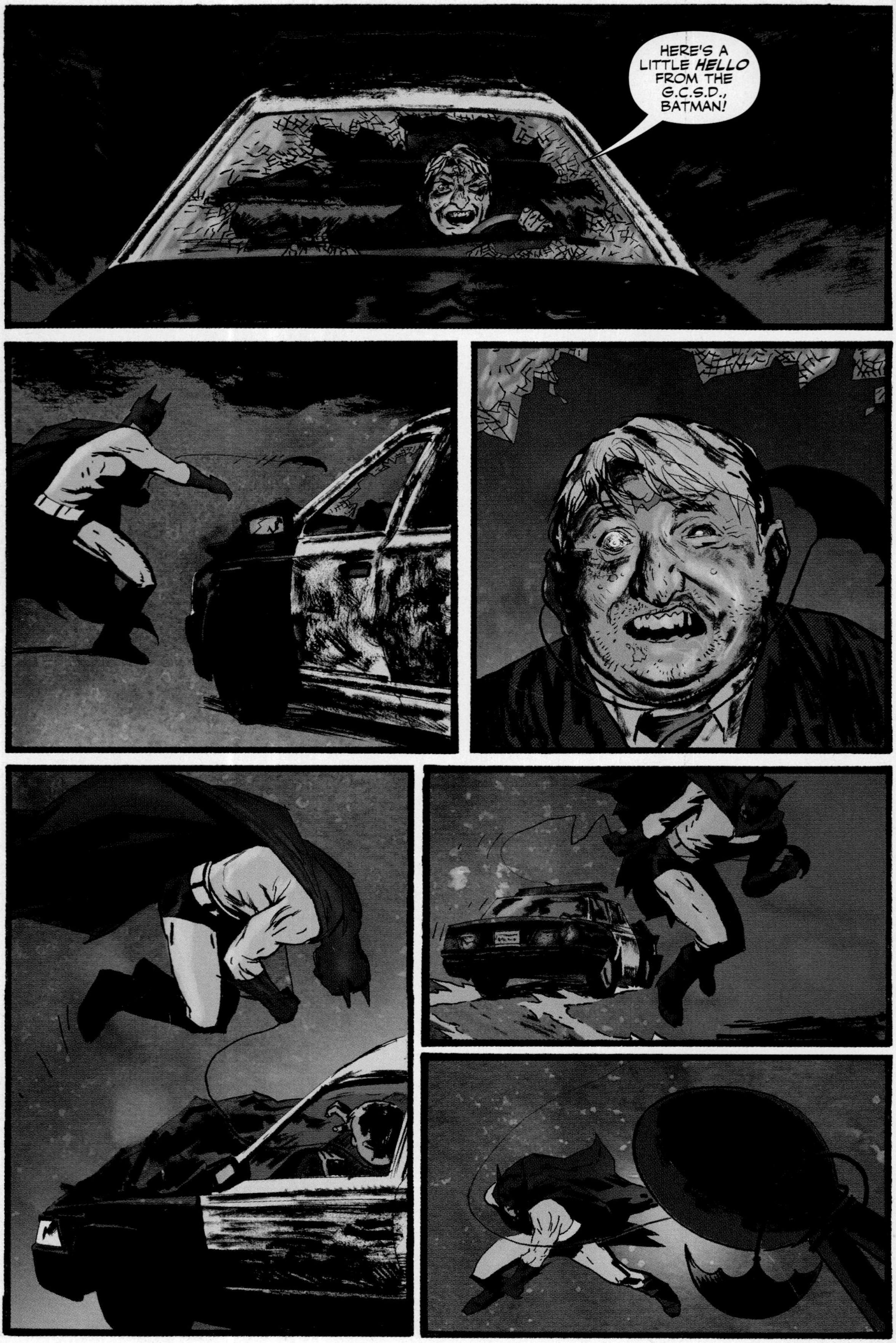
HERE'S A LITTLE *HELLO* FROM THE G.C.S.D., BATMAN!

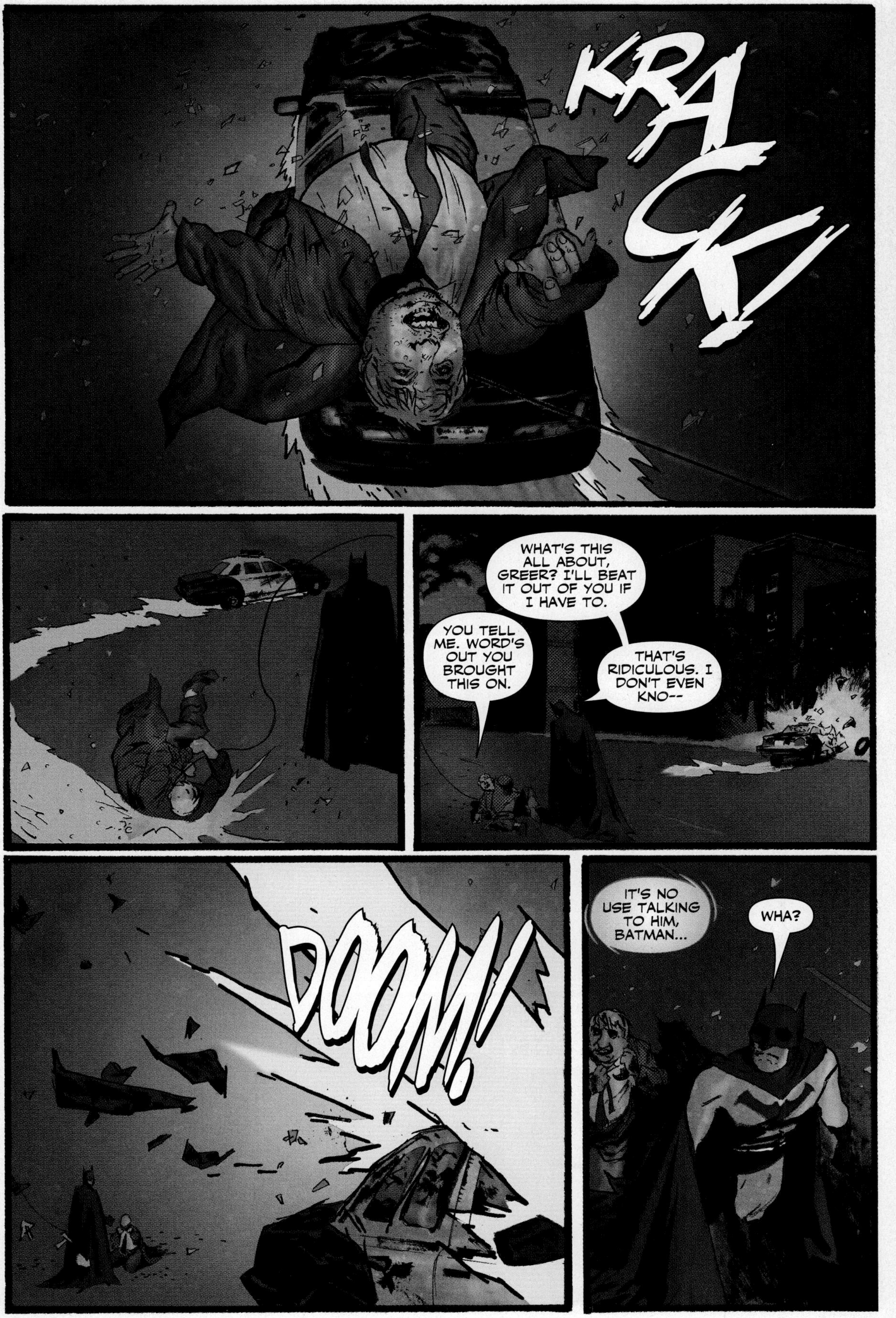
KRACK!
WHAT'S THIS ALL ABOUT, GREER? I'LL BEAT IT OUT OF YOU IF I HAVE TO.
YOU TELL ME. WORD'S OUT YOU BROUGHT THIS ON.
THAT'S RIDICULOUS. I DON'T EVEN KNO--
DOOM!
IT'S NO USE TALKING TO HIM, BATMAN...
WHA?

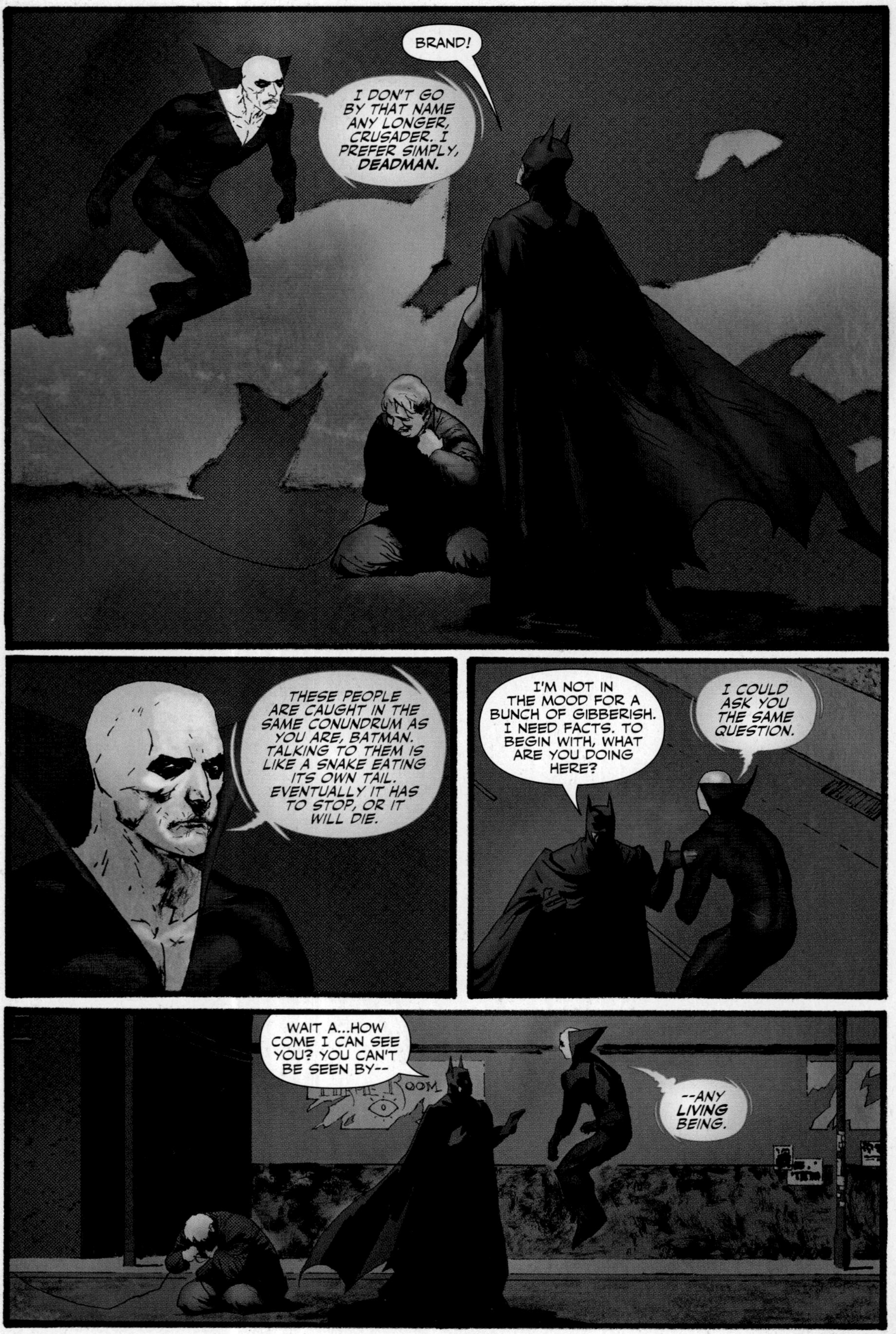
BRAND!
I DON'T GO BY THAT NAME ANY LONGER, CRUSADER. I PREFER SIMPLY, DEADMAN.
THESE PEOPLE ARE CAUGHT IN THE SAME CONUNDRUM AS YOU ARE, BATMAN. TALKING TO THEM IS LIKE A SNAKE EATING ITS OWN TAIL. EVENTUALLY IT HAS TO STOP, OR IT WILL DIE.
I'M NOT IN THE MOOD FOR A BUNCH OF GIBBERISH. I NEED FACTS. TO BEGIN WITH, WHAT ARE YOU DOING HERE?
I COULD ASK YOU THE SAME QUESTION.
WAIT A...HOW COME I CAN SEE YOU? YOU CAN'T BE SEEN BY--
--ANY LIVING BEING.

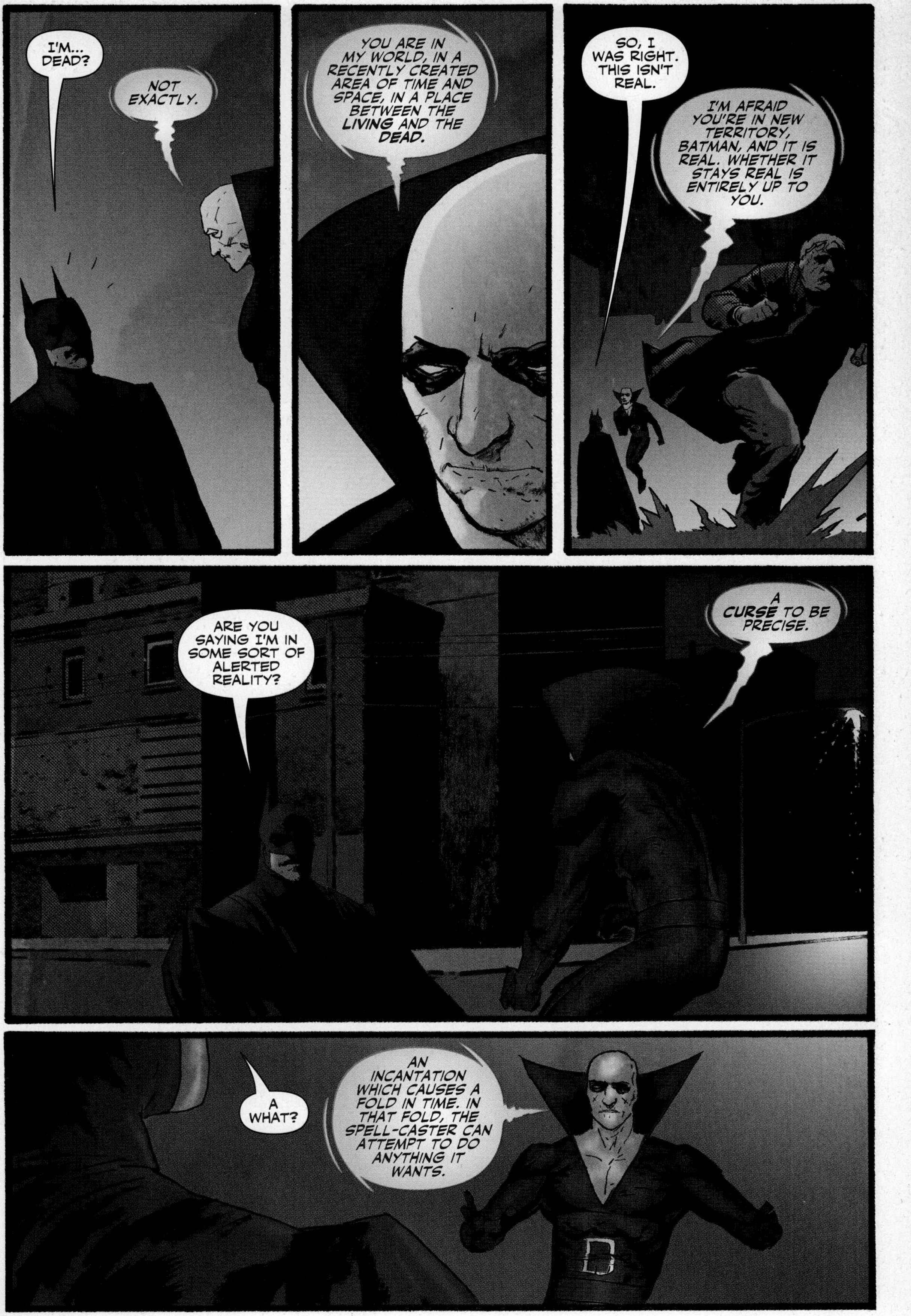
I'M... DEAD?
NOT EXACTLY.
YOU ARE IN MY WORLD, IN A RECENTLY CREATED AREA OF TIME AND SPACE, IN A PLACE BETWEEN THE LIVING AND THE DEAD.
SO, I WAS RIGHT. THIS ISN'T REAL.
I'M AFRAID YOU'RE IN NEW TERRITORY, BATMAN, AND IT IS REAL. WHETHER IT STAYS REAL IS ENTIRELY UP TO YOU.
ARE YOU SAYING I'M IN SOME SORT OF ALERTED REALITY?
A CURSE TO BE PRECISE.
A WHAT?
AN INCANTATION WHICH CAUSES A FOLD IN TIME. IN THAT FOLD, THE SPELL-CASTER CAN ATTEMPT TO DO ANYTHING IT WANTS.

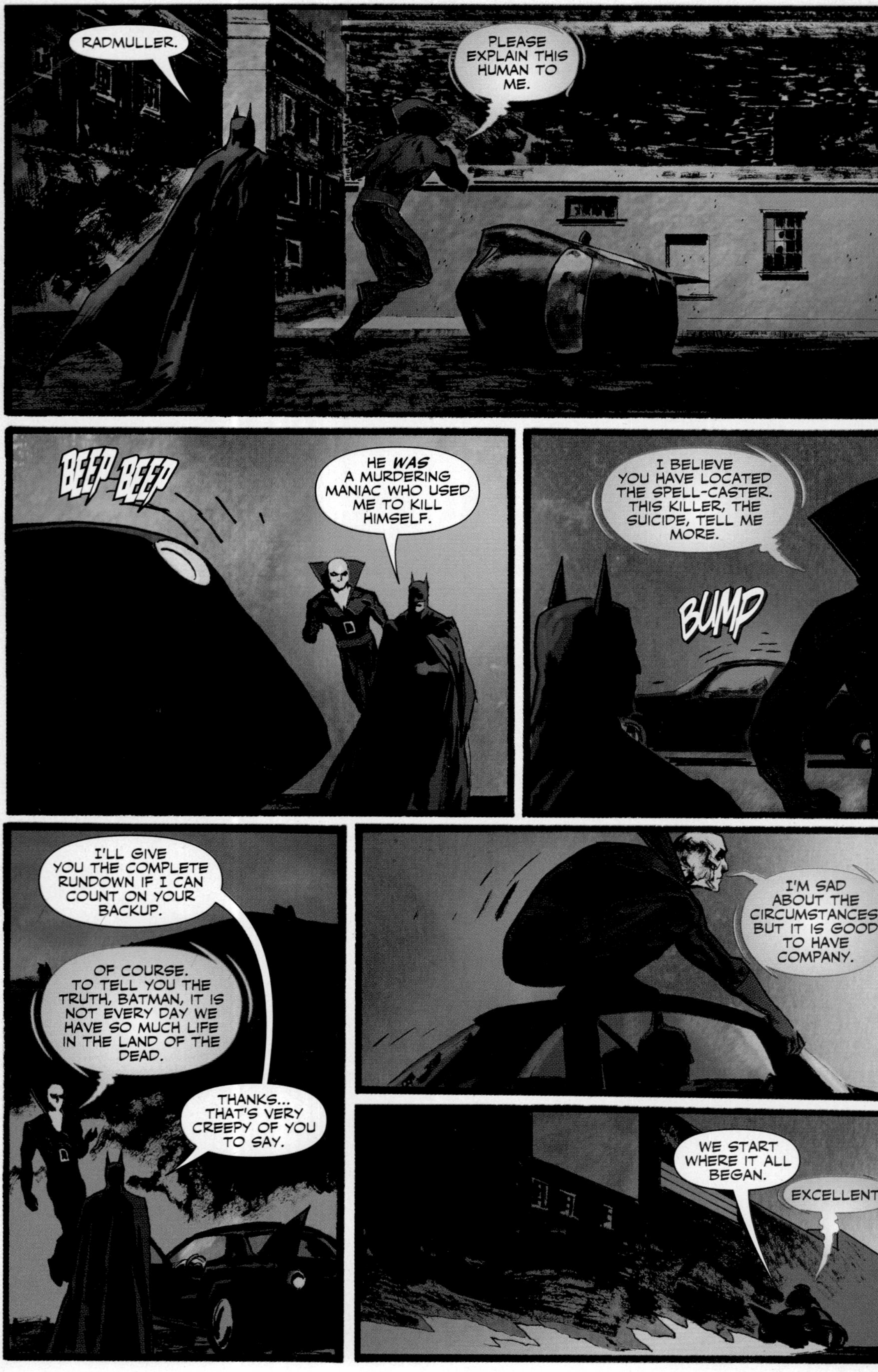
RADMULLER.
PLEASE EXPLAIN THIS HUMAN TO ME.
BEEP BEEP
HE WAS A MURDERING MANIAC WHO USED ME TO KILL HIMSELF.
I BELIEVE YOU HAVE LOCATED THE SPELL-CASTER. THIS KILLER, THE SUICIDE, TELL ME MORE.
BUMP
I'LL GIVE YOU THE COMPLETE RUNDOWN IF I CAN COUNT ON YOUR BACKUP.
OF COURSE. TO TELL YOU THE TRUTH, BATMAN, IT IS NOT EVERY DAY WE HAVE SO MUCH LIFE IN THE LAND OF THE DEAD.
THANKS... THAT'S VERY CREEPY OF YOU TO SAY.
I'M SAD ABOUT THE CIRCUMSTANCES, BUT IT IS GOOD TO HAVE COMPANY.
WE START WHERE IT ALL BEGAN.
EXCELLENT.

WHAT IS THIS PLACE?

WHERE RADMULLER LIVED, WHERE HE DUPED ME INTO KILLING HIM.

YOU SEEM IN HIGHER SPIRITS.

I KNOW MORE THAN I DID TEN MINUTES AGO. FACTS MAKE ME HAPPY.

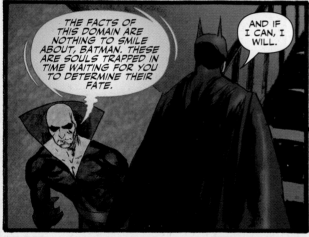

THE FACTS OF THIS DOMAIN ARE NOTHING TO SMILE ABOUT, BATMAN. THESE ARE SOULS TRAPPED IN TIME WAITING FOR YOU TO DETERMINE THEIR FATE.

AND IF I CAN, I WILL.

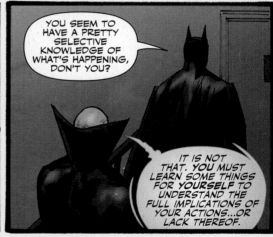

YOU SEEM TO HAVE A PRETTY SELECTIVE KNOWLEDGE OF WHAT'S HAPPENING, DON'T YOU?

IT IS NOT THAT. YOU MUST LEARN SOME THINGS FOR YOURSELF TO UNDERSTAND THE FULL IMPLICATIONS OF YOUR ACTIONS...OR LACK THEREOF.

YOU LIVE IN A VERY SMALL WORLD FOR A MAN OF SUCH KNOWLEDGE. YOU ARE TOO CONFINED BY YOUR OWN IMAGINATION, RULES AND BOUNDARIES WHICH HAVE NOTHING TO DO WITH THE SITUATION YOU ARE COMBATING.

BUT YOU WILL SEE FOR YOURSELF...

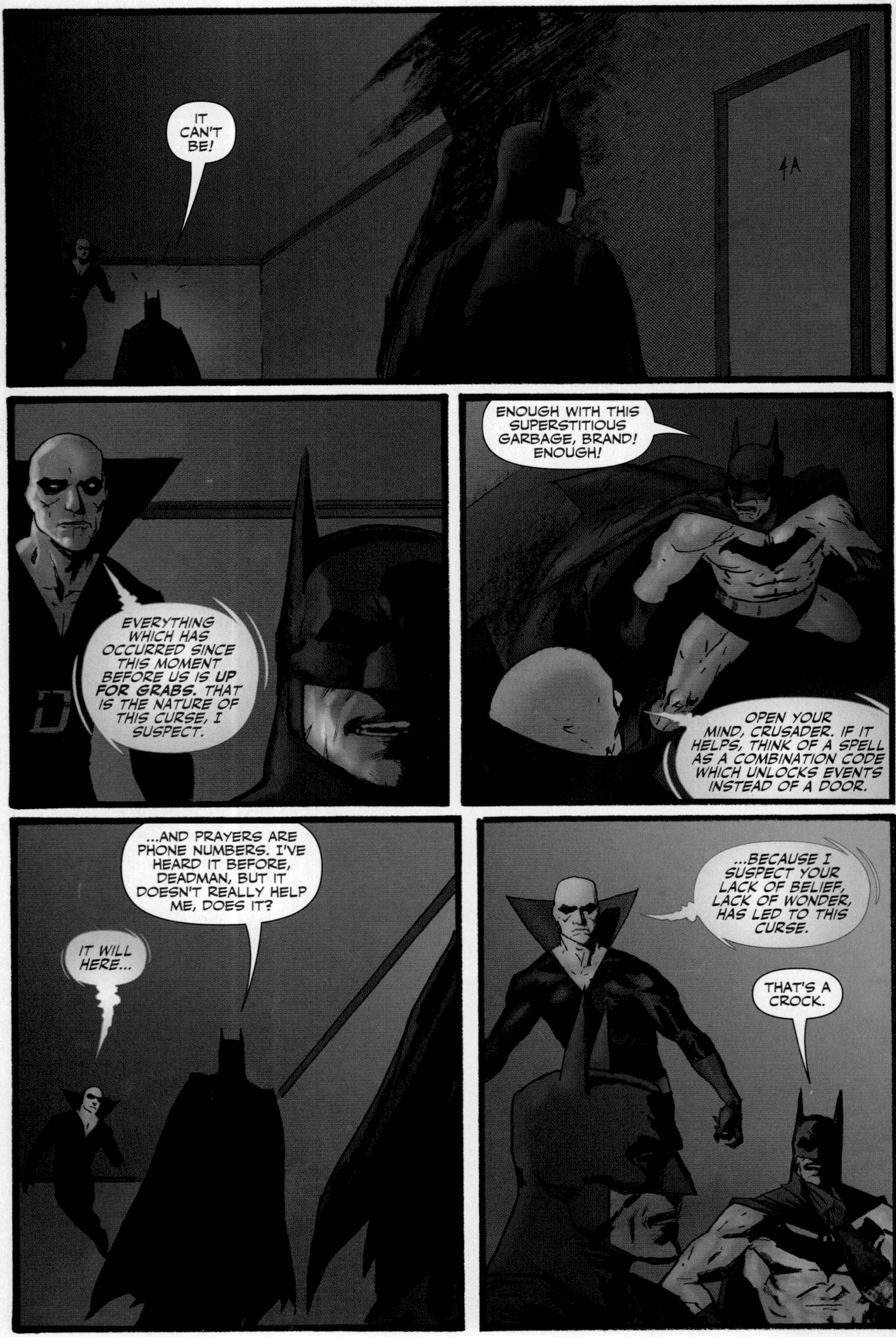
IT CAN'T BE!
EVERYTHING WHICH HAS OCCURRED SINCE THIS MOMENT BEFORE US IS UP FOR GRABS. THAT IS THE NATURE OF THIS CURSE, I SUSPECT.
ENOUGH WITH THIS SUPERSTITIOUS GARBAGE, BRAND! ENOUGH!
OPEN YOUR MIND, CRUSADER. IF IT HELPS, THINK OF A SPELL AS A COMBINATION CODE WHICH UNLOCKS EVENTS INSTEAD OF A DOOR.
...AND PRAYERS ARE PHONE NUMBERS. I'VE HEARD IT BEFORE, DEADMAN, BUT IT DOESN'T REALLY HELP ME, DOES IT?
IT WILL HERE...
...BECAUSE I SUSPECT YOUR LACK OF BELIEF, LACK OF WONDER, HAS LED TO THIS CURSE.
THAT'S A CROCK.

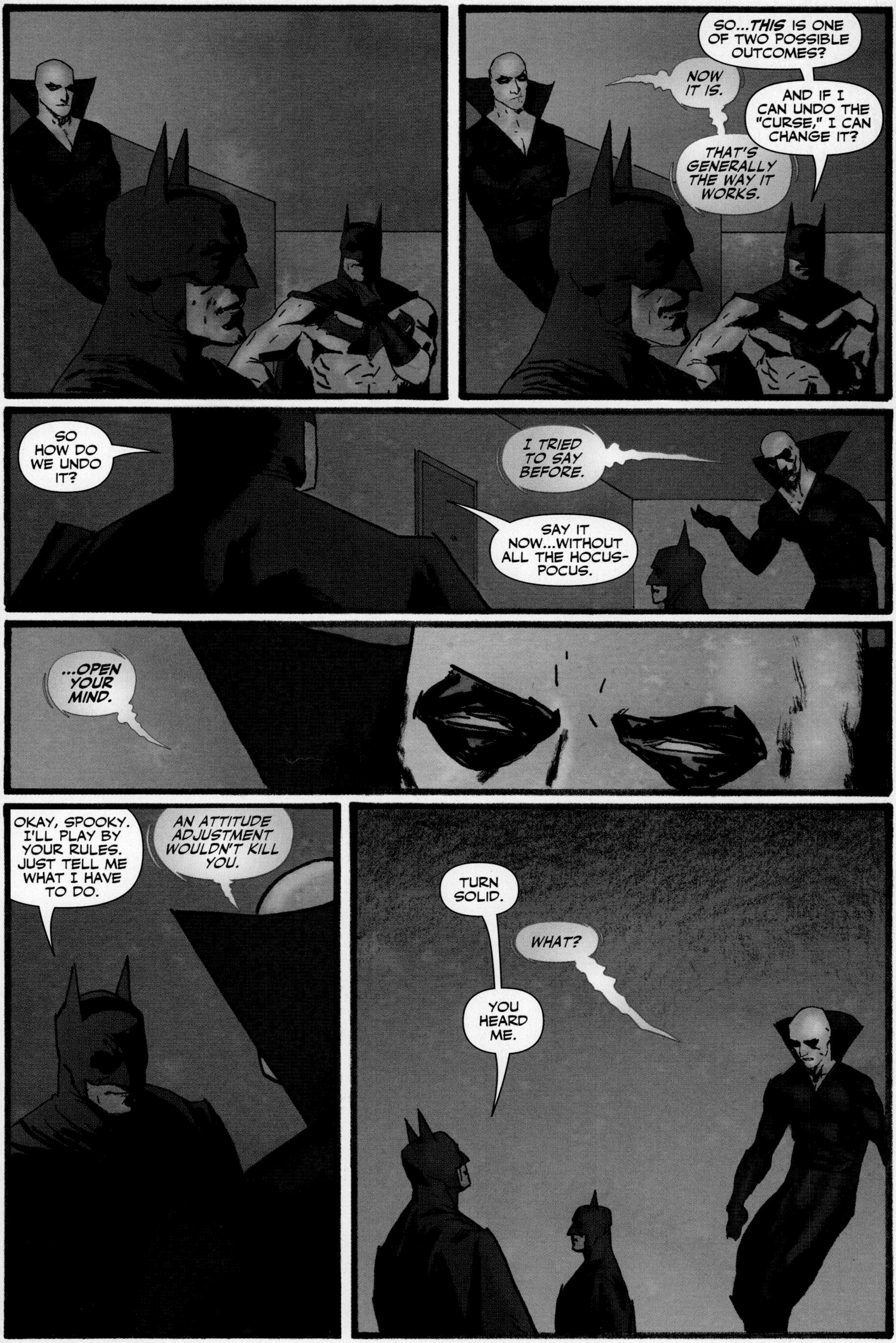
SO...THIS IS ONE OF TWO POSSIBLE OUTCOMES?
NOW IT IS.
AND IF I CAN UNDO THE "CURSE," I CAN CHANGE IT?
THAT'S GENERALLY THE WAY IT WORKS.
SO HOW DO WE UNDO IT?
I TRIED TO SAY BEFORE.
SAY IT NOW...WITHOUT ALL THE HOCUS-POCUS.
...OPEN YOUR MIND.
OKAY, SPOOKY. I'LL PLAY BY YOUR RULES. JUST TELL ME WHAT I HAVE TO DO.
AN ATTITUDE ADJUSTMENT WOULDN'T KILL YOU.
TURN SOLID.
WHAT?
YOU HEARD ME.

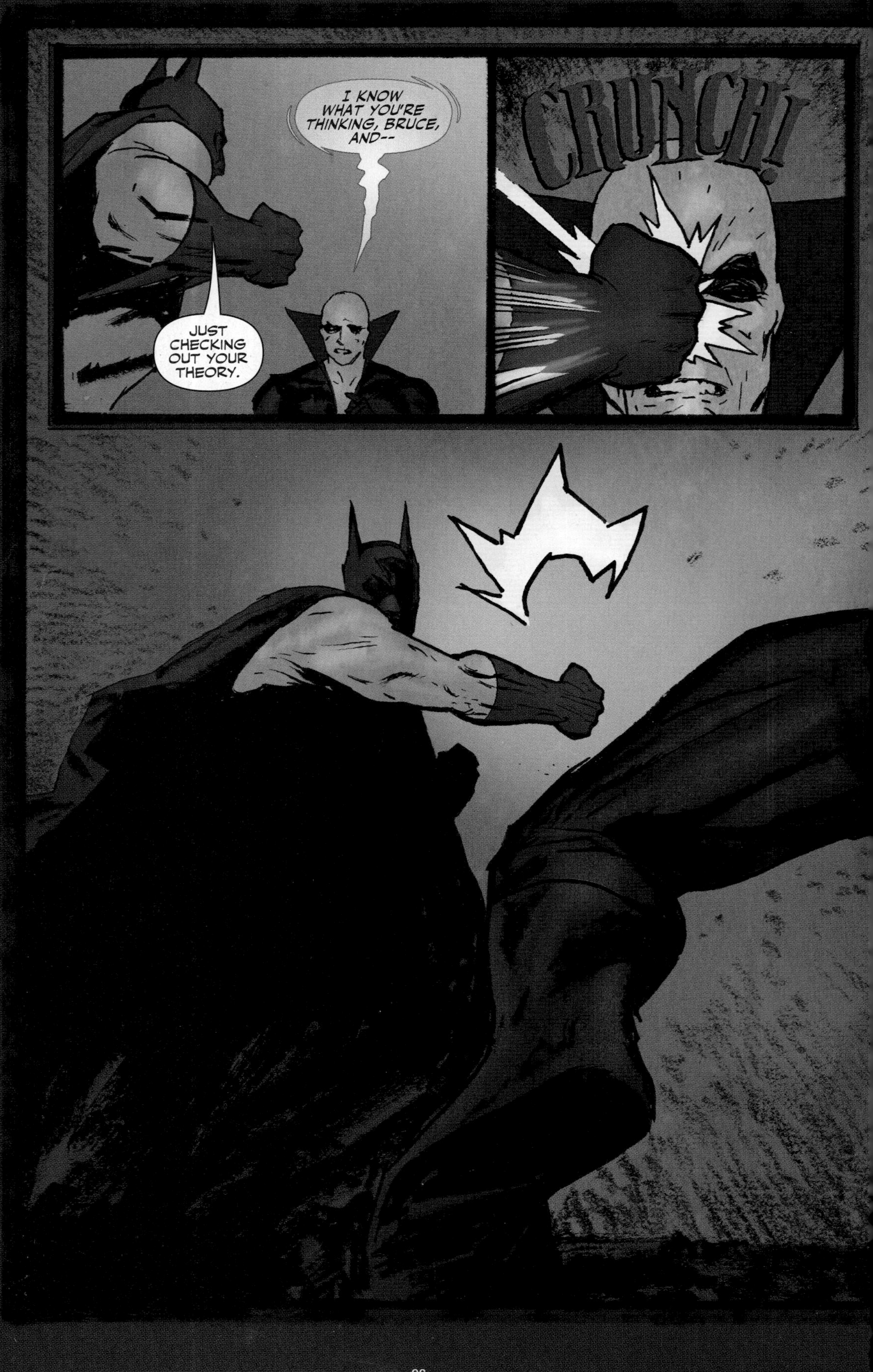
I KNOW WHAT YOU'RE THINKING, BRUCE, AND--
JUST CHECKING OUT YOUR THEORY.
CRUNCH!

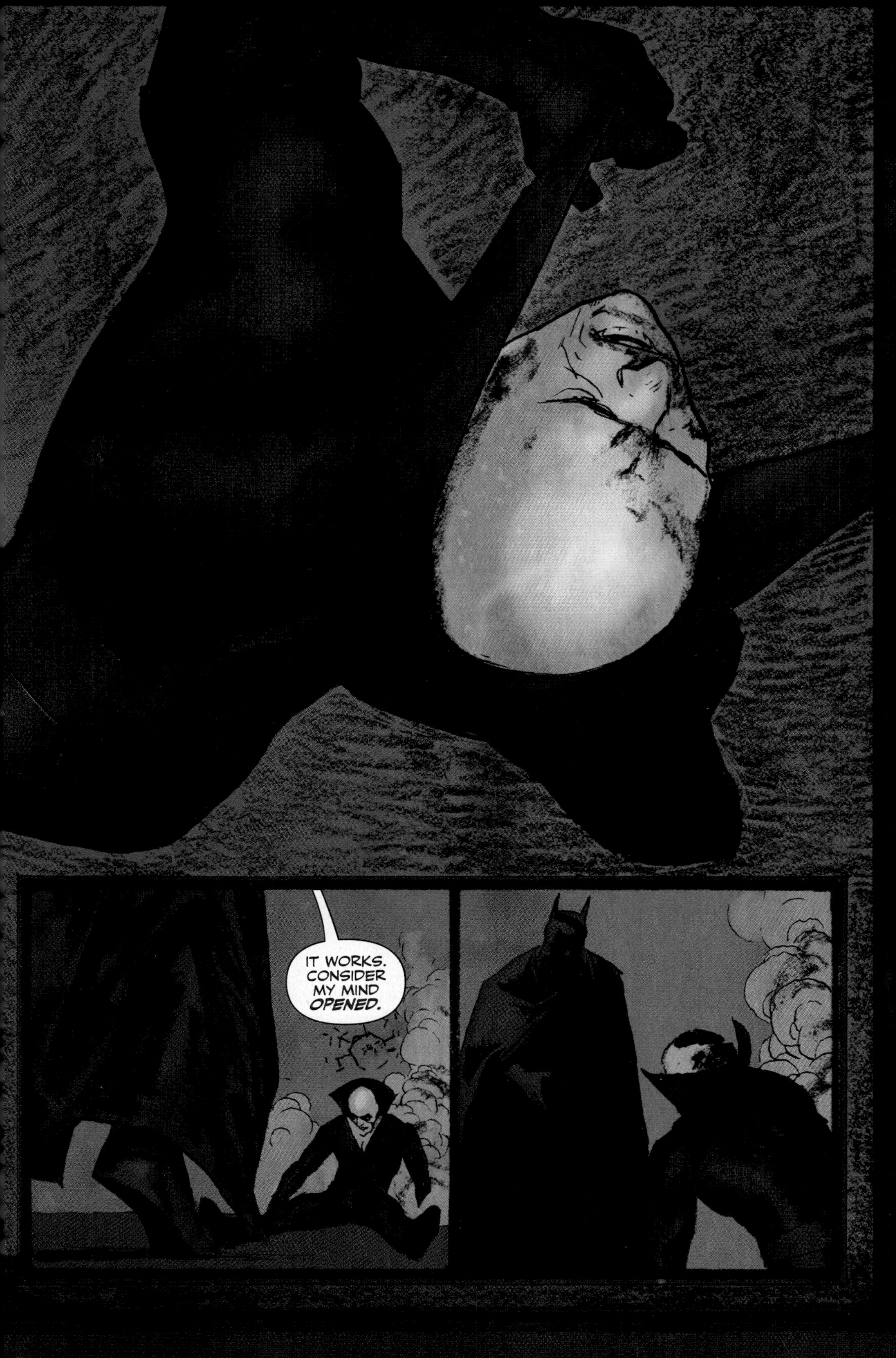
IT WORKS. CONSIDER MY MIND *OPENED*.

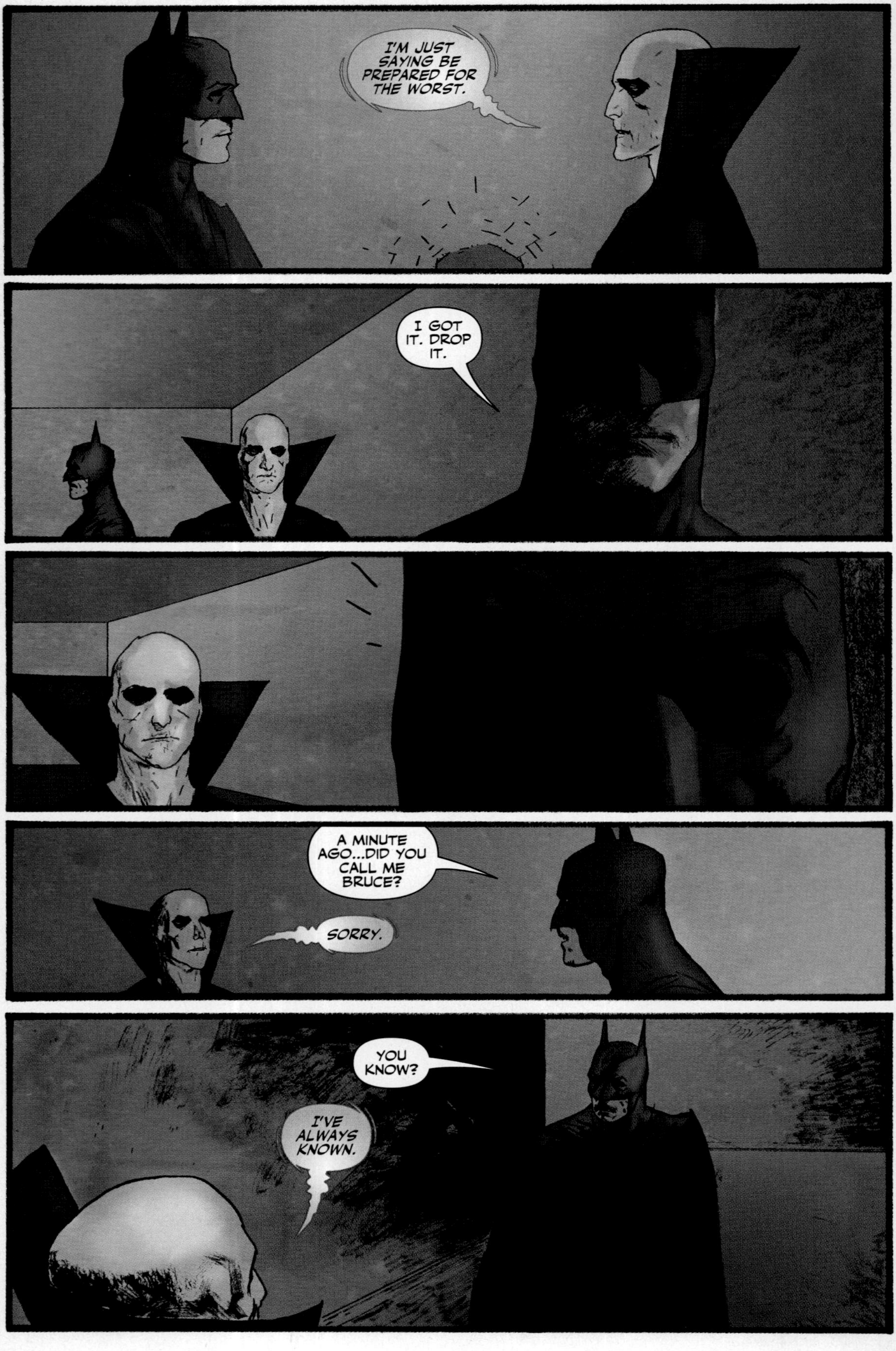
I'M JUST SAYING BE PREPARED FOR THE WORST.
I GOT IT. DROP IT.
A MINUTE AGO...DID YOU CALL ME BRUCE?
SORRY.
YOU KNOW?
I'VE ALWAYS KNOWN.

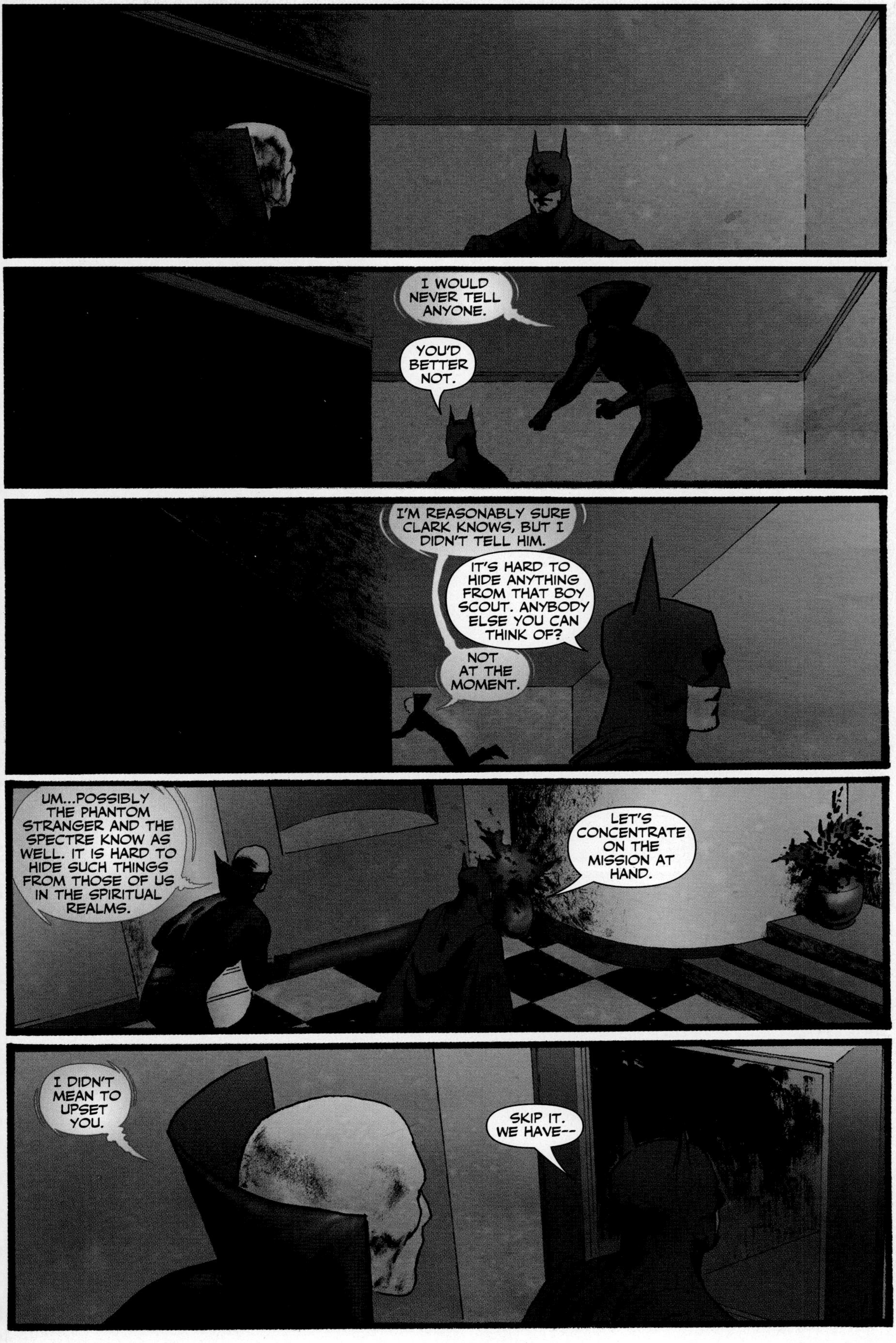
I WOULD NEVER TELL ANYONE.
YOU'D BETTER NOT.
I'M REASONABLY SURE CLARK KNOWS, BUT I DIDN'T TELL HIM.
IT'S HARD TO HIDE ANYTHING FROM THAT BOY SCOUT. ANYBODY ELSE YOU CAN THINK OF?
NOT AT THE MOMENT.
UM...POSSIBLY THE PHANTOM STRANGER AND THE SPECTRE KNOW AS WELL. IT IS HARD TO HIDE SUCH THINGS FROM THOSE OF US IN THE SPIRITUAL REALMS.
LET'S CONCENTRATE ON THE MISSION AT HAND.
I DIDN'T MEAN TO UPSET YOU.
SKIP IT. WE HAVE--

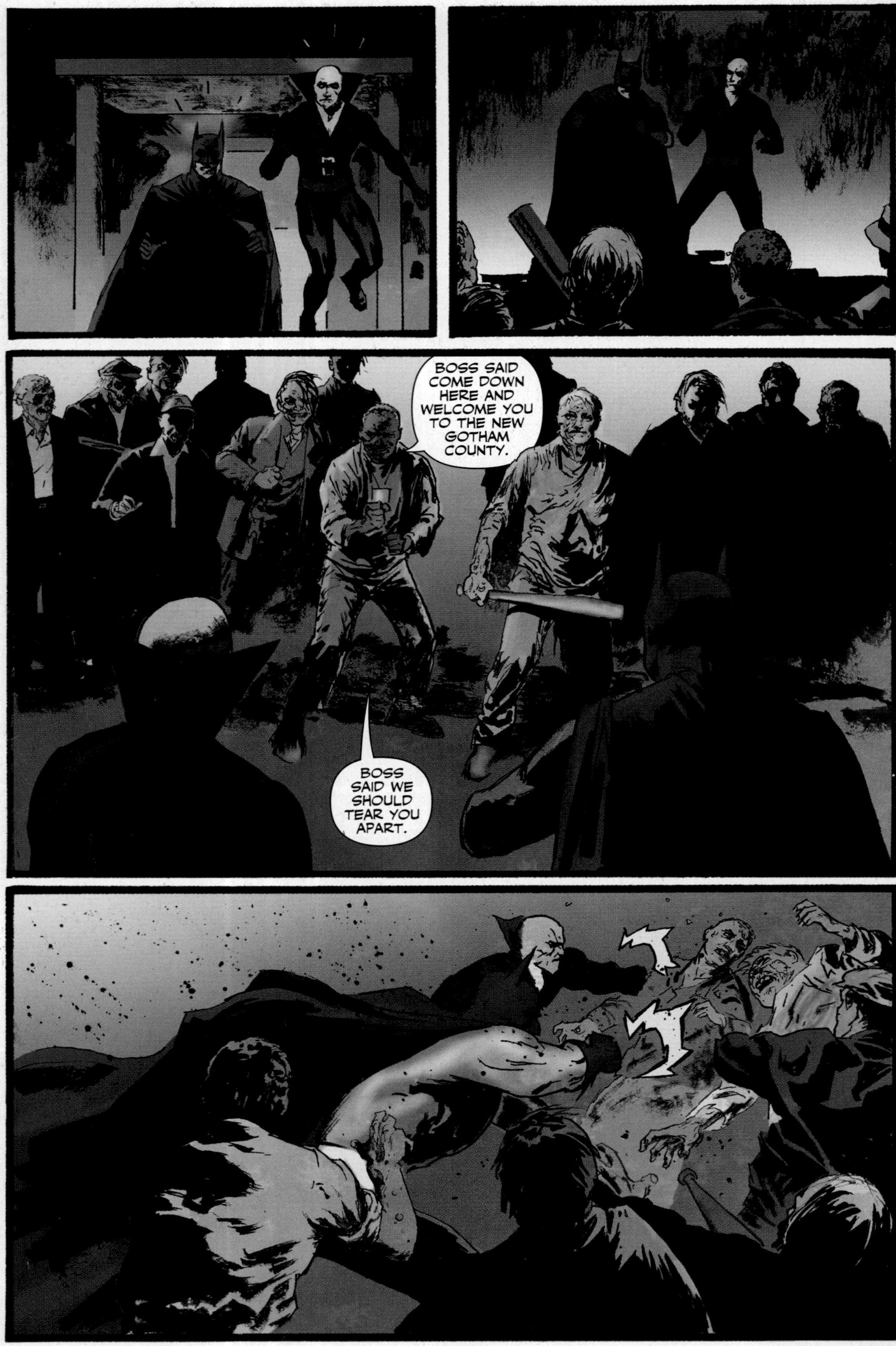
BOSS SAID COME DOWN HERE AND WELCOME YOU TO THE NEW GOTHAM COUNTY.
BOSS SAID WE SHOULD TEAR YOU APART.

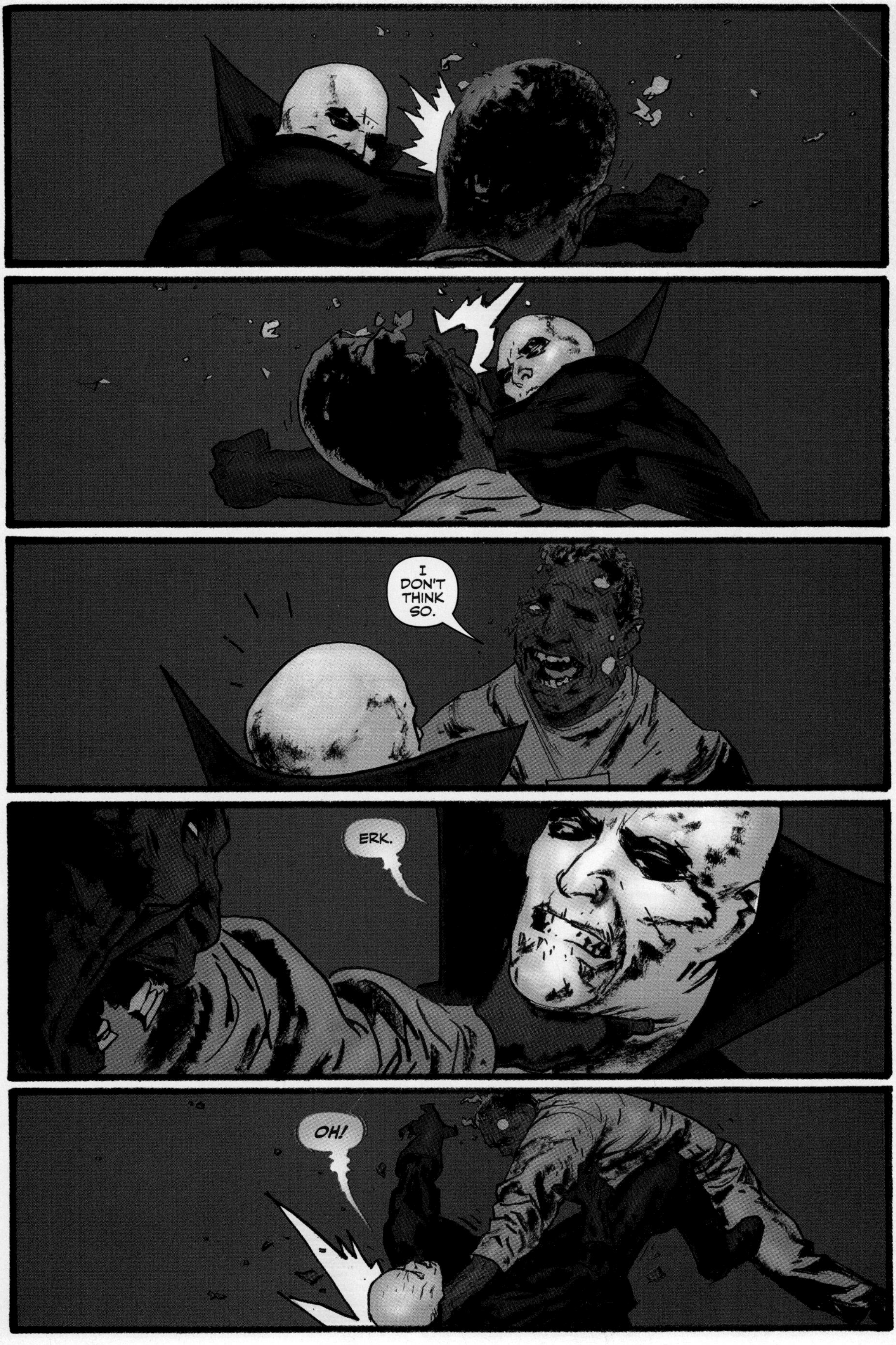
I DON'T THINK SO.
ERK.
OH!

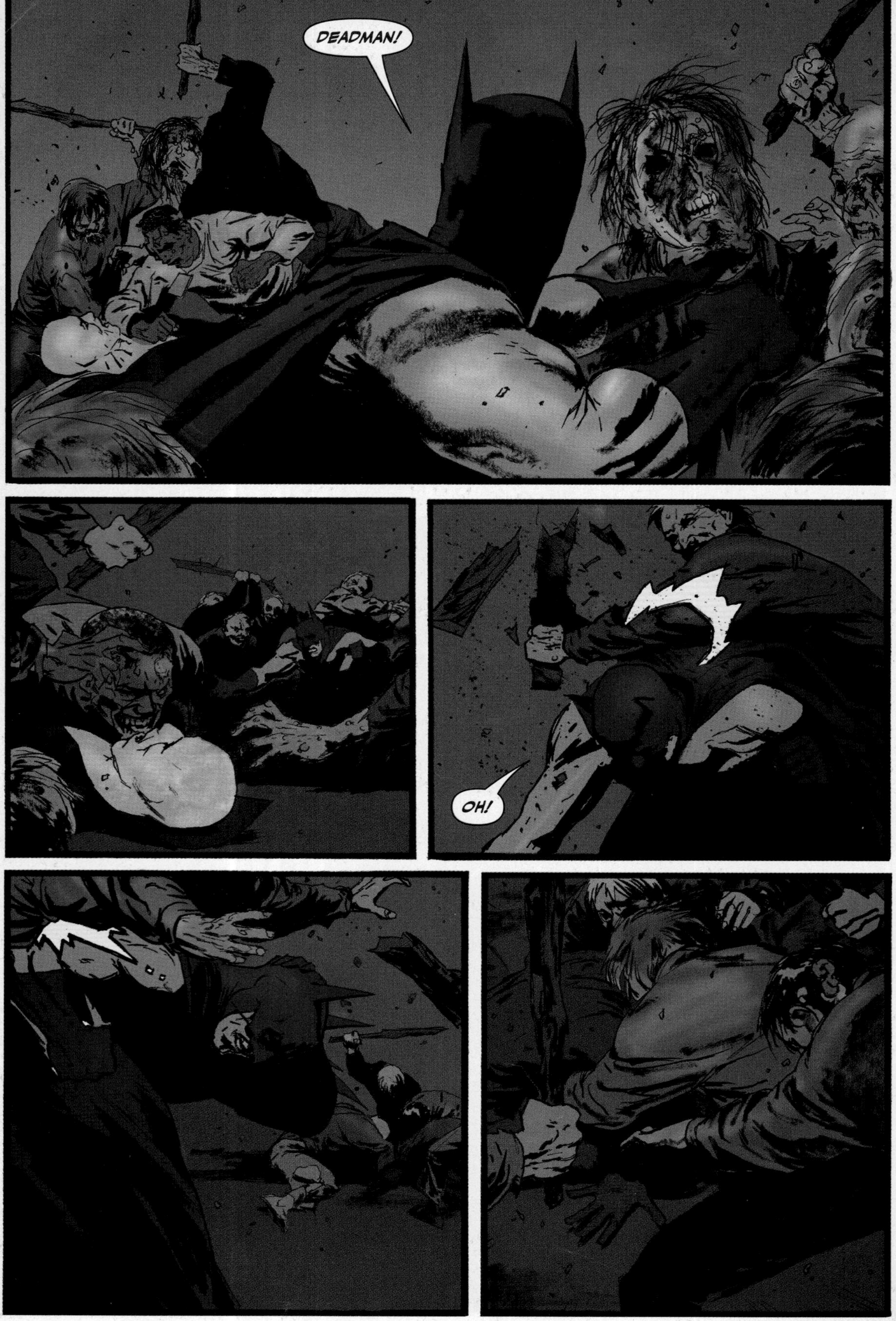
DEADMAN!
OH!

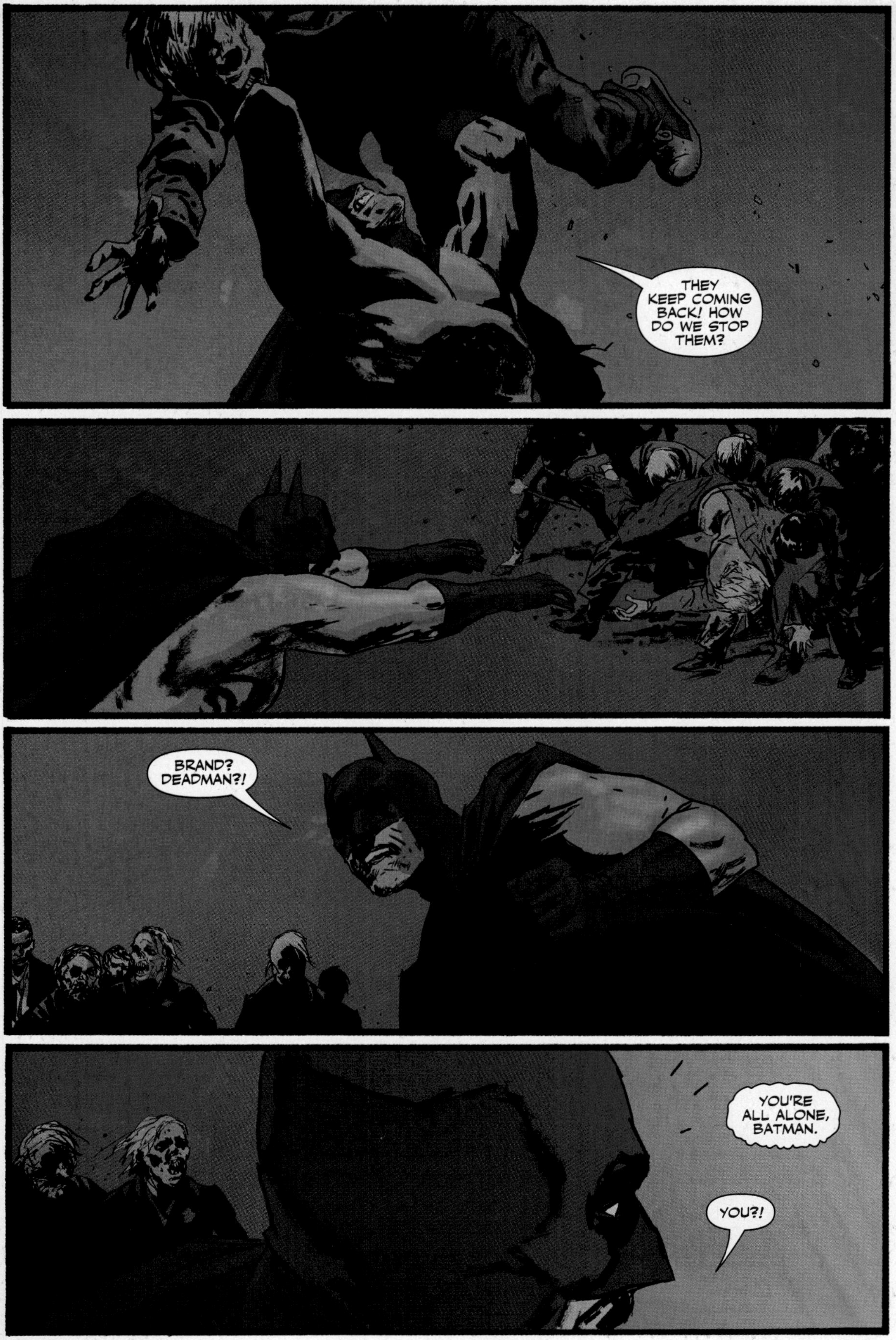
THEY KEEP COMING BACK! HOW DO WE STOP THEM?
BRAND? DEADMAN?!
YOU'RE ALL ALONE, BATMAN.
YOU?!

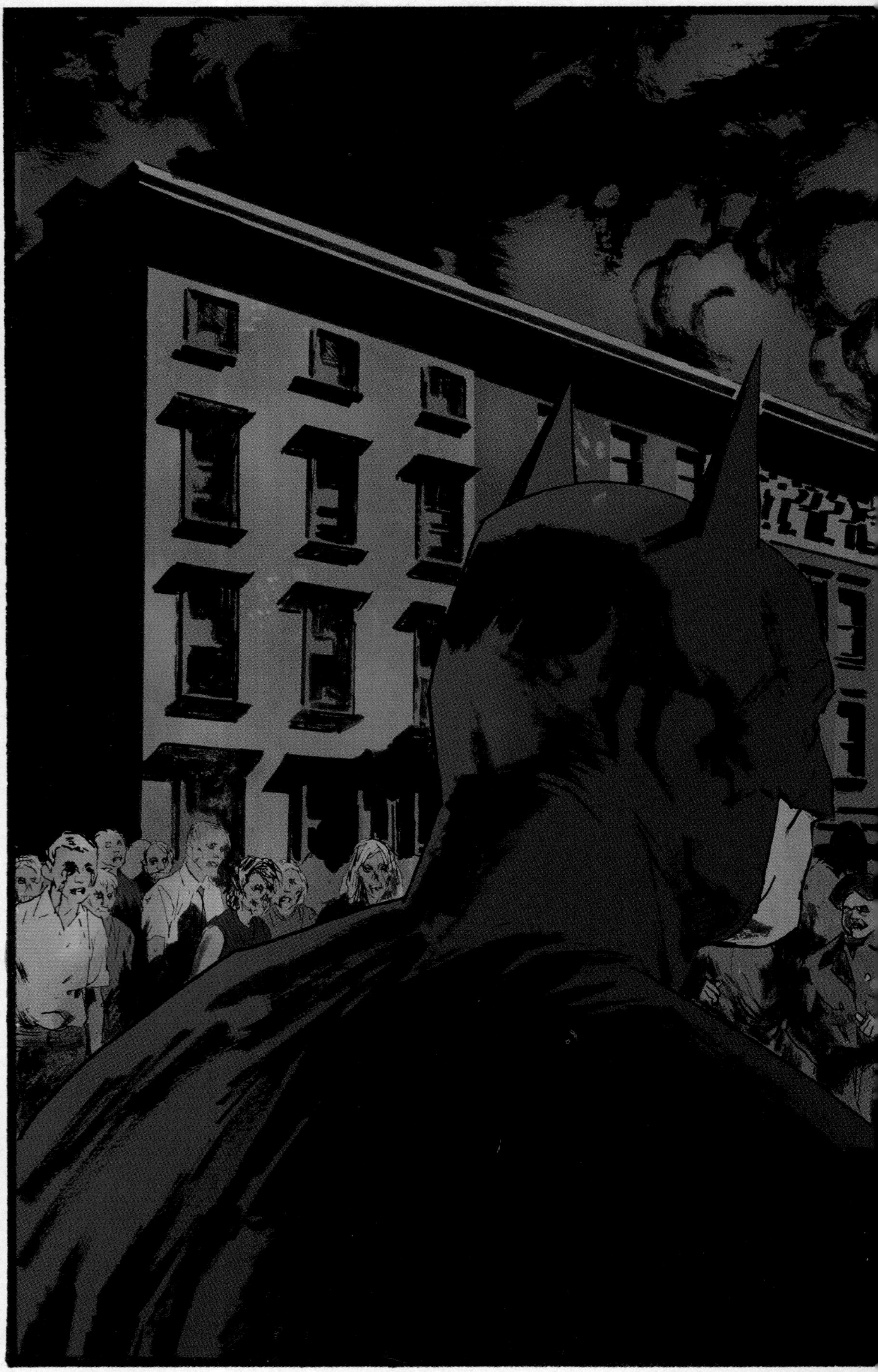

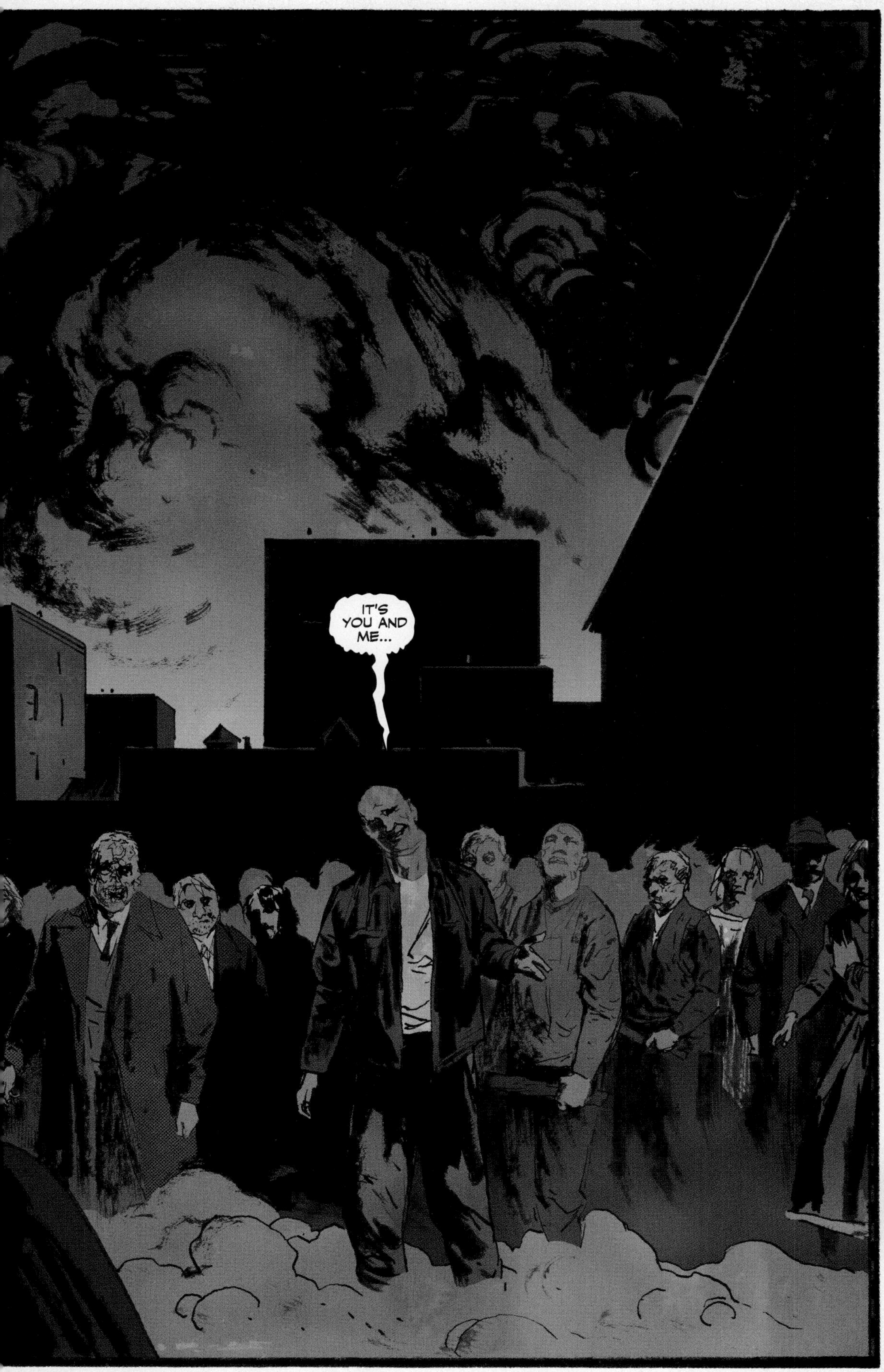
IT'S YOU AND ME...

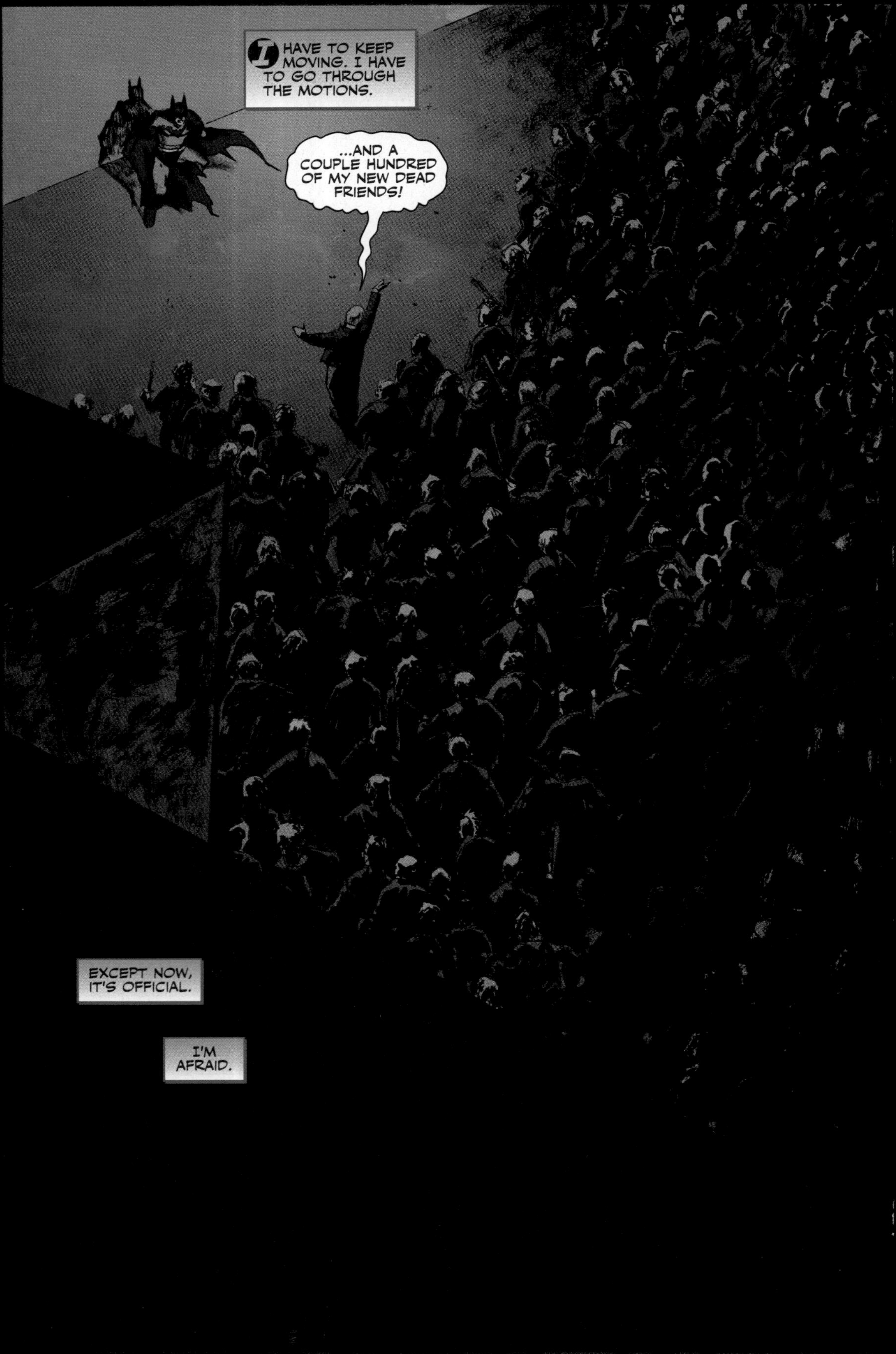
I HAVE TO KEEP MOVING. I HAVE TO GO THROUGH THE MOTIONS.
...AND A COUPLE HUNDRED OF MY NEW DEAD FRIENDS!
EXCEPT NOW, IT'S OFFICIAL.
I'M AFRAID.

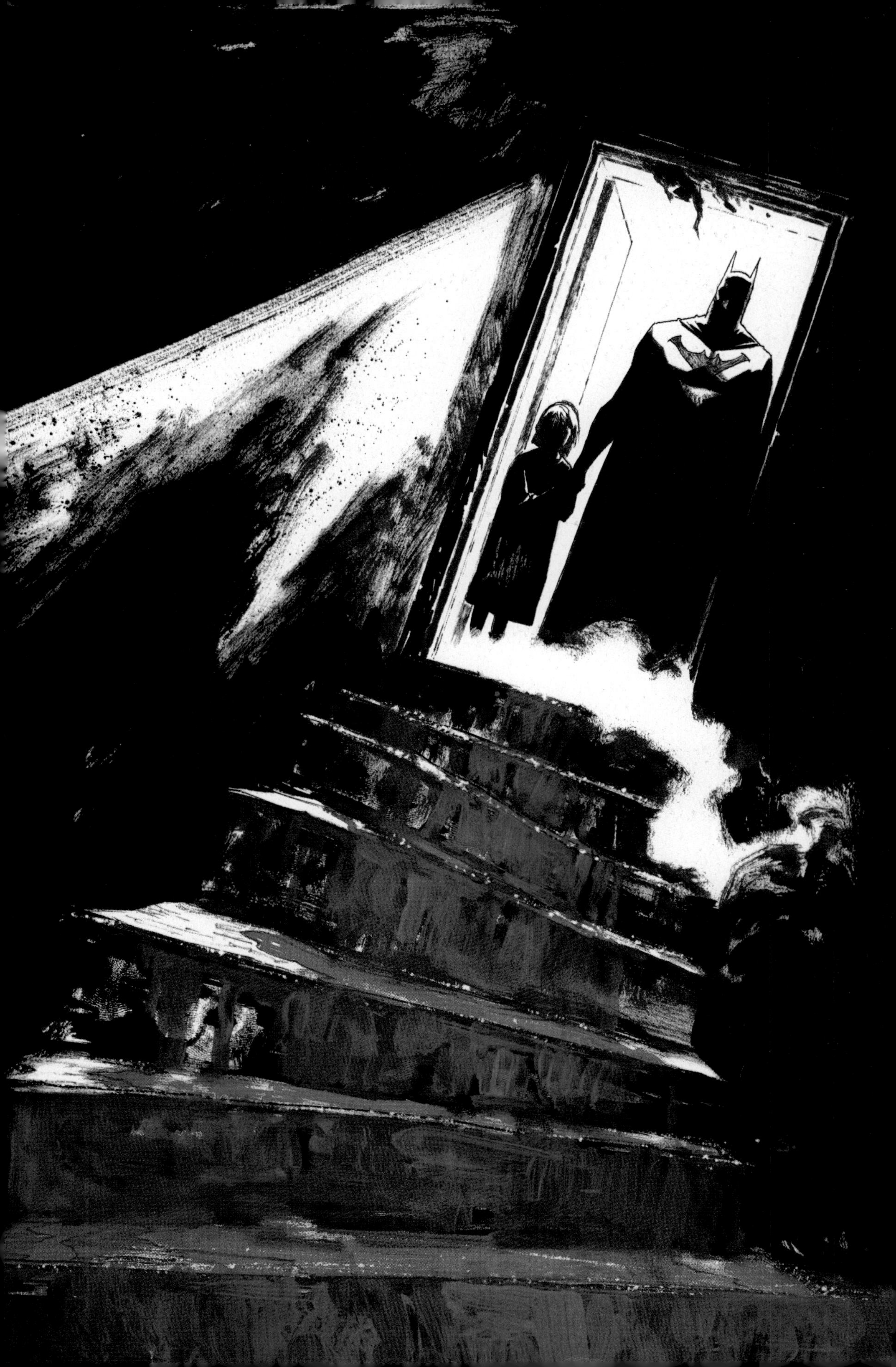

BOOK THREE:
NIGHT OF THE LIVING DEATH

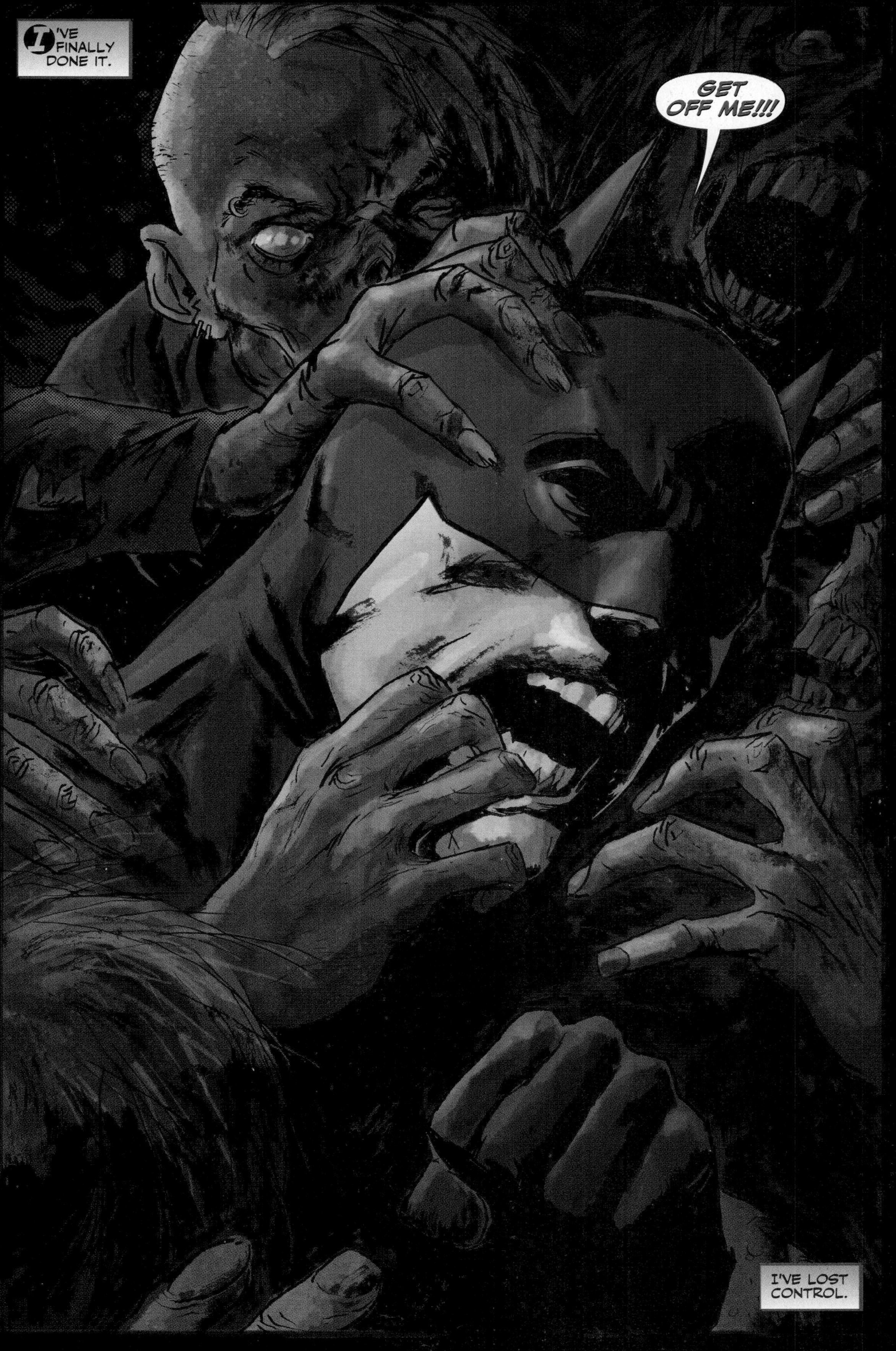
I'VE FINALLY DONE IT.
GET OFF ME!!!
I'VE LOST CONTROL.

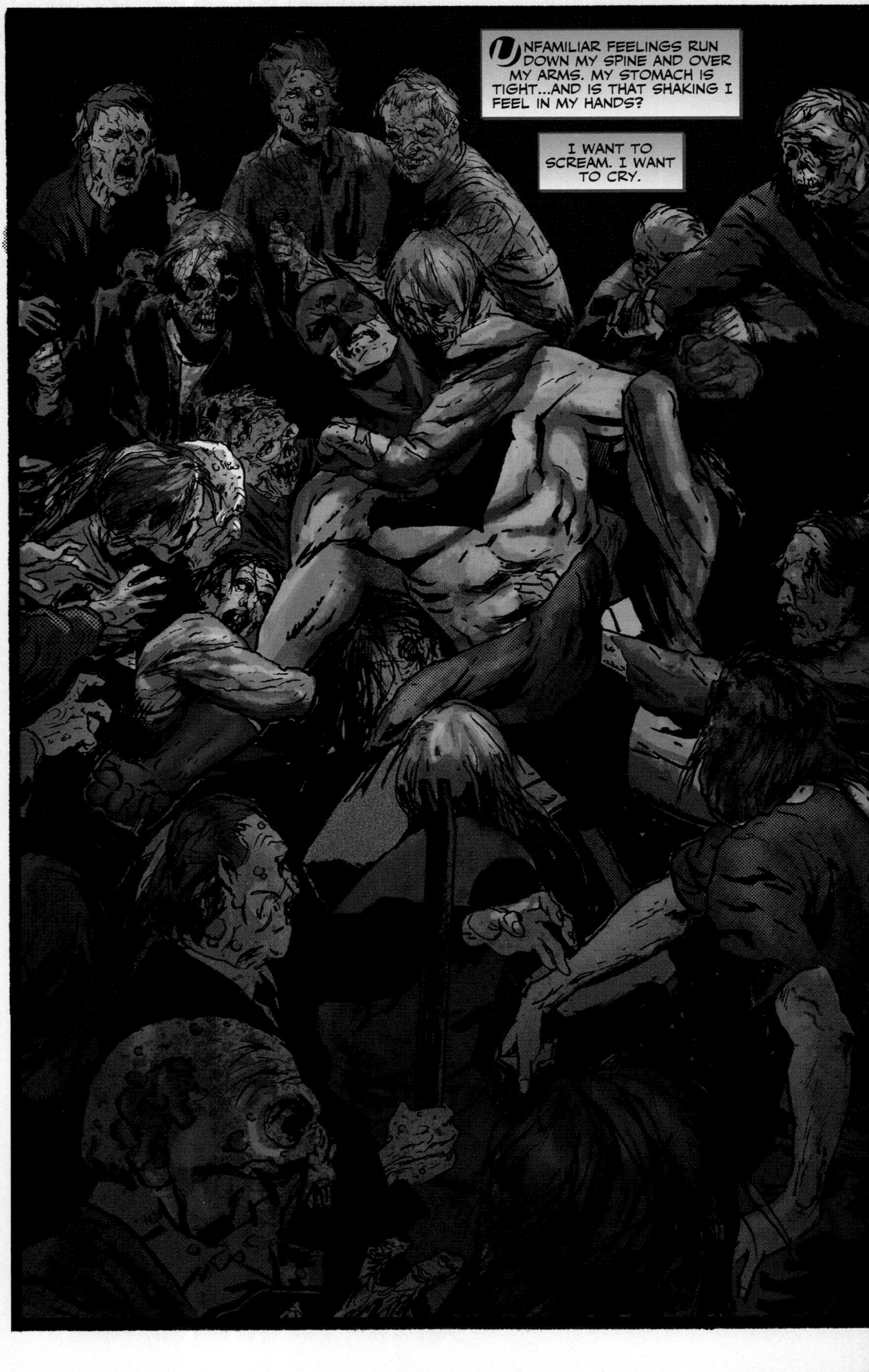
UNFAMILIAR FEELINGS RUN DOWN MY SPINE AND OVER MY ARMS. MY STOMACH IS TIGHT...AND IS THAT SHAKING I FEEL IN MY HANDS?
I WANT TO SCREAM. I WANT TO CRY.

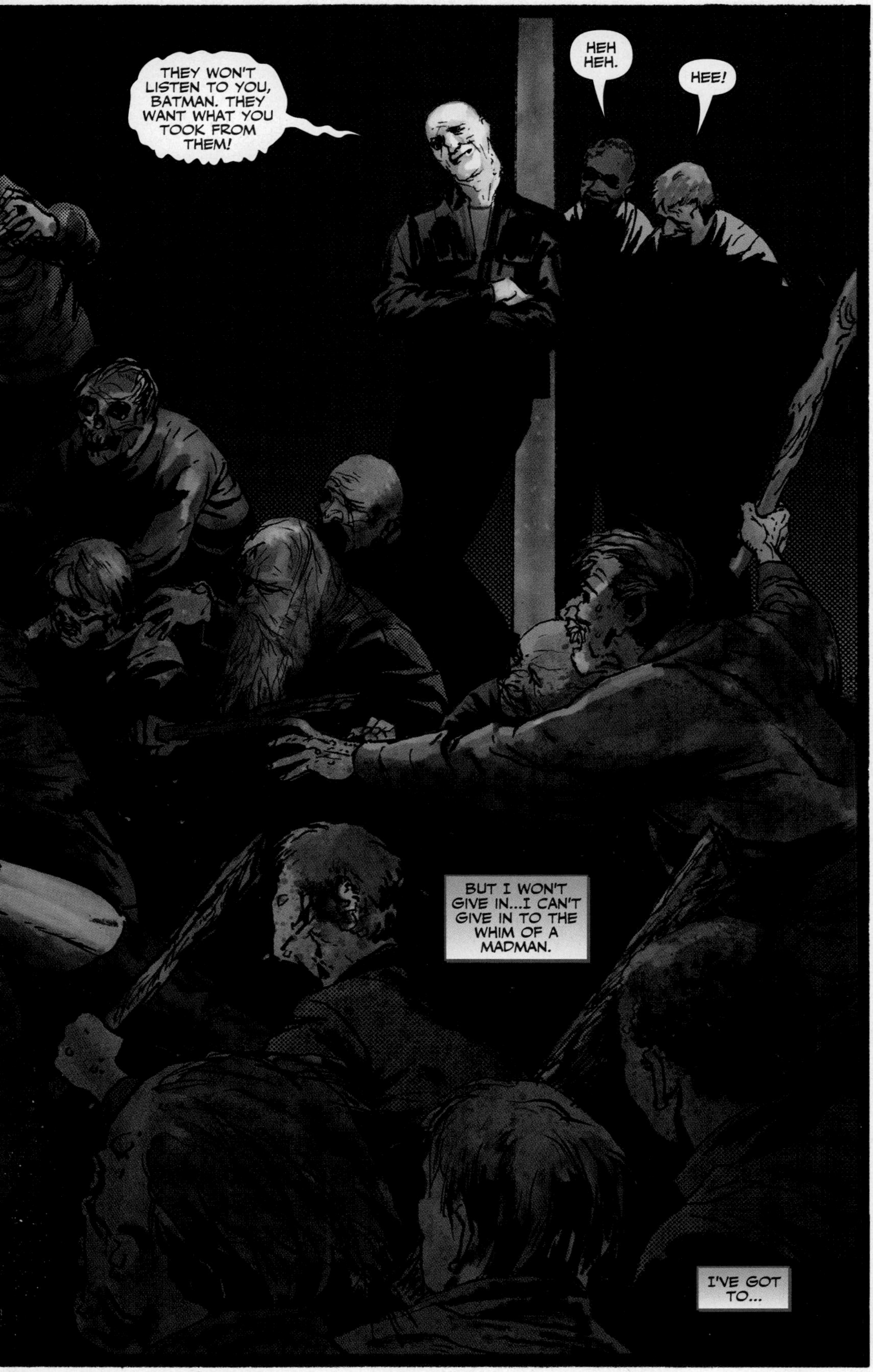
THEY WON'T LISTEN TO YOU, BATMAN. THEY WANT WHAT YOU TOOK FROM THEM!
HEH HEH.
HEE!
BUT I WON'T GIVE IN...I CAN'T GIVE IN TO THE WHIM OF A MADMAN.
I'VE GOT TO...

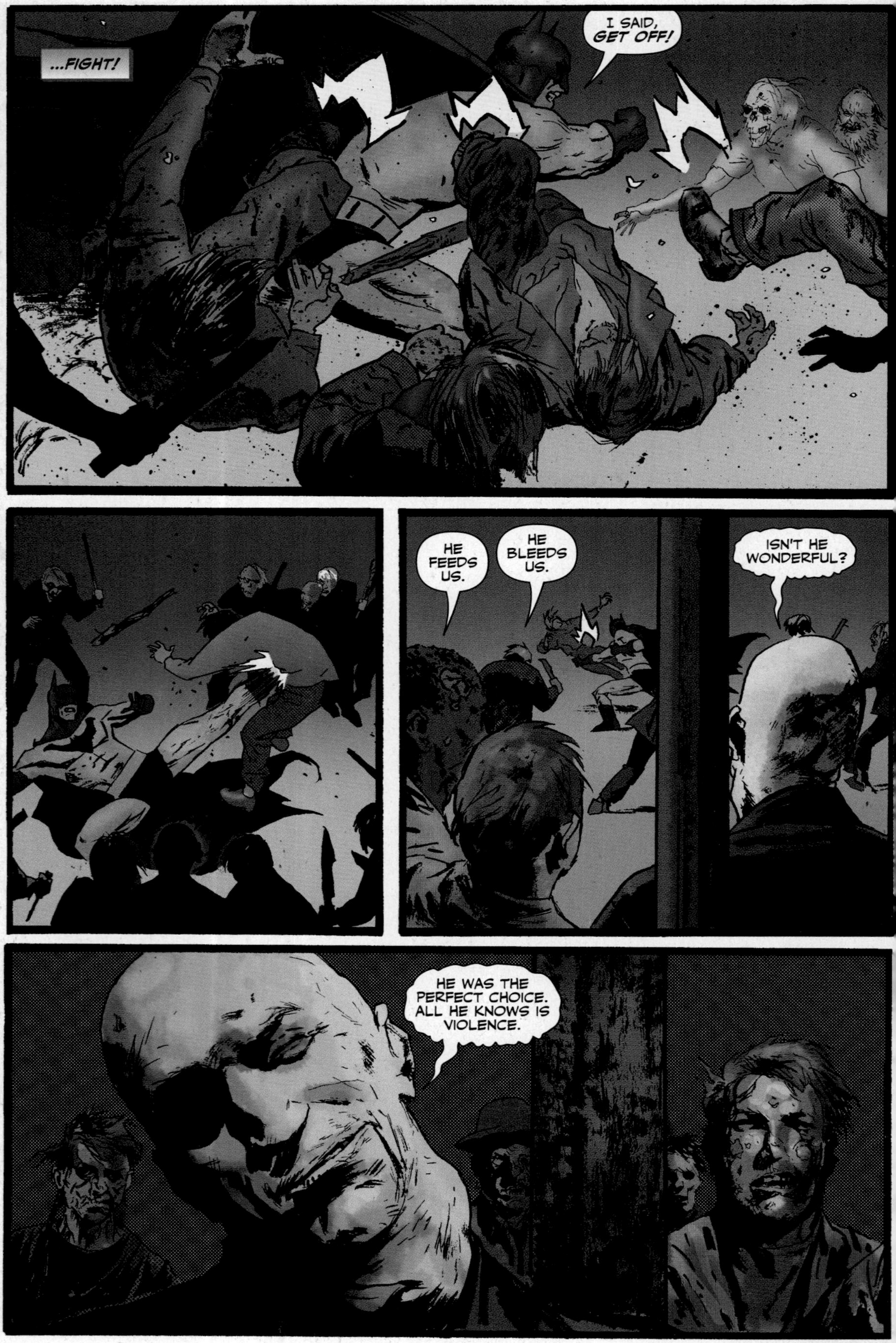
...FIGHT!
I SAID, GET OFF!
HE FEEDS US.
HE BLEEDS US.
ISN'T HE WONDERFUL?
HE WAS THE PERFECT CHOICE. ALL HE KNOWS IS VIOLENCE.

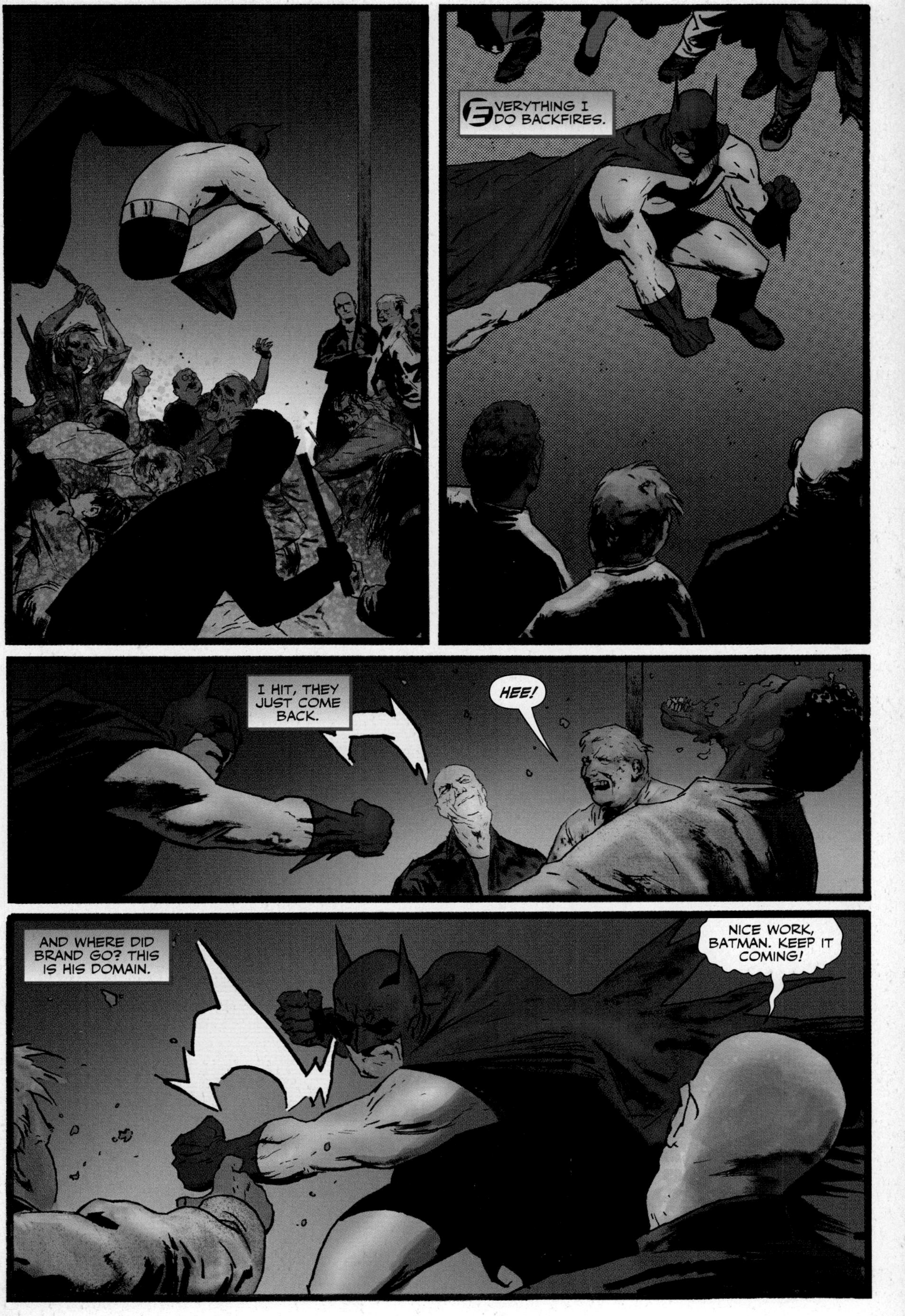
EVERYTHING I DO BACKFIRES.
I HIT, THEY JUST COME BACK.
HEE!
AND WHERE DID BRAND GO? THIS IS HIS DOMAIN.
NICE WORK, BATMAN. KEEP IT COMING!

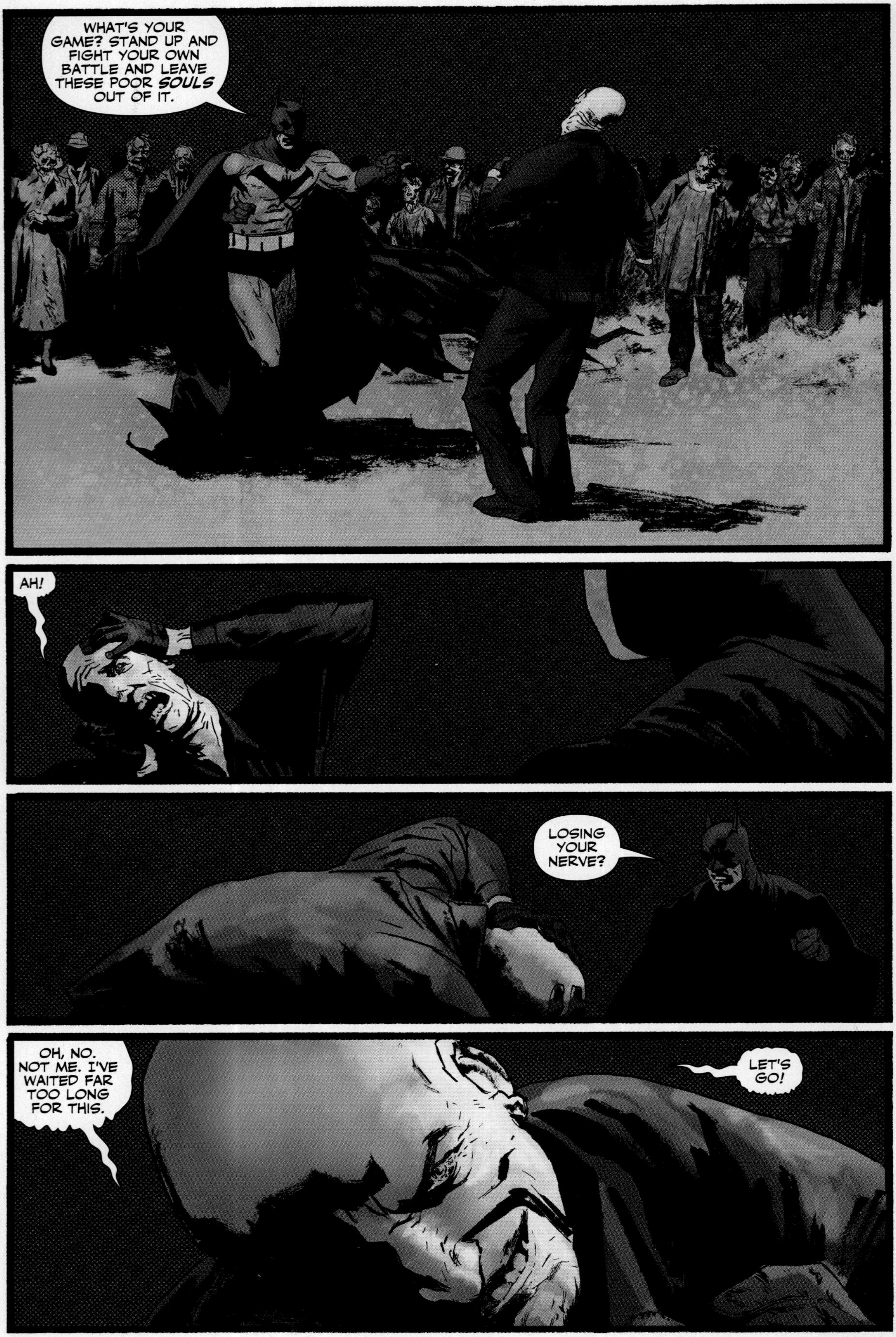
WHAT'S YOUR GAME? STAND UP AND FIGHT YOUR OWN BATTLE AND LEAVE THESE POOR SOULS OUT OF IT.
AH!
LOSING YOUR NERVE?
OH, NO. NOT ME. I'VE WAITED FAR TOO LONG FOR THIS.
LET'S GO!

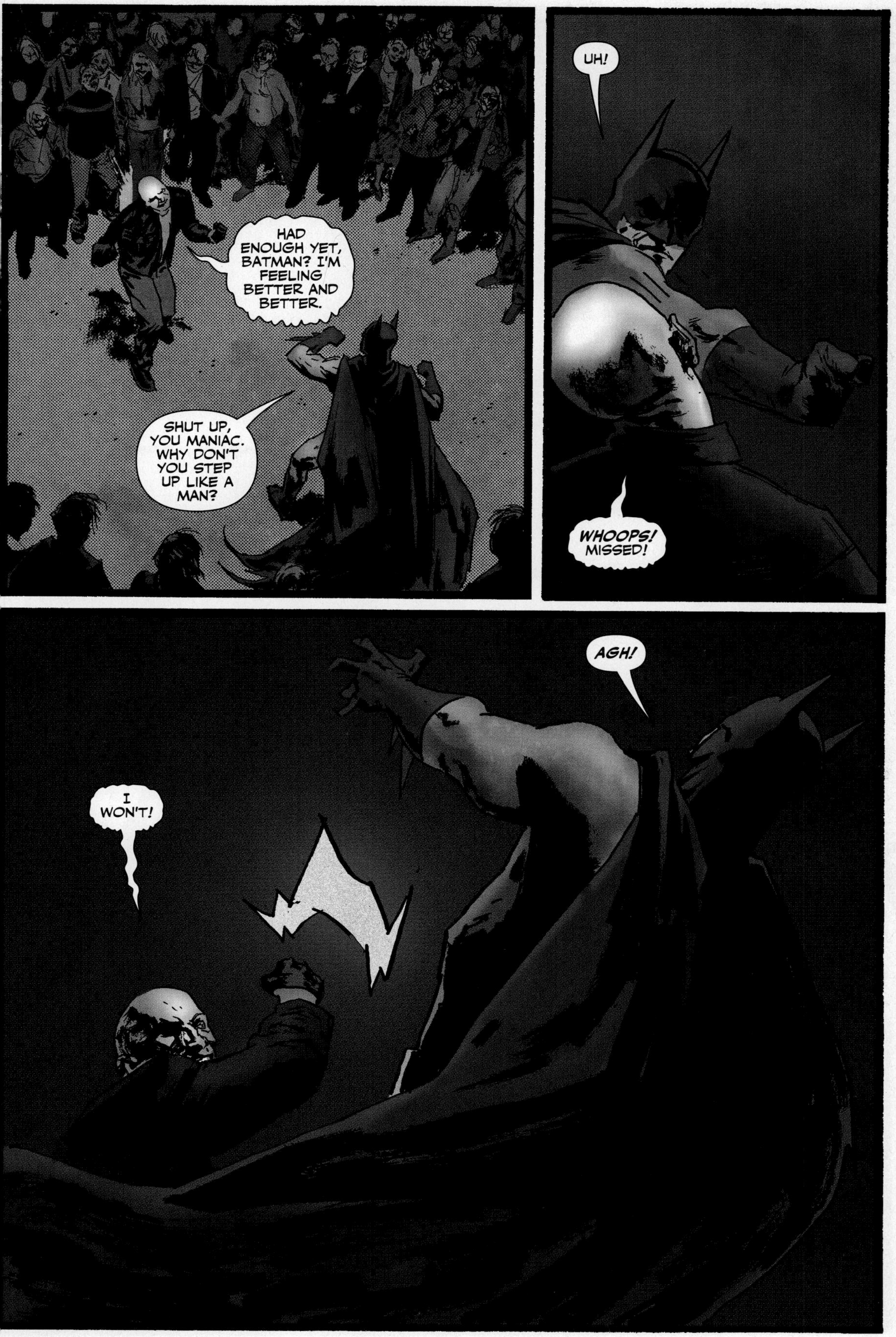
HAD ENOUGH YET, BATMAN? I'M FEELING BETTER AND BETTER.
SHUT UP, YOU MANIAC. WHY DON'T YOU STEP UP LIKE A MAN?
UH!
WHOOPS! MISSED!
AGH!
I WON'T!

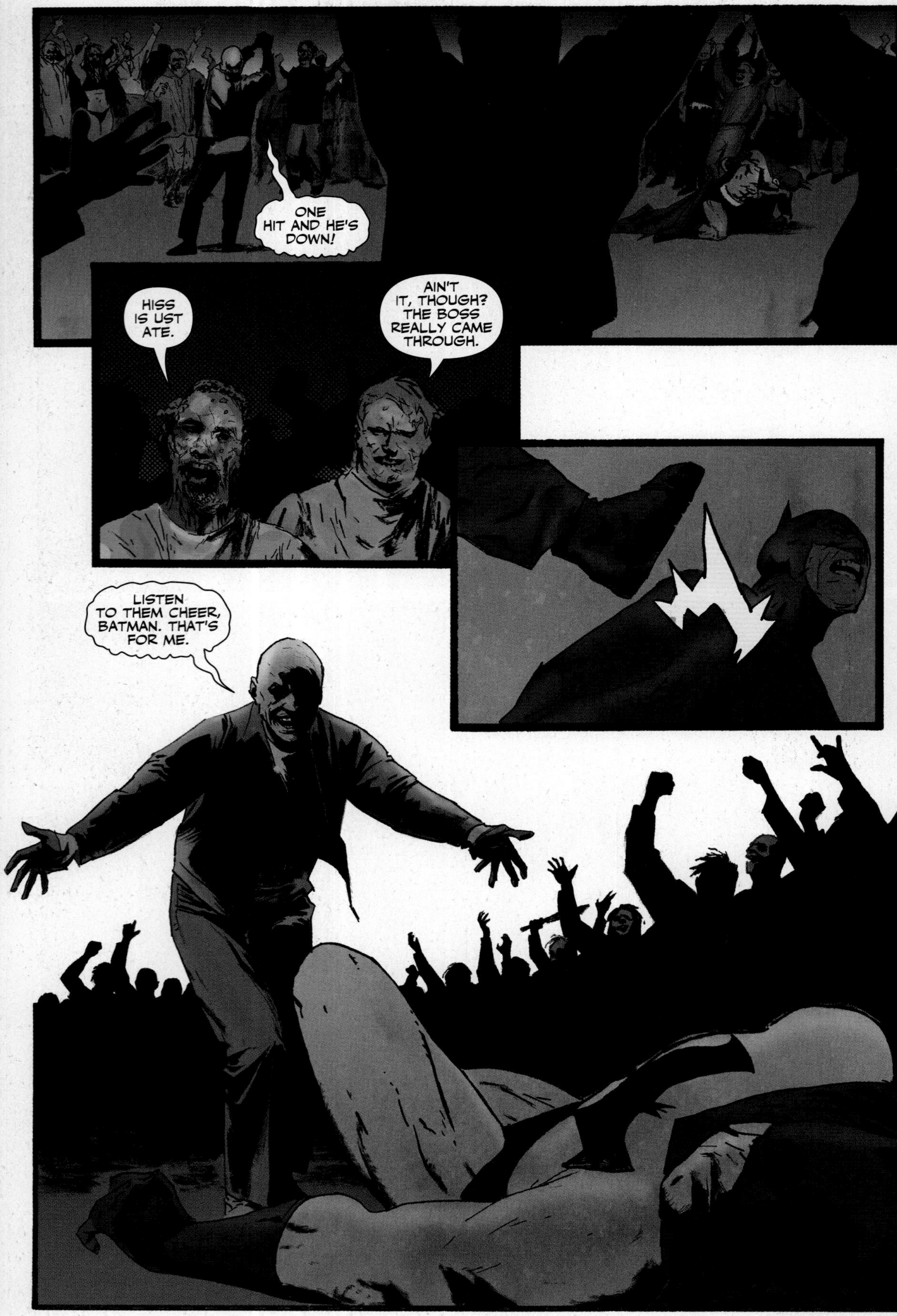
ONE HIT AND HE'S DOWN!
HISS IS UST ATE.
AIN'T IT, THOUGH? THE BOSS REALLY CAME THROUGH.
LISTEN TO THEM CHEER, BATMAN. THAT'S FOR ME.

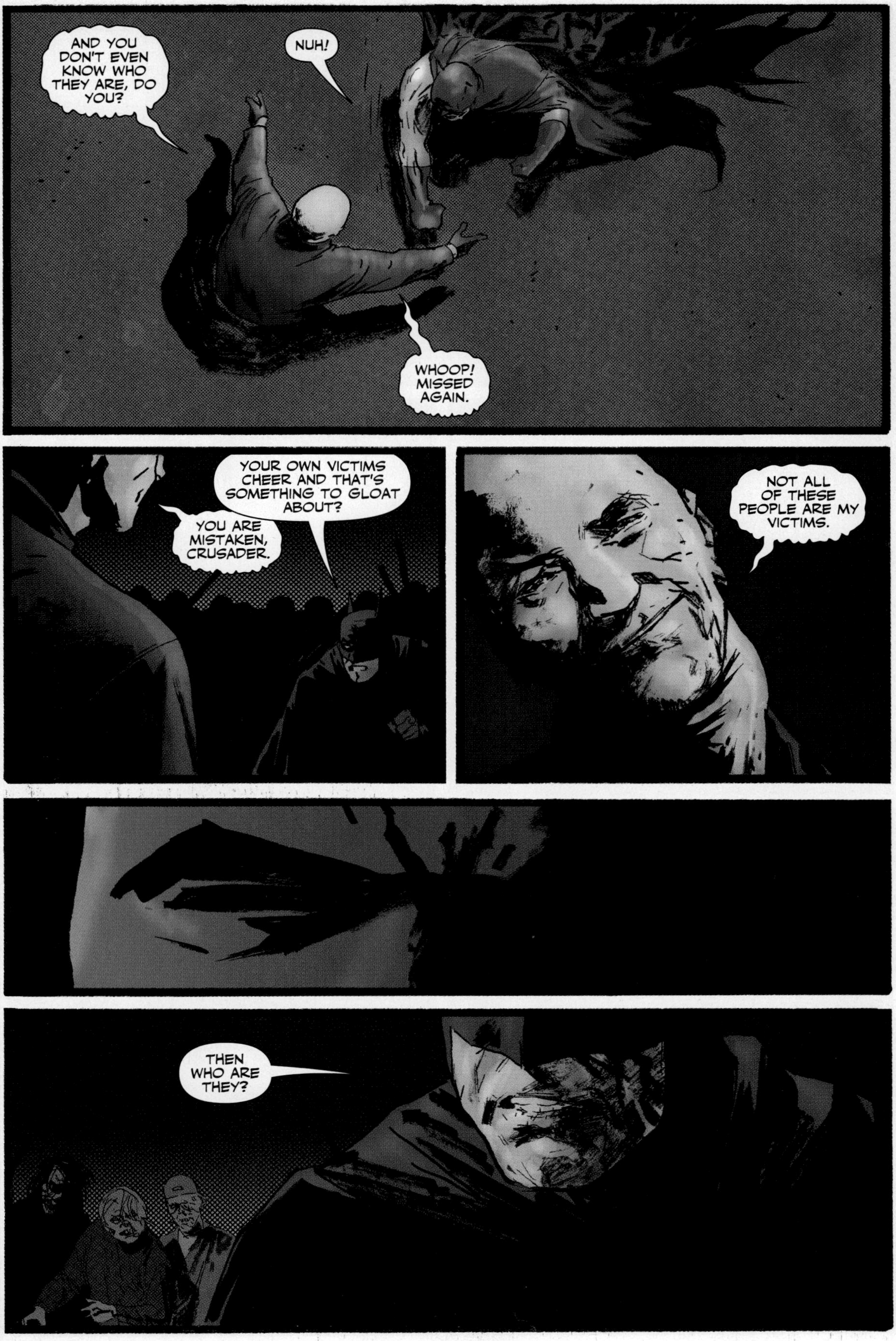
AND YOU DON'T EVEN KNOW WHO THEY ARE, DO YOU?
NUH!
WHOOP! MISSED AGAIN.
YOUR OWN VICTIMS CHEER AND THAT'S SOMETHING TO GLOAT ABOUT?
YOU ARE MISTAKEN, CRUSADER.
NOT ALL OF THESE PEOPLE ARE MY VICTIMS.
THEN WHO ARE THEY?

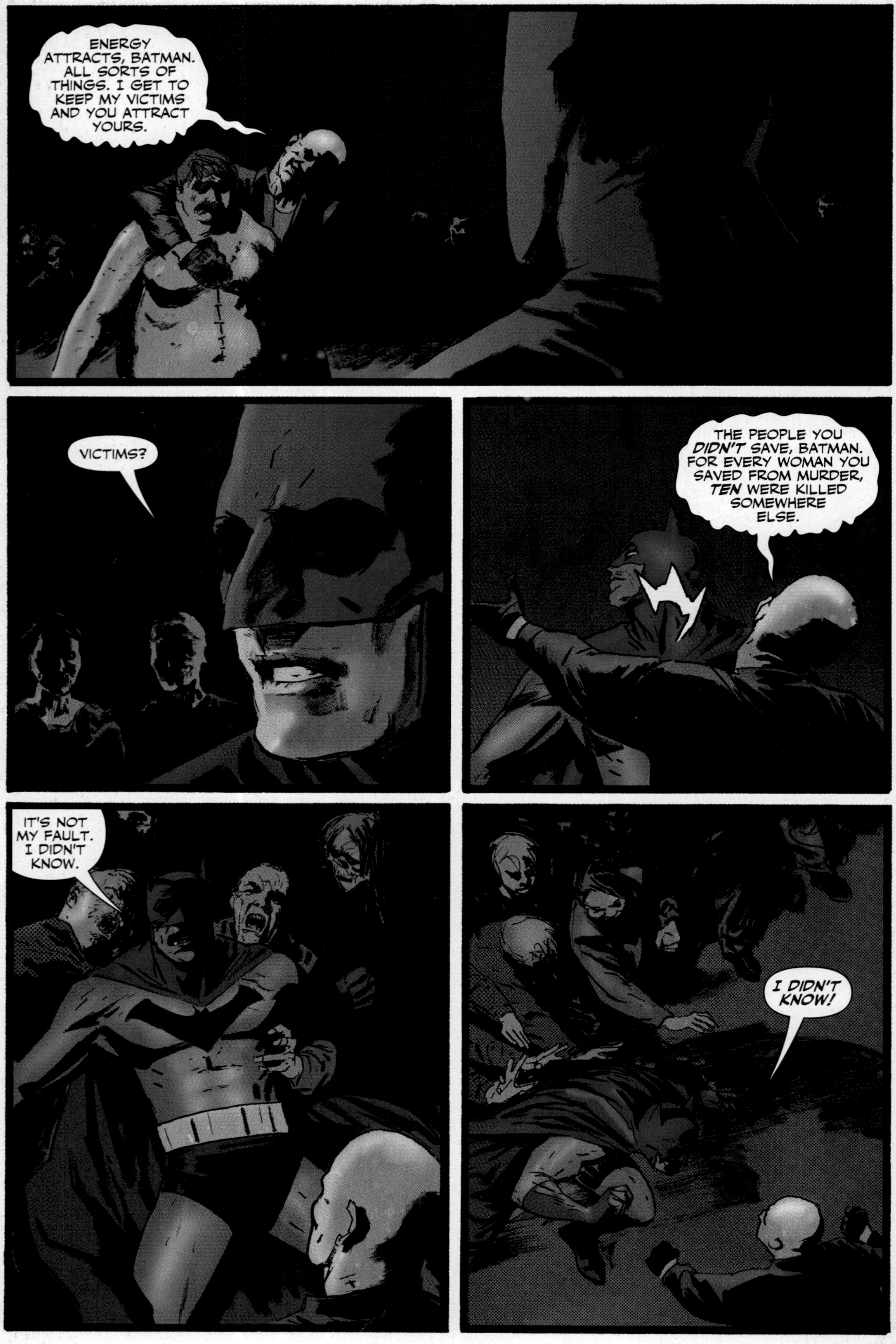
ENERGY ATTRACTS, BATMAN. ALL SORTS OF THINGS. I GET TO KEEP MY VICTIMS AND YOU ATTRACT YOURS.
VICTIMS?
THE PEOPLE YOU *DIDN'T* SAVE, BATMAN. FOR EVERY WOMAN YOU SAVED FROM MURDER, ***TEN*** WERE KILLED SOMEWHERE ELSE.
IT'S NOT MY FAULT. I DIDN'T KNOW.
I DIDN'T KNOW!

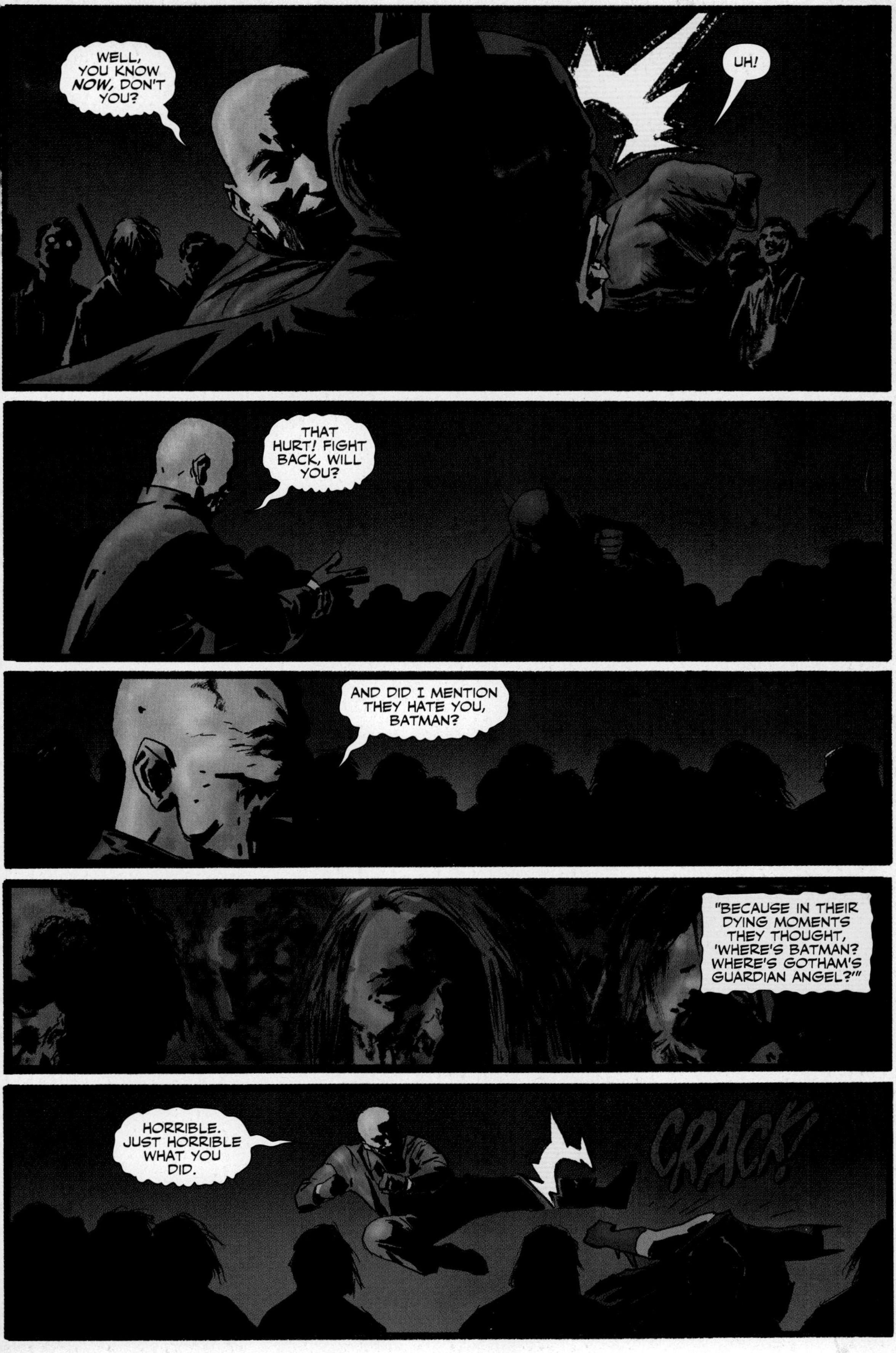
WELL, YOU KNOW *NOW*, DON'T YOU?
UH!
THAT HURT! FIGHT BACK, WILL YOU?
AND DID I MENTION THEY HATE YOU, BATMAN?
"BECAUSE IN THEIR DYING MOMENTS THEY THOUGHT, 'WHERE'S BATMAN? WHERE'S GOTHAM'S GUARDIAN ANGEL?'"
HORRIBLE. JUST HORRIBLE WHAT YOU DID.
CRACK!

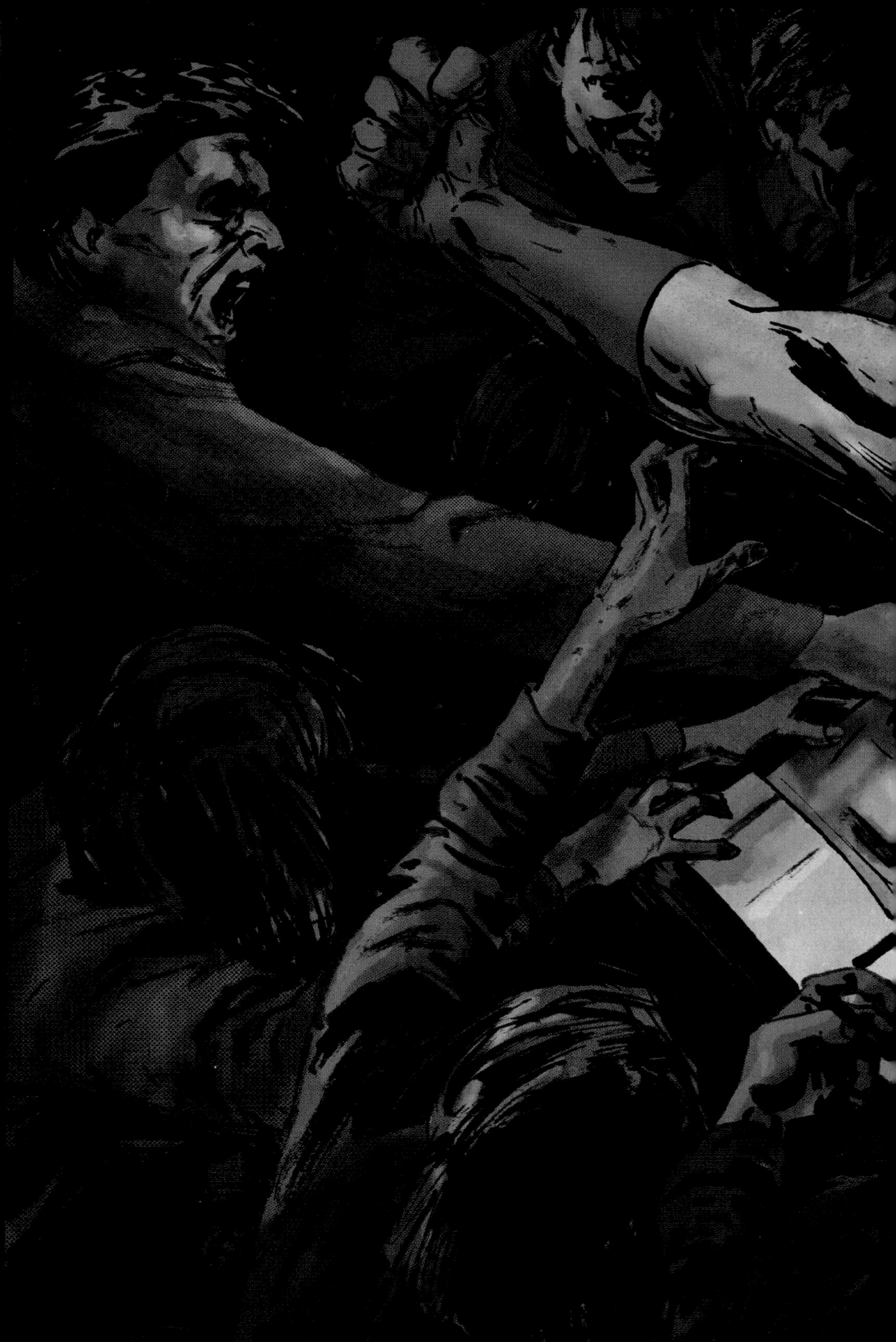

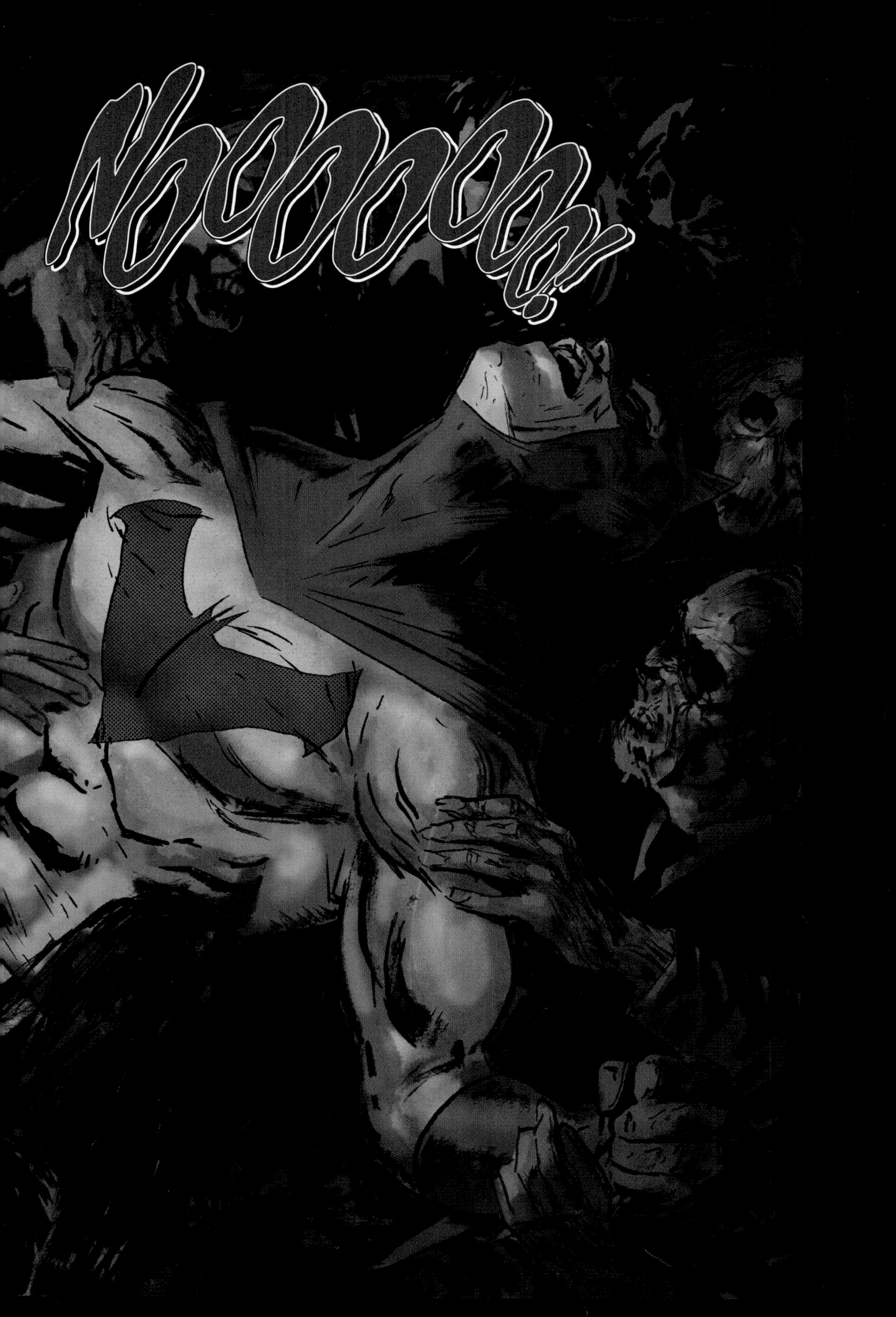
Nhooooo!

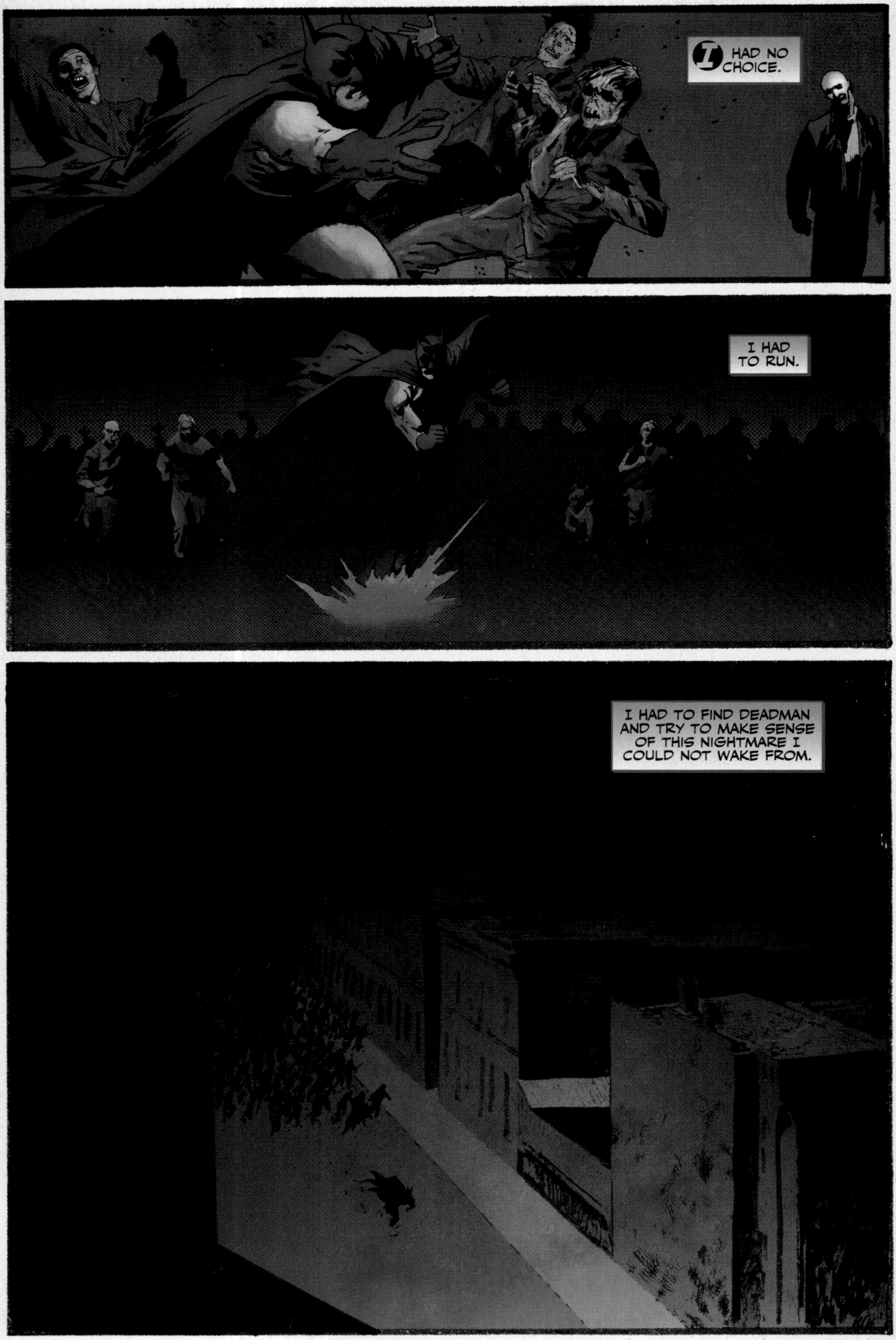
I HAD NO CHOICE.
I HAD TO RUN.
I HAD TO FIND DEADMAN AND TRY TO MAKE SENSE OF THIS NIGHTMARE I COULD NOT WAKE FROM.

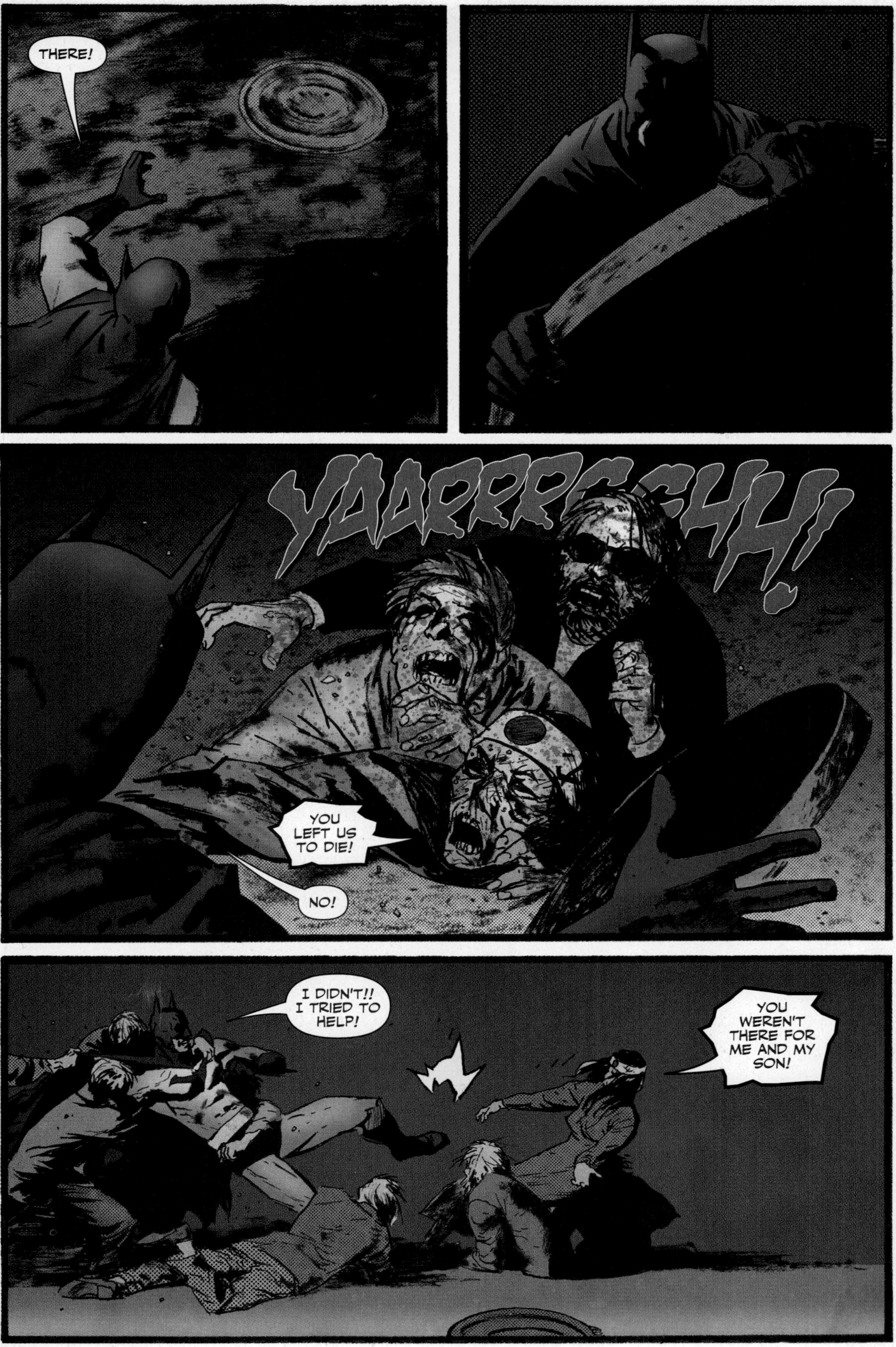
THERE!
YAARRRGGHH!!
YOU LEFT US TO DIE!
NO!
I DIDN'T!! I TRIED TO HELP!
YOU WEREN'T THERE FOR ME AND MY SON!

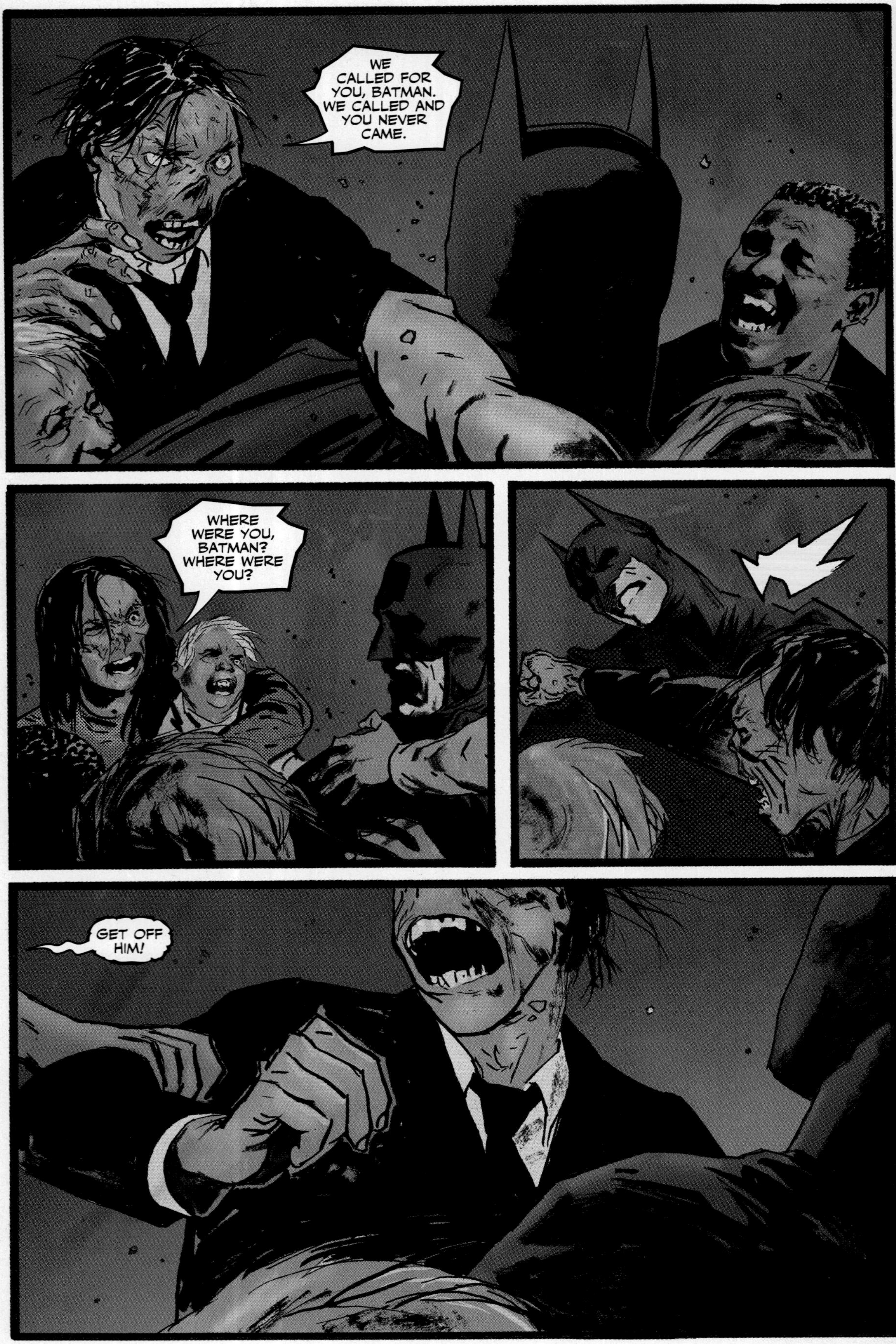
WE CALLED FOR YOU, BATMAN. WE CALLED AND YOU NEVER CAME.
WHERE WERE YOU, BATMAN? WHERE WERE YOU?
GET OFF HIM!

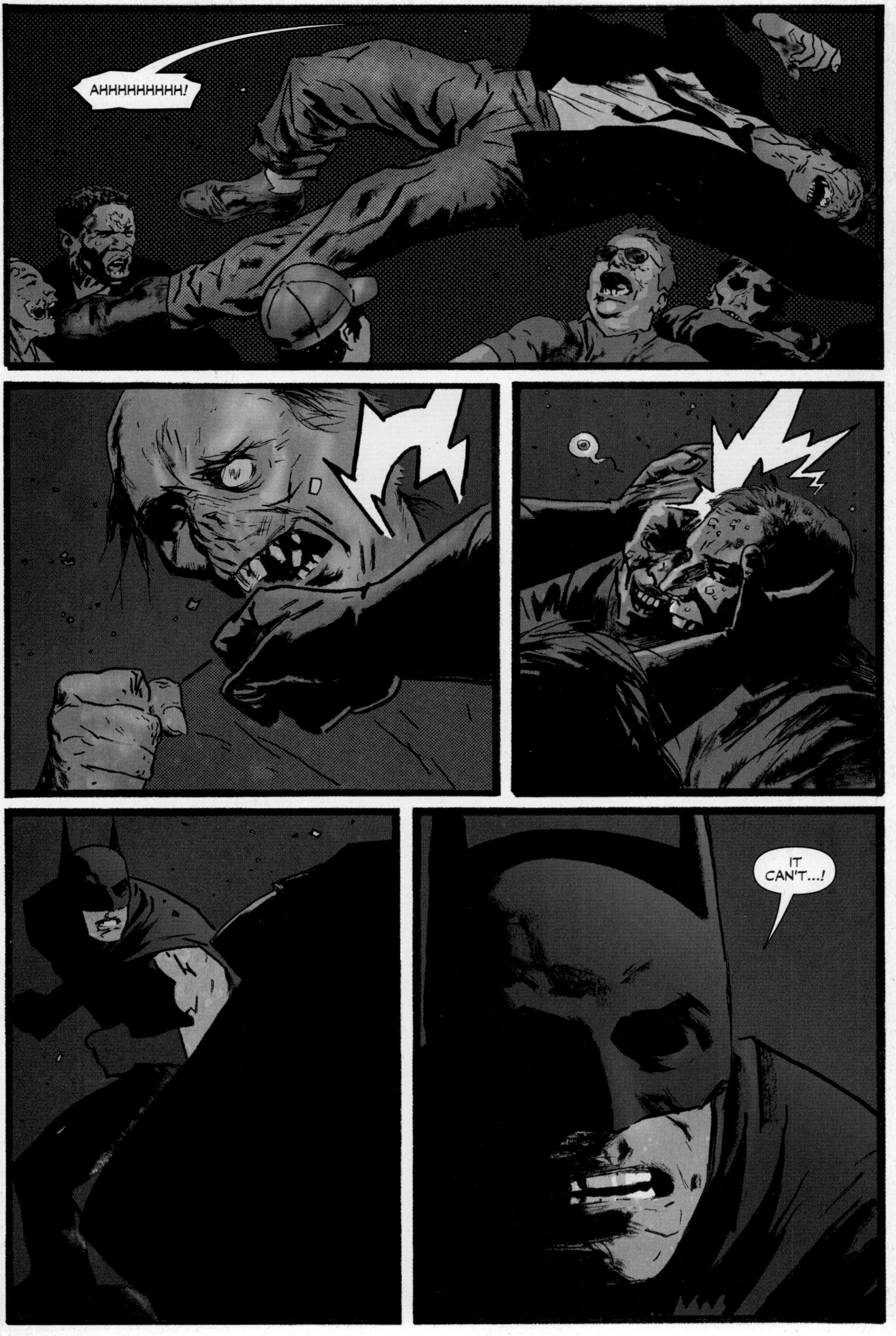
AHHHHHHHHH!
IT CAN'T...!

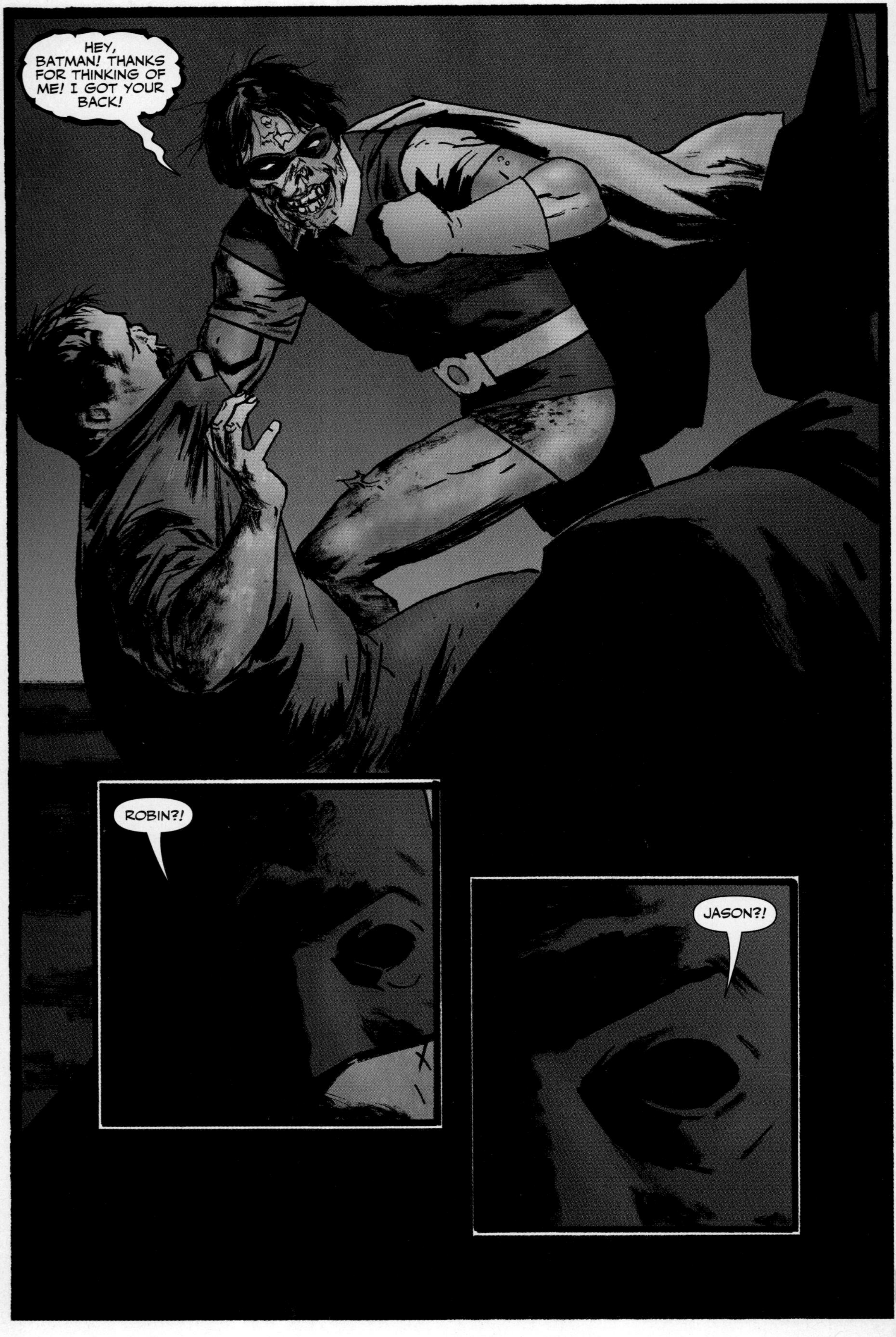
HEY, BATMAN! THANKS FOR THINKING OF ME! I GOT YOUR BACK!
ROBIN?!
JASON?!

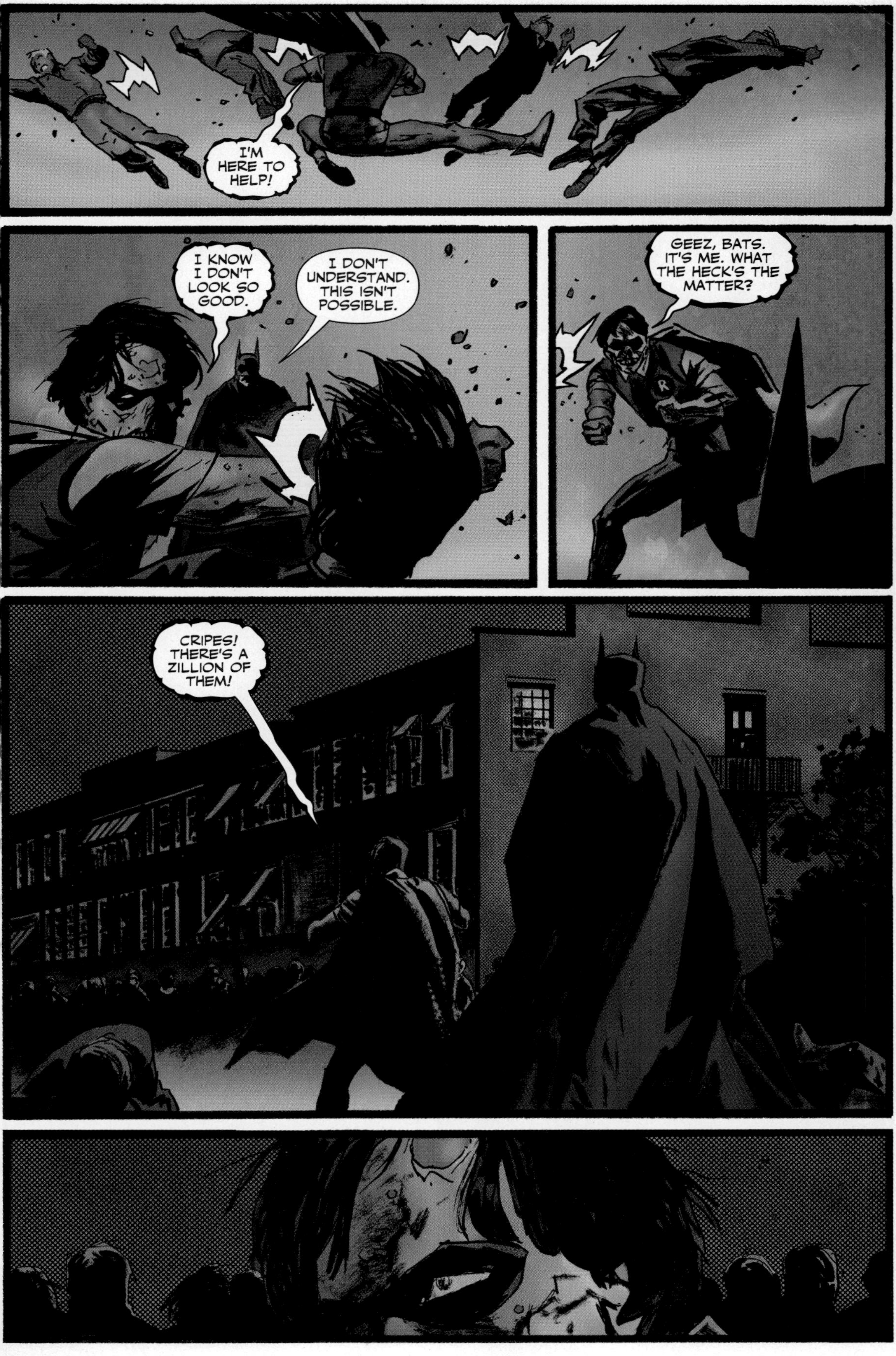
I'M HERE TO HELP!
I KNOW I DON'T LOOK SO GOOD.
I DON'T UNDERSTAND. THIS ISN'T POSSIBLE.
GEEZ, BATS. IT'S ME. WHAT THE HECK'S THE MATTER?
CRIPES! THERE'S A ZILLION OF THEM!

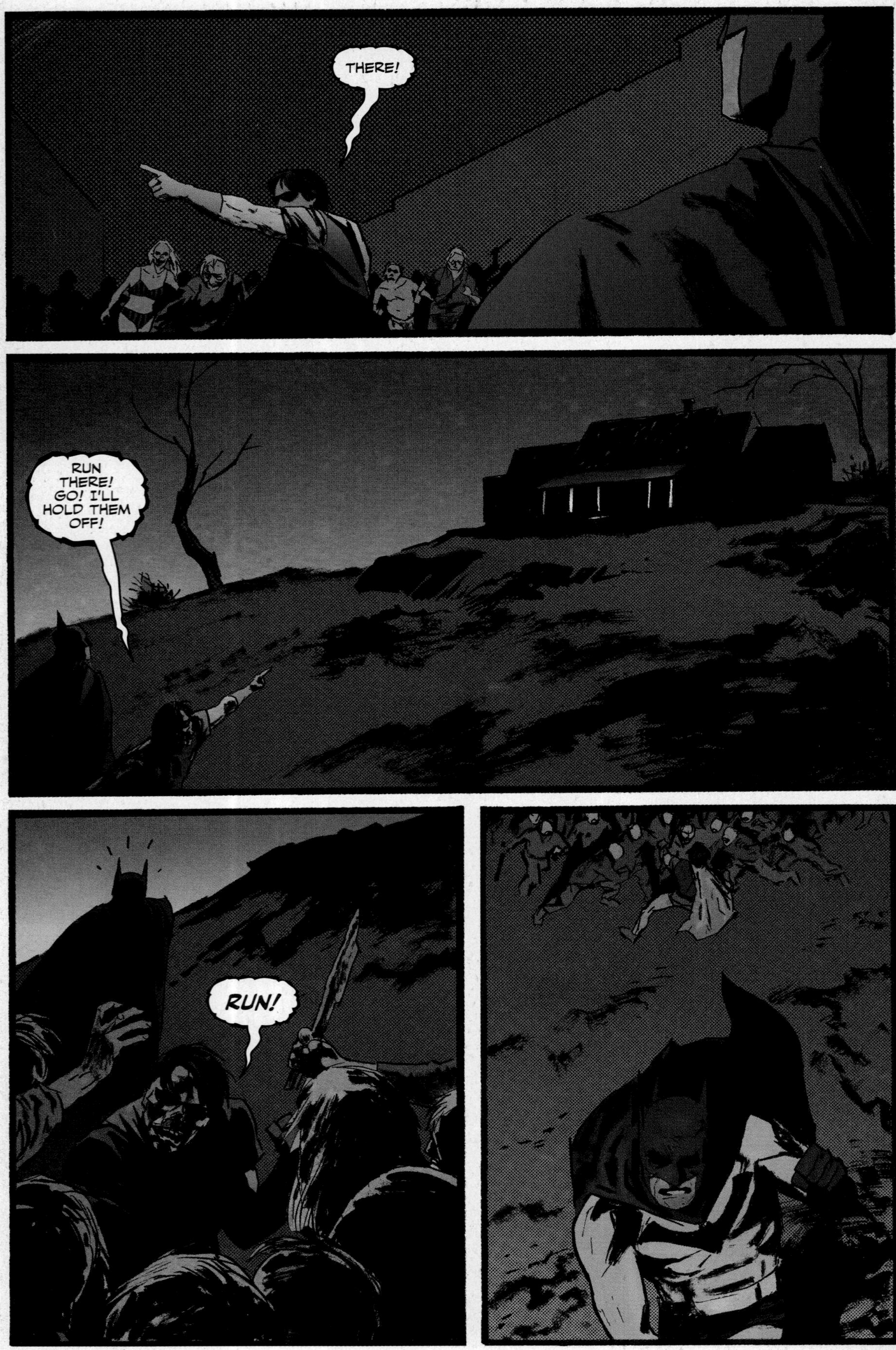
THERE!
RUN THERE! GO! I'LL HOLD THEM OFF!
RUN!

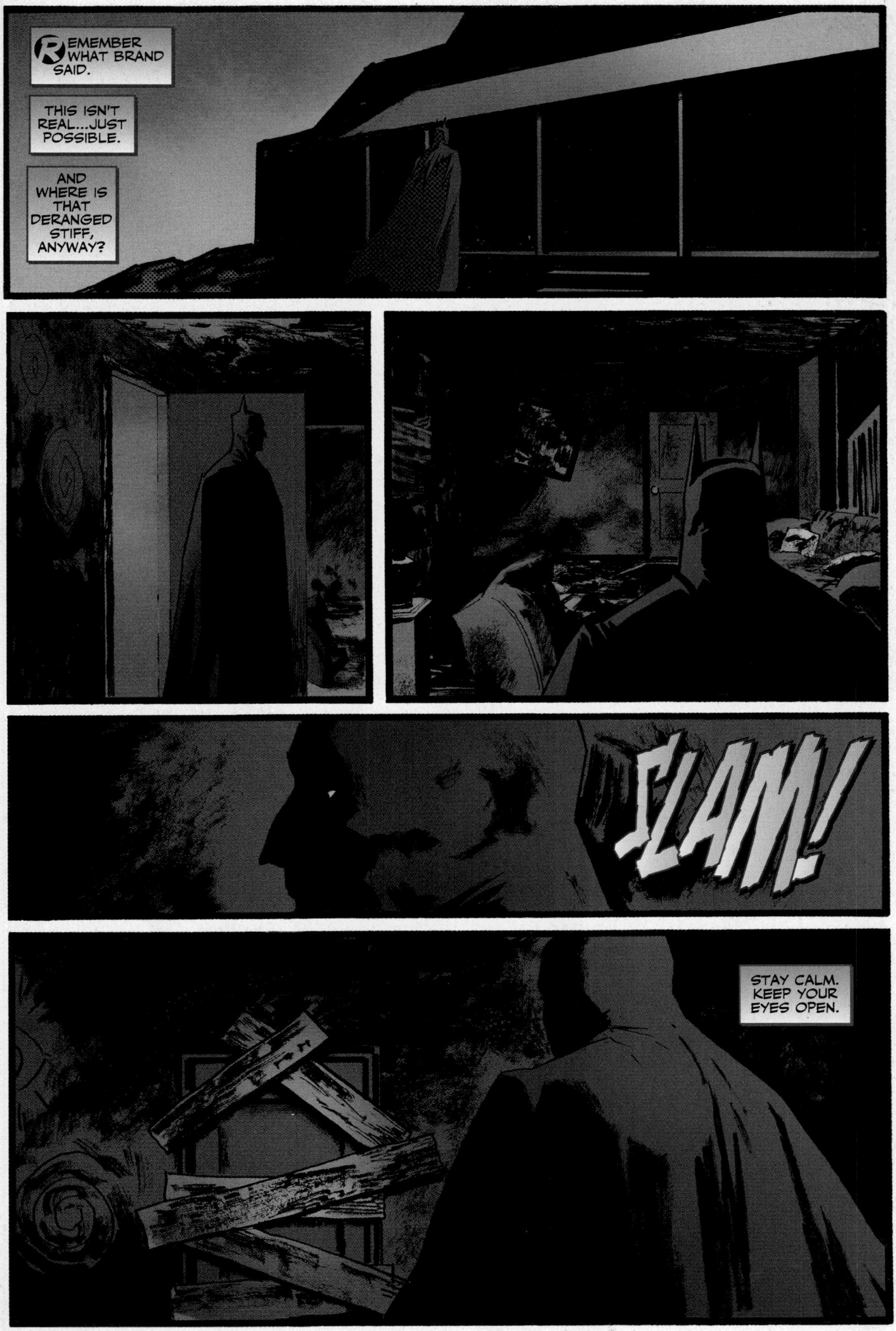
REMEMBER WHAT BRAND SAID.
THIS ISN'T REAL...JUST POSSIBLE.
AND WHERE IS THAT DERANGED STIFF, ANYWAY?
SLAM!
STAY CALM. KEEP YOUR EYES OPEN.

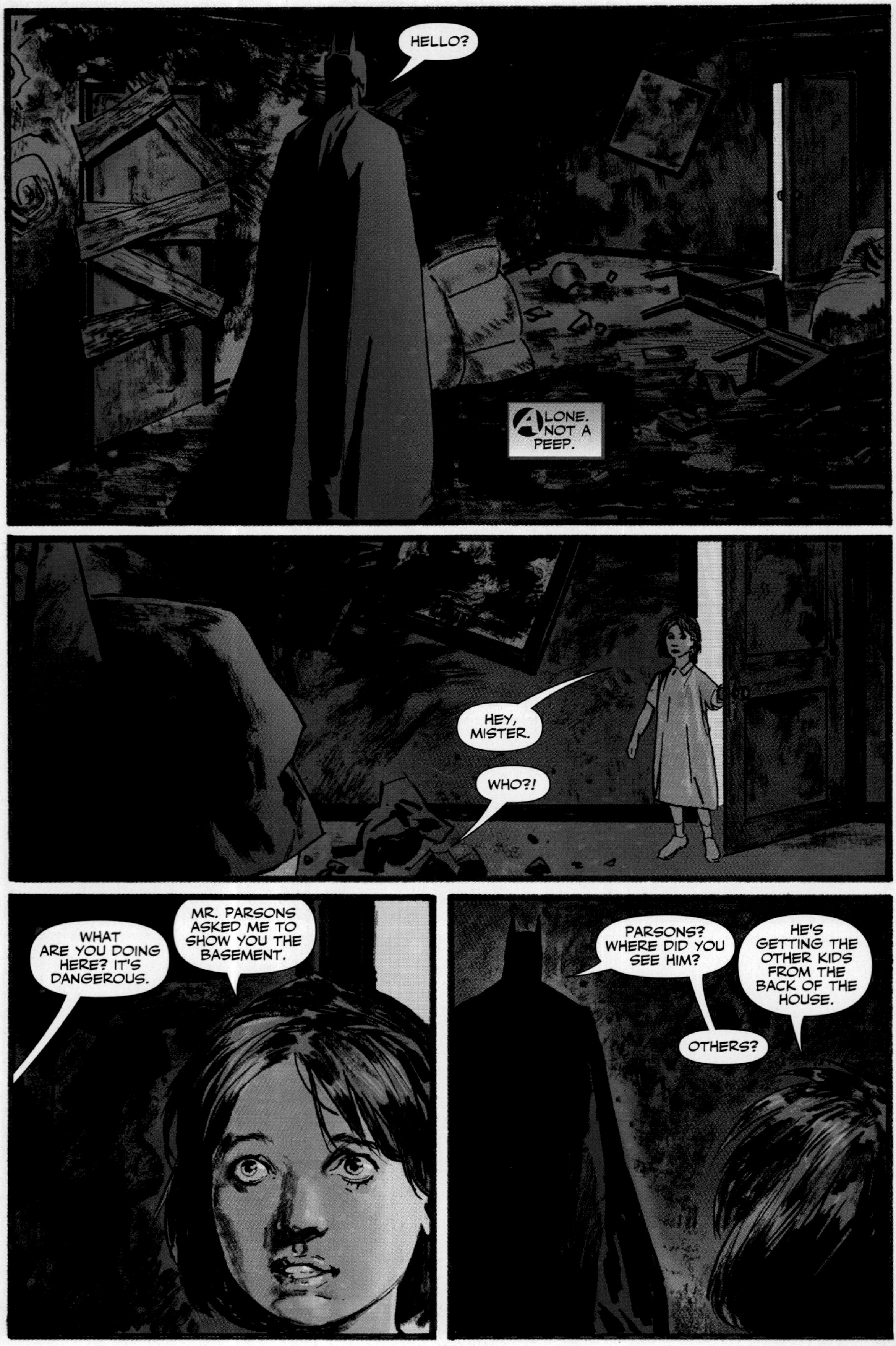

HELLO?
ALONE. NOT A PEEP.
HEY, MISTER.
WHO?!
WHAT ARE YOU DOING HERE? IT'S DANGEROUS.
MR. PARSONS ASKED ME TO SHOW YOU THE BASEMENT.
PARSONS? WHERE DID YOU SEE HIM?
HE'S GETTING THE OTHER KIDS FROM THE BACK OF THE HOUSE.
OTHERS?

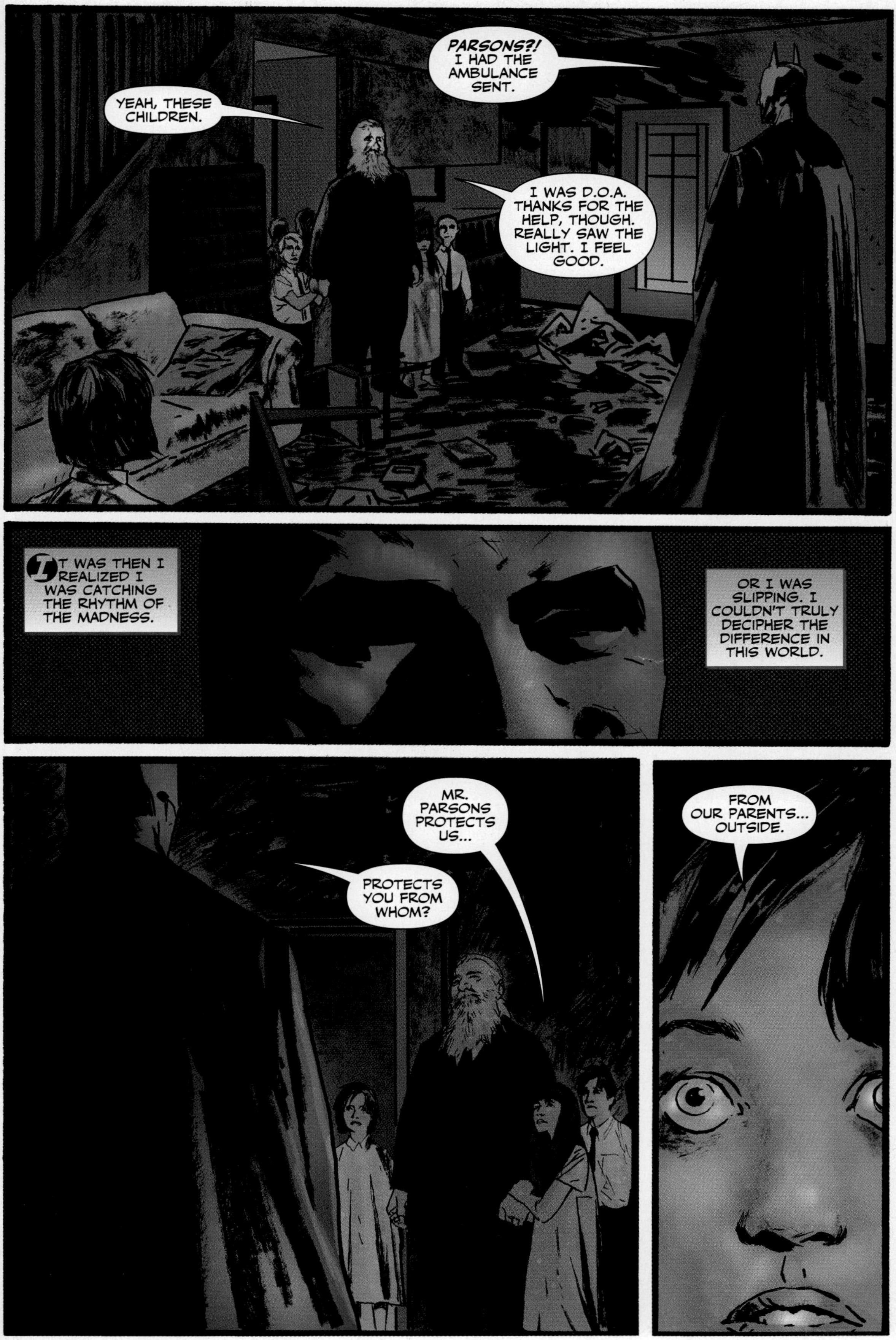
YEAH, THESE CHILDREN.
PARSONS?! I HAD THE AMBULANCE SENT.
I WAS D.O.A. THANKS FOR THE HELP, THOUGH. REALLY SAW THE LIGHT. I FEEL GOOD.
IT WAS THEN I REALIZED I WAS CATCHING THE RHYTHM OF THE MADNESS.
OR I WAS SLIPPING. I COULDN'T TRULY DECIPHER THE DIFFERENCE IN THIS WORLD.
MR. PARSONS PROTECTS US...
PROTECTS YOU FROM WHOM?
FROM OUR PARENTS... OUTSIDE.

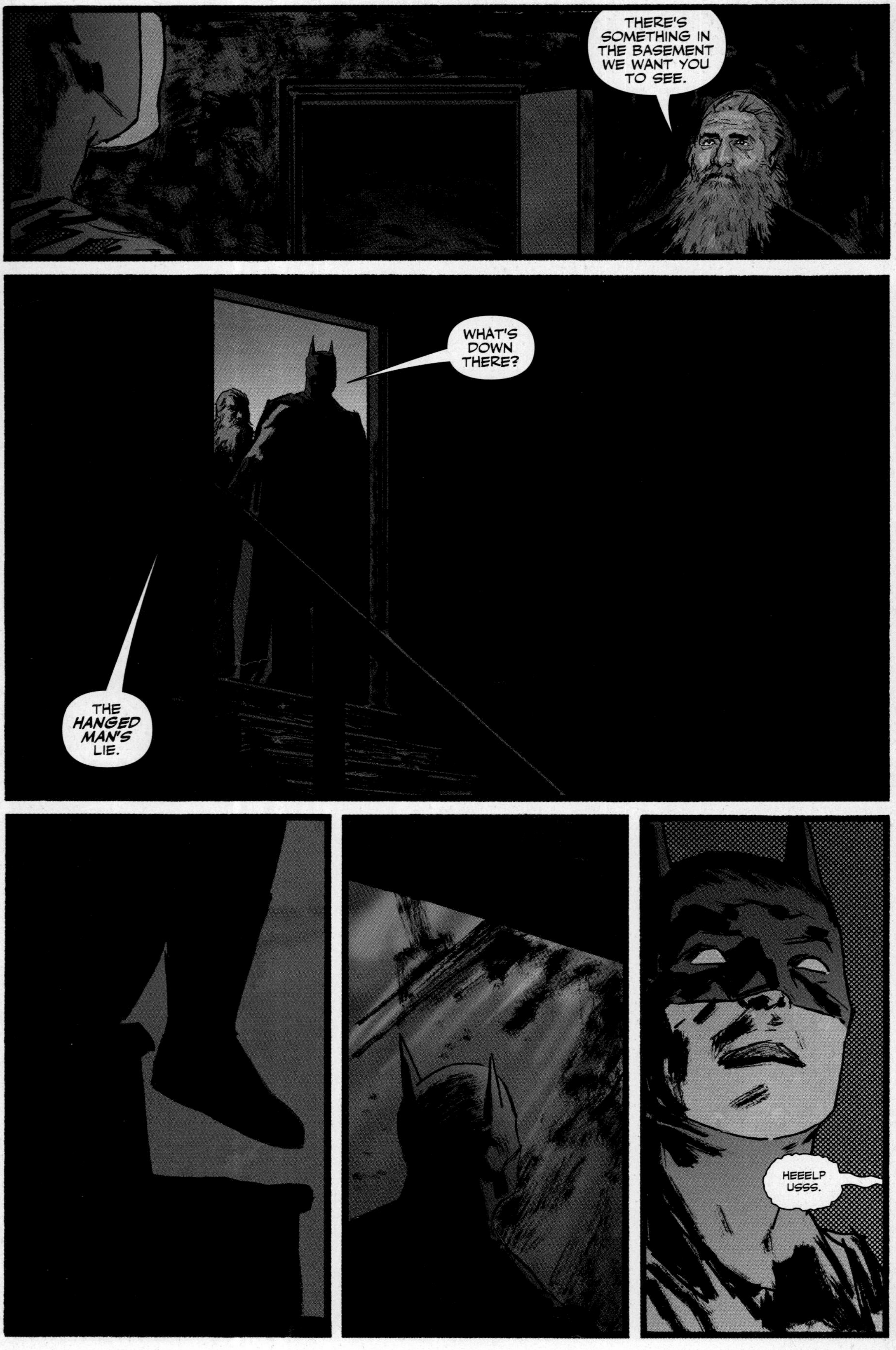
THERE'S SOMETHING IN THE BASEMENT WE WANT YOU TO SEE.
WHAT'S DOWN THERE?
THE HANGED MAN'S LIE.
HEEELP USSS.

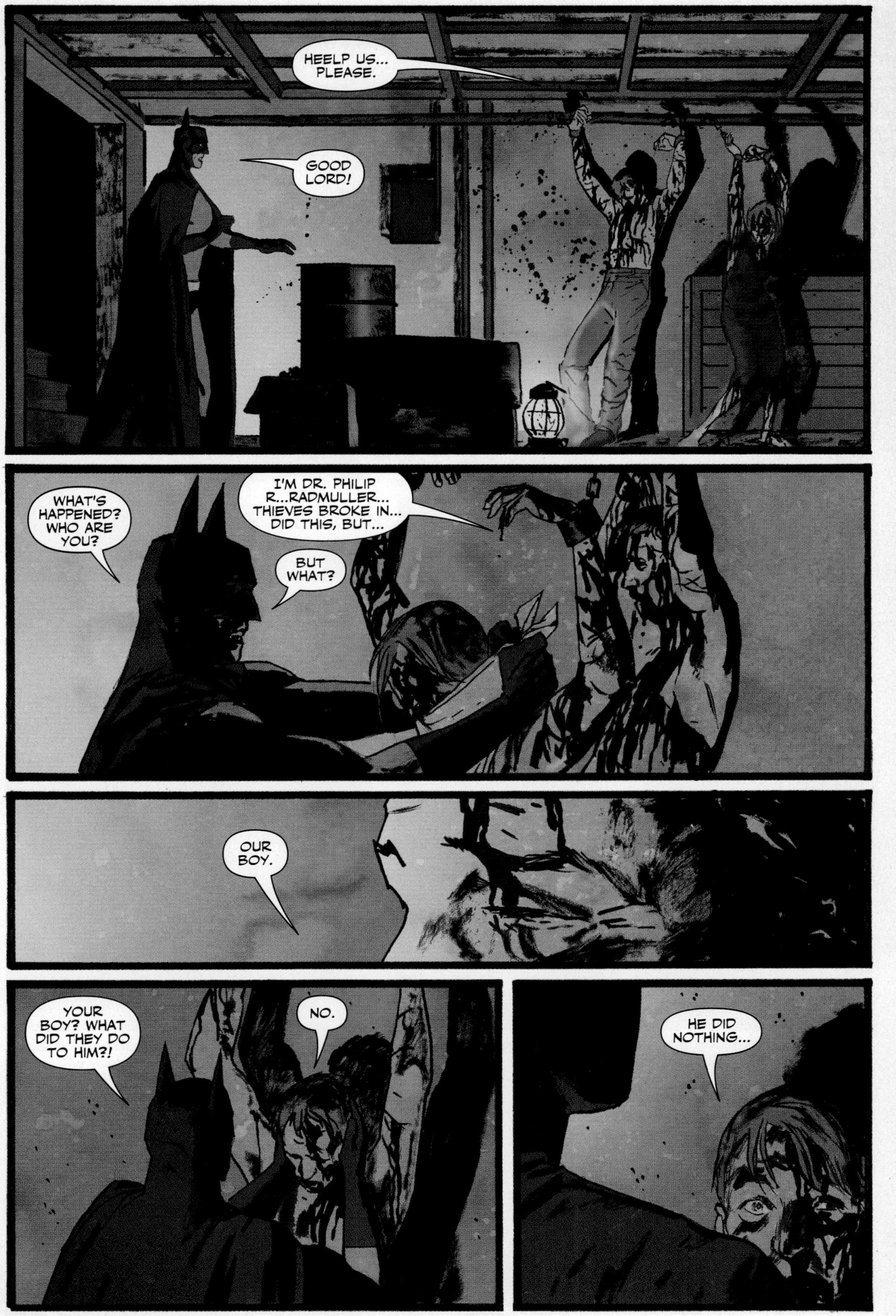
HEELP US... PLEASE.
GOOD LORD!
WHAT'S HAPPENED? WHO ARE YOU?
I'M DR. PHILIP R...RADMULLER... THIEVES BROKE IN... DID THIS, BUT...
BUT WHAT?
OUR BOY.
YOUR BOY? WHAT DID THEY DO TO HIM?!
NO.
HE DID NOTHING...

HE WATCHED US DIE! HE WATCHED THEM!

HE WATCHED!!

I GUESS I BLOCKED OUT THIS PART, BATMAN.

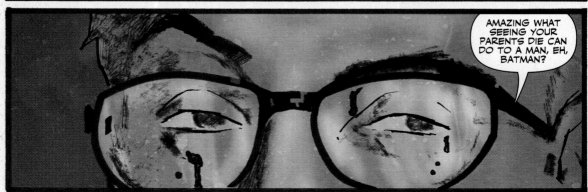

AMAZING WHAT SEEING YOUR PARENTS DIE CAN DO TO A MAN, EH, BATMAN?

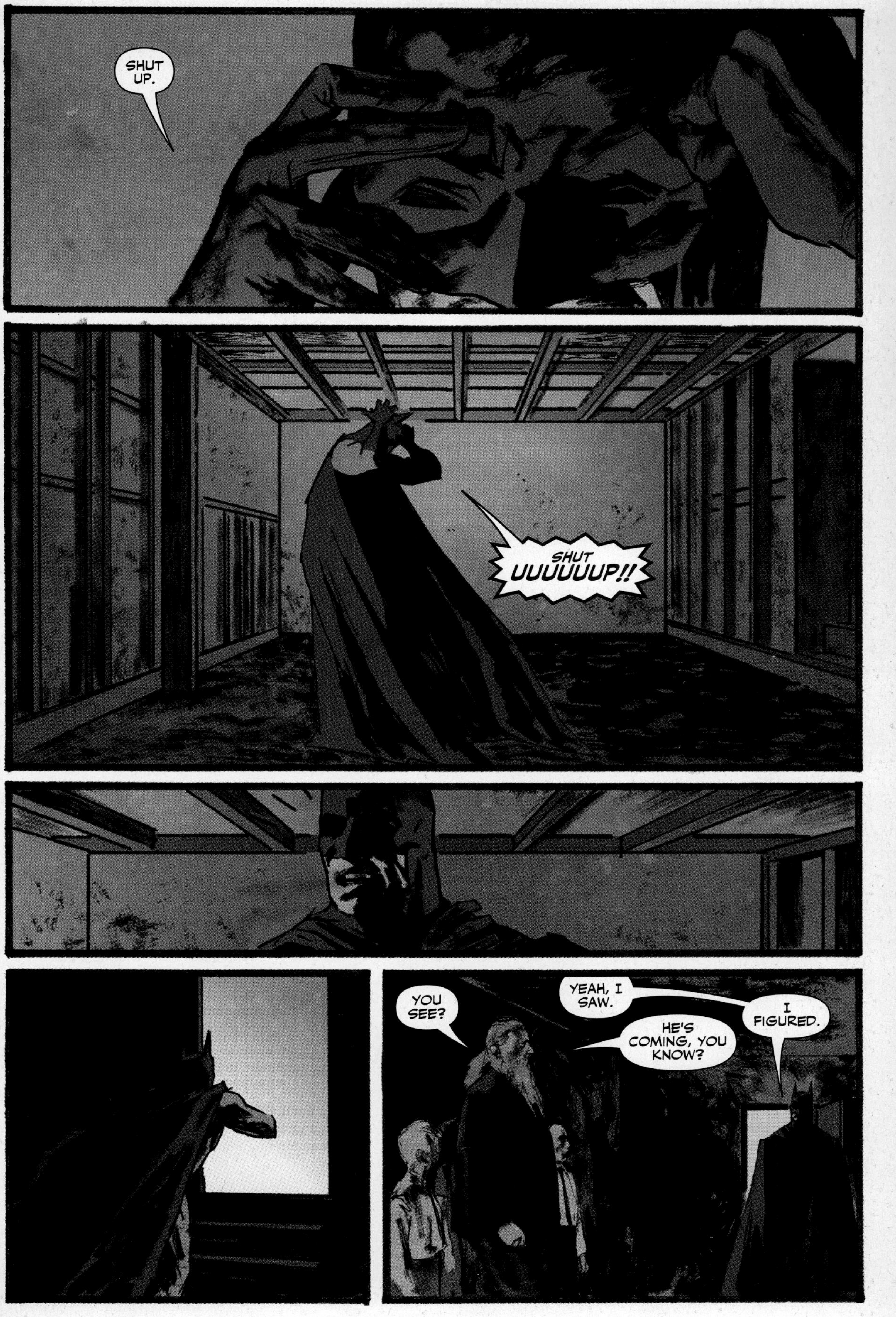
SHUT UP.
SHUT UUUUUUP!!
YOU SEE?
YEAH, I SAW.
HE'S COMING, YOU KNOW?
I FIGURED.

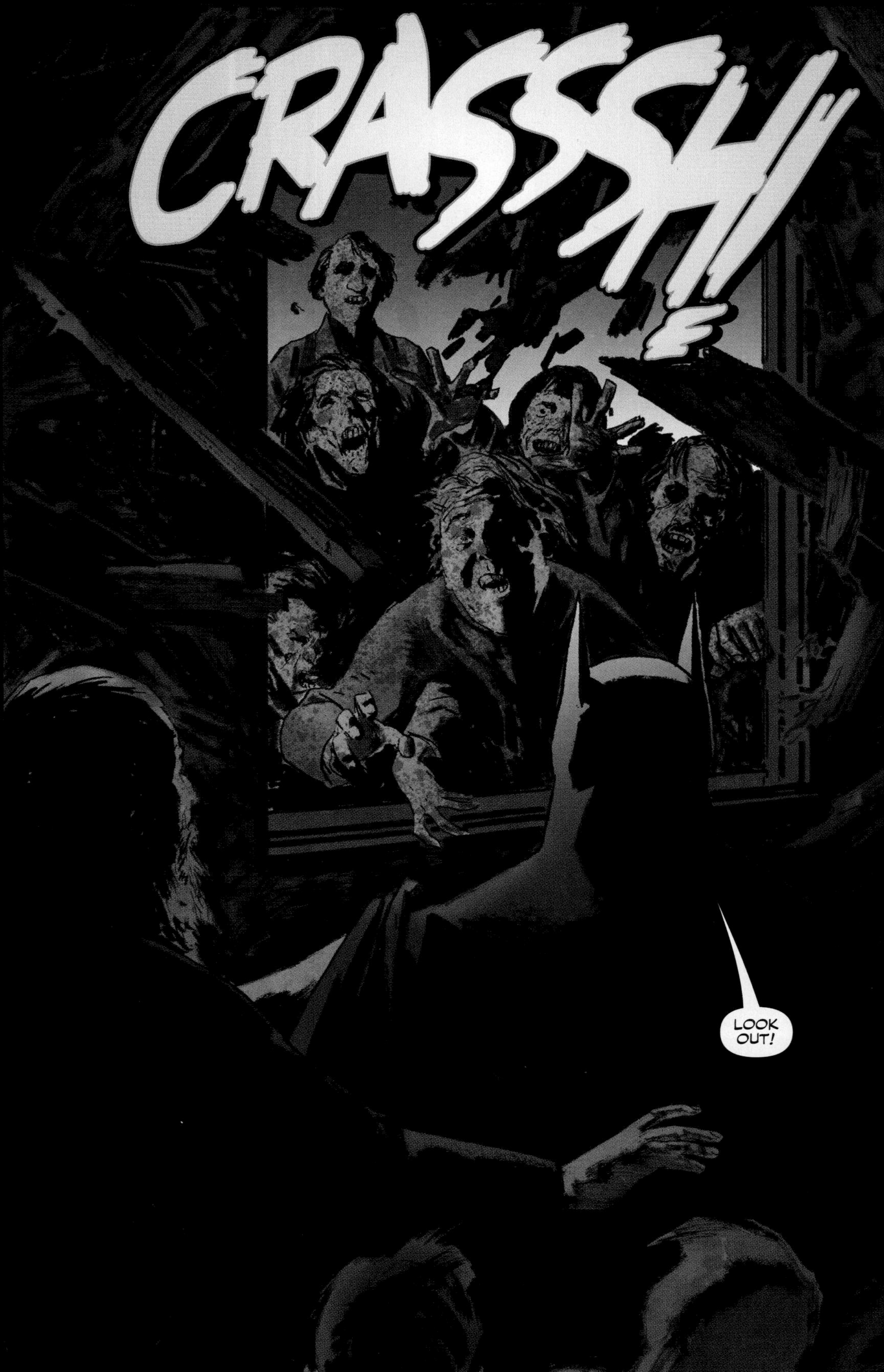
CRASSSH!
LOOK OUT!

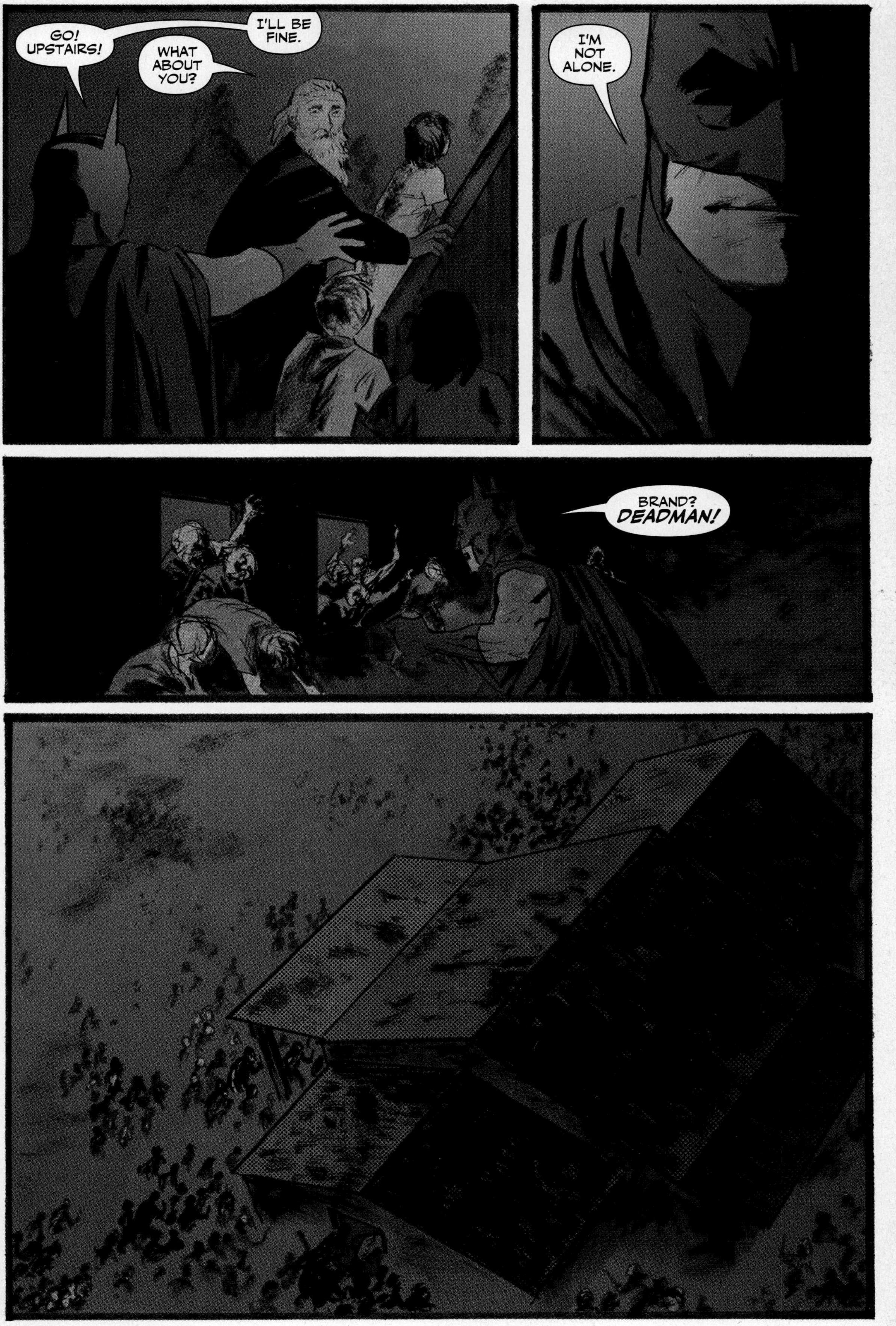
GO! UPSTAIRS!
WHAT ABOUT YOU?
I'LL BE FINE.
I'M NOT ALONE.
BRAND? DEADMAN!

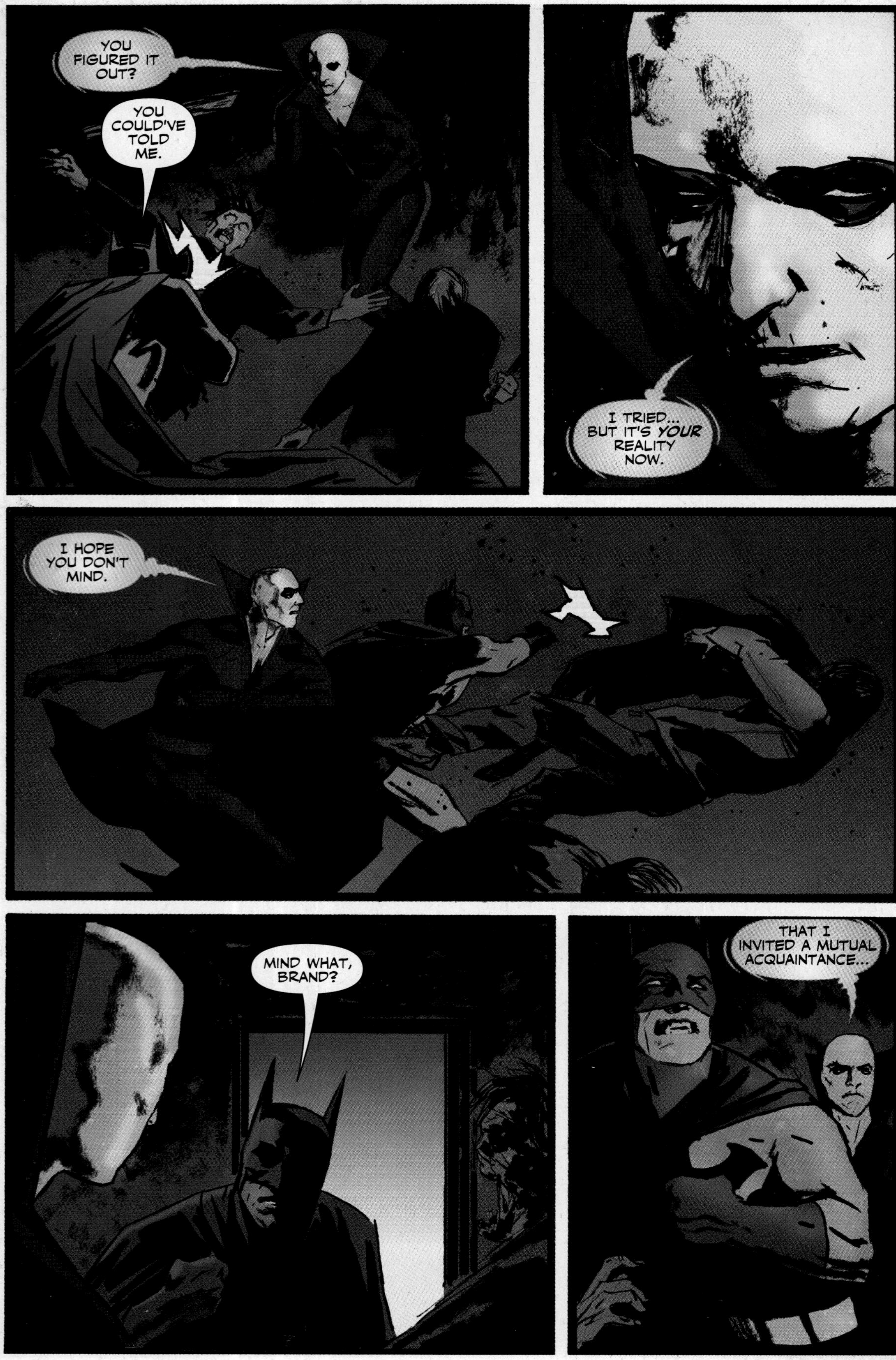
YOU FIGURED IT OUT?
YOU COULD'VE TOLD ME.
I TRIED... BUT IT'S *YOUR* REALITY NOW.
I HOPE YOU DON'T MIND.
MIND WHAT, BRAND?
THAT I INVITED A MUTUAL ACQUAINTANCE...

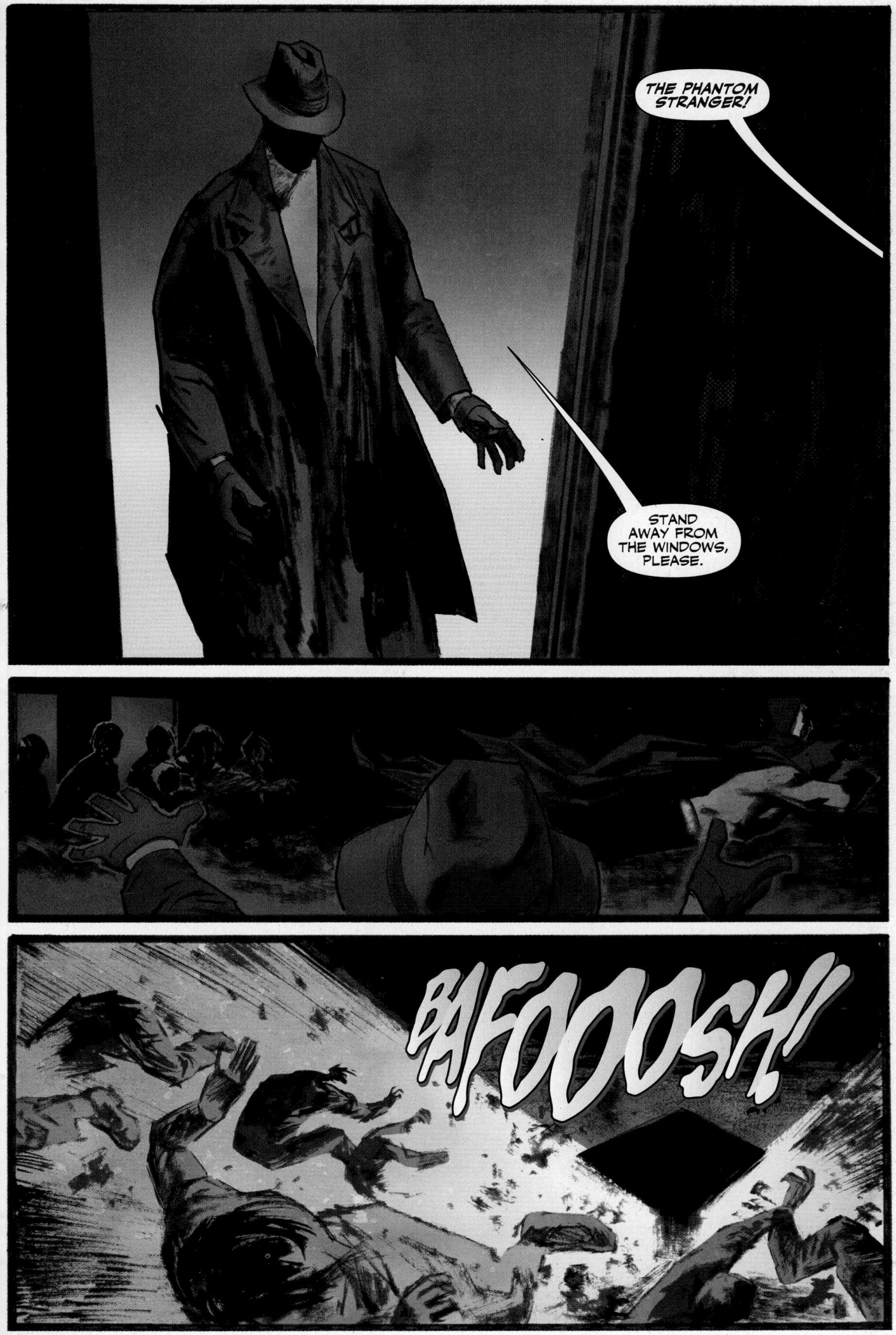

THE PHANTOM STRANGER!
STAND AWAY FROM THE WINDOWS, PLEASE.
BAFOOOSH!

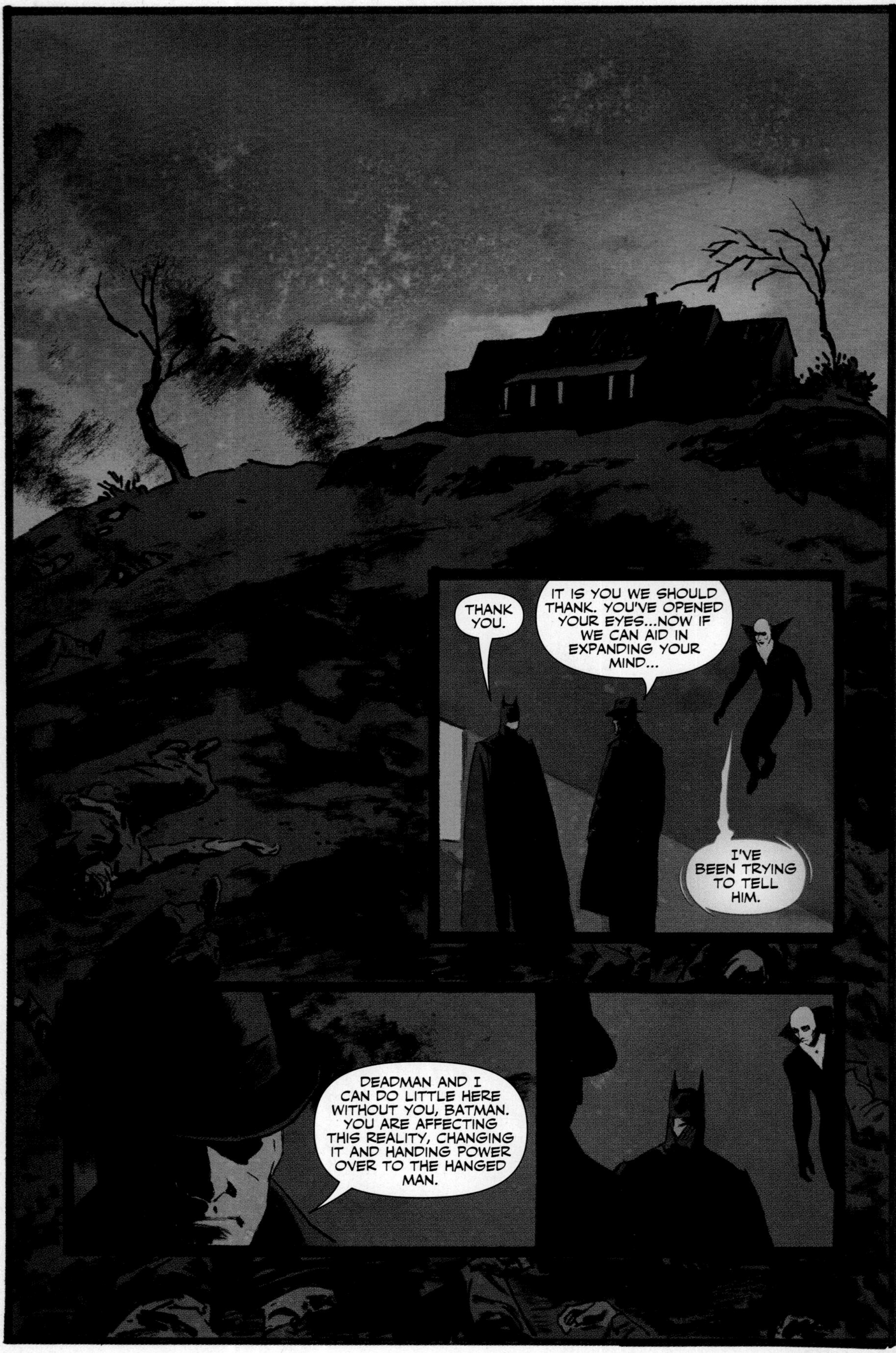
THANK YOU.
IT IS YOU WE SHOULD THANK. YOU'VE OPENED YOUR EYES...NOW IF WE CAN AID IN EXPANDING YOUR MIND...
I'VE BEEN TRYING TO TELL HIM.
DEADMAN AND I CAN DO LITTLE HERE WITHOUT YOU, BATMAN. YOU ARE AFFECTING THIS REALITY, CHANGING IT AND HANDING POWER OVER TO THE HANGED MAN.

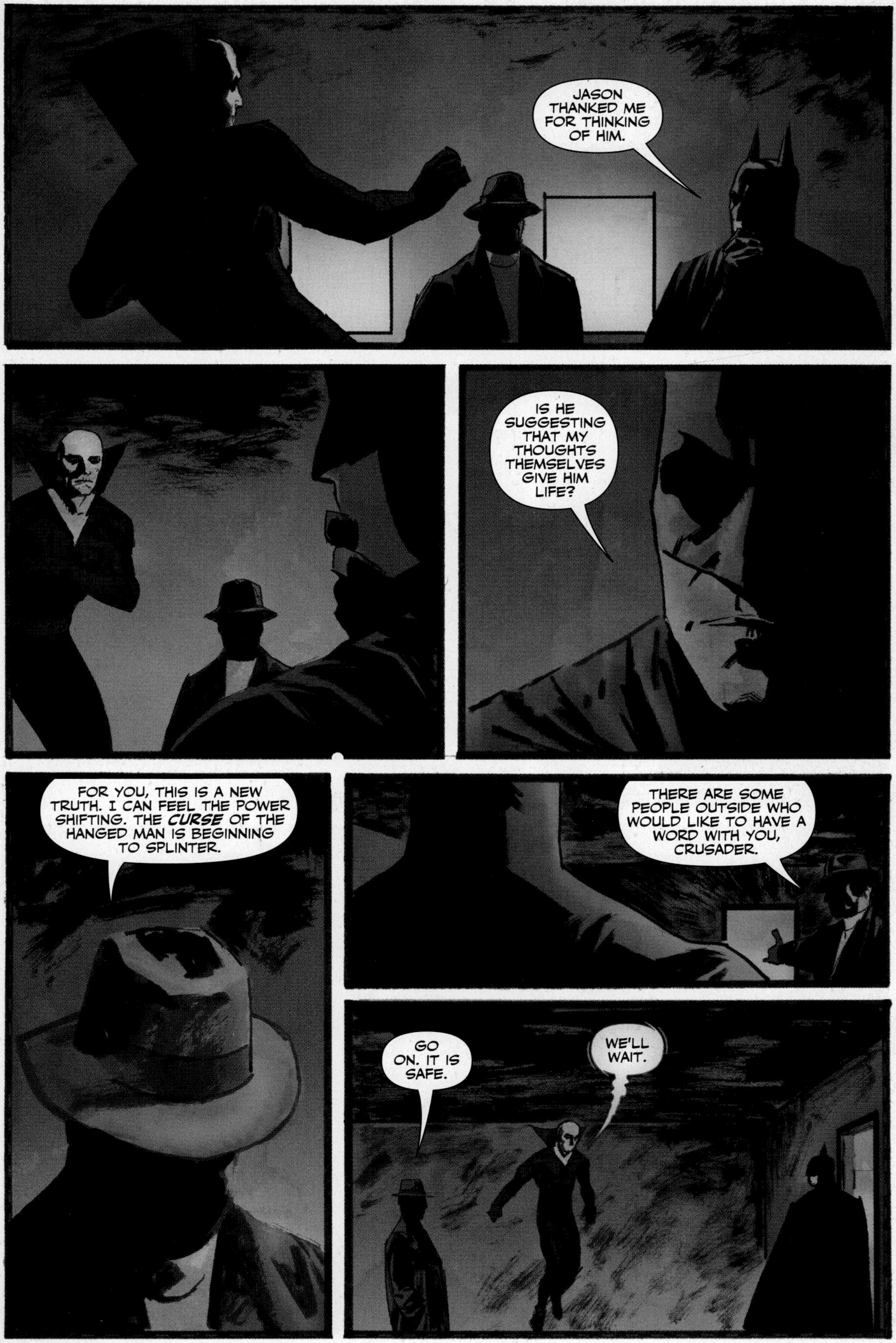
JASON THANKED ME FOR THINKING OF HIM.
IS HE SUGGESTING THAT MY THOUGHTS THEMSELVES GIVE HIM LIFE?
FOR YOU, THIS IS A NEW TRUTH. I CAN FEEL THE POWER SHIFTING. THE *CURSE* OF THE HANGED MAN IS BEGINNING TO SPLINTER.
THERE ARE SOME PEOPLE OUTSIDE WHO WOULD LIKE TO HAVE A WORD WITH YOU, CRUSADER.
GO ON. IT IS SAFE.
WE'LL WAIT.

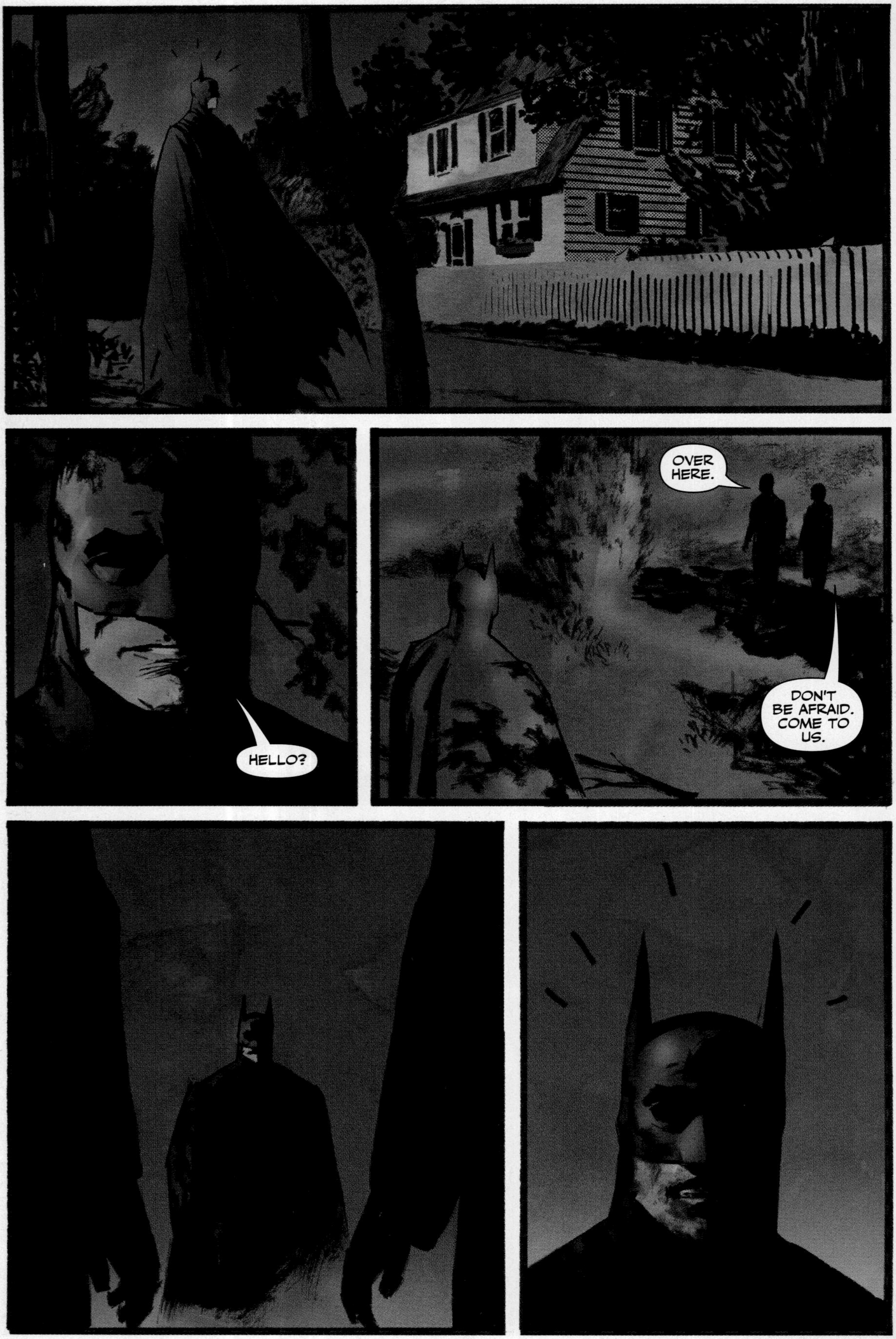
HELLO?
OVER HERE.
DON'T BE AFRAID. COME TO US.

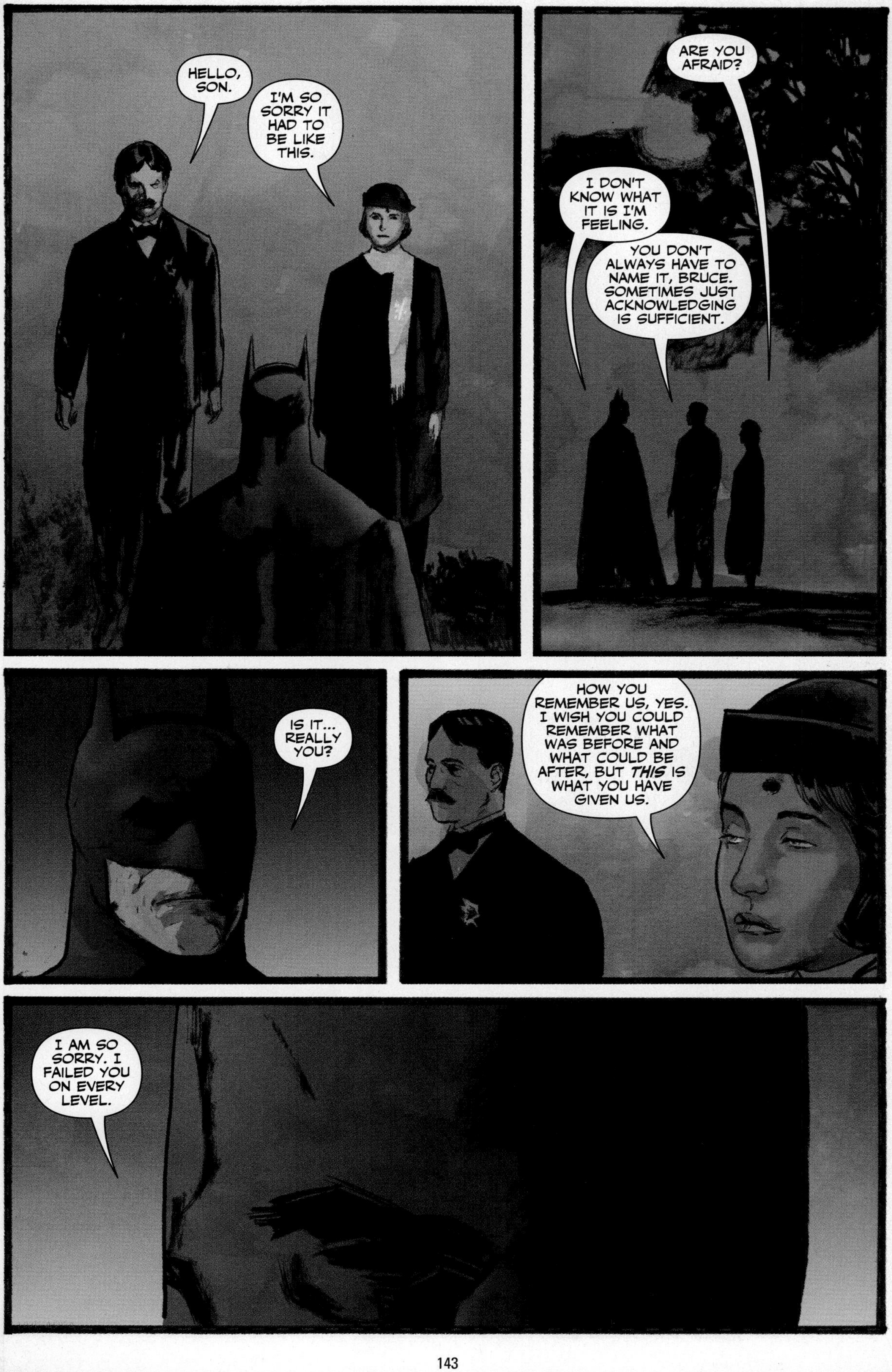
HELLO, SON.
I'M SO SORRY IT HAD TO BE LIKE THIS.
ARE YOU AFRAID?
I DON'T KNOW WHAT IT IS I'M FEELING.
YOU DON'T ALWAYS HAVE TO NAME IT, BRUCE. SOMETIMES JUST ACKNOWLEDGING IS SUFFICIENT.
IS IT... REALLY YOU?
HOW YOU REMEMBER US, YES. I WISH YOU COULD REMEMBER WHAT WAS BEFORE AND WHAT COULD BE AFTER, BUT *THIS* IS WHAT YOU HAVE GIVEN US.
I AM SO SORRY. I FAILED YOU ON EVERY LEVEL.

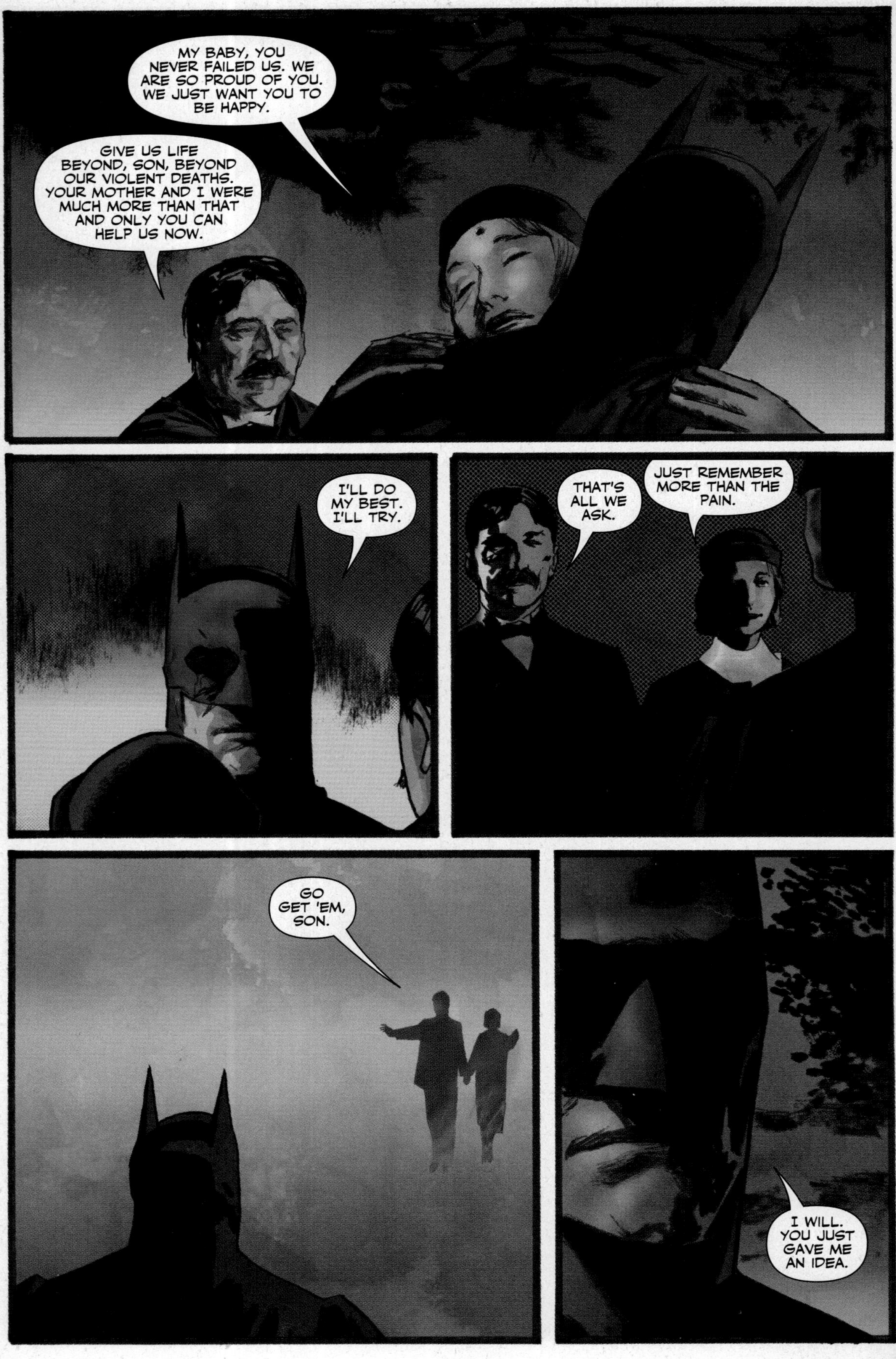
MY BABY, YOU NEVER FAILED US. WE ARE SO PROUD OF YOU. WE JUST WANT YOU TO BE HAPPY.
GIVE US LIFE BEYOND, SON, BEYOND OUR VIOLENT DEATHS. YOUR MOTHER AND I WERE MUCH MORE THAN THAT AND ONLY YOU CAN HELP US NOW.
I'LL DO MY BEST. I'LL TRY.
THAT'S ALL WE ASK.
JUST REMEMBER MORE THAN THE PAIN.
GO GET 'EM, SON.
I WILL. YOU JUST GAVE ME AN IDEA.

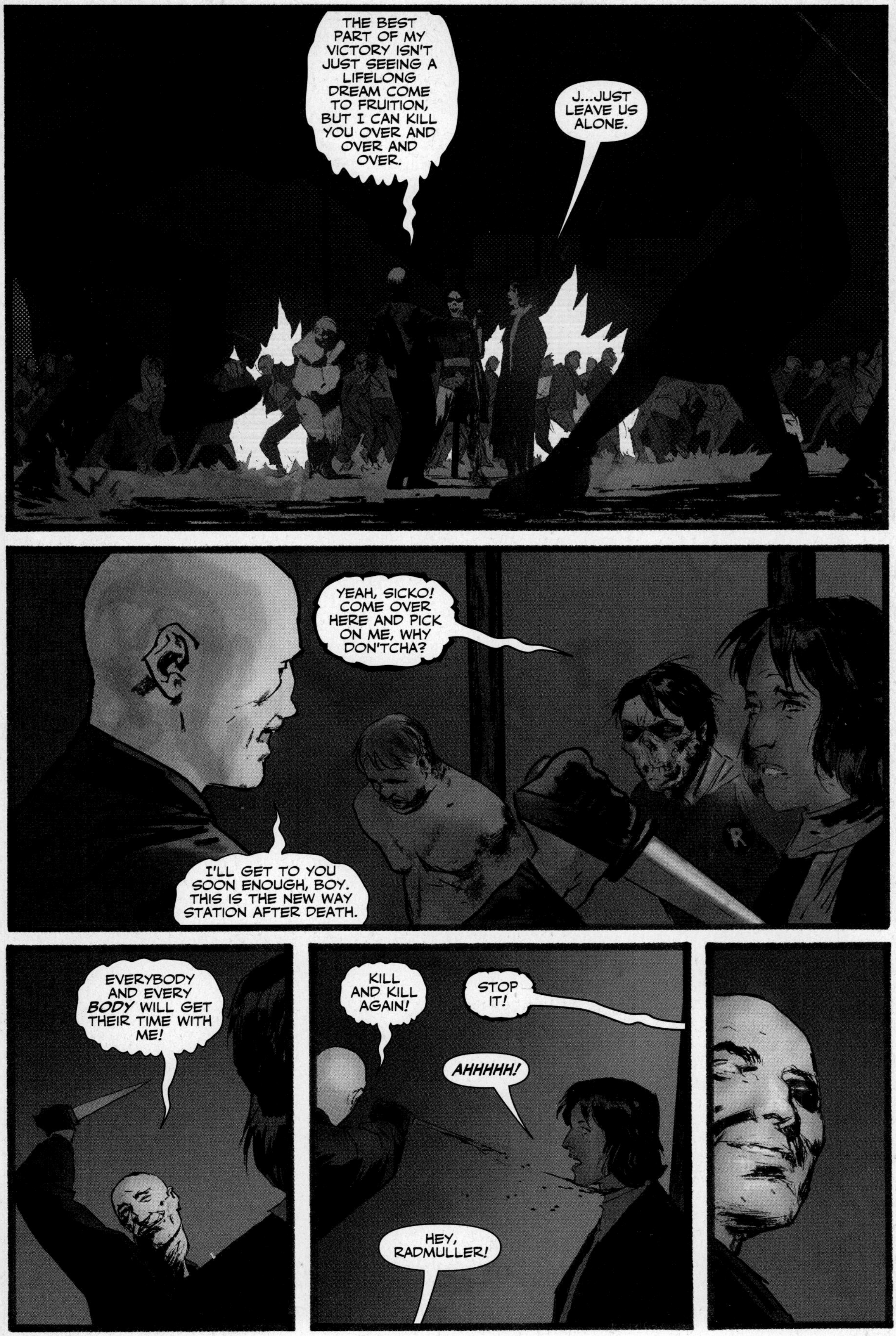
THE BEST PART OF MY VICTORY ISN'T JUST SEEING A LIFELONG DREAM COME TO FRUITION, BUT I CAN KILL YOU OVER AND OVER AND OVER.
J...JUST LEAVE US ALONE.
YEAH, SICKO! COME OVER HERE AND PICK ON ME, WHY DON'TCHA?
I'LL GET TO YOU SOON ENOUGH, BOY. THIS IS THE NEW WAY STATION AFTER DEATH.
EVERYBODY AND EVERY *BODY* WILL GET THEIR TIME WITH ME!
KILL AND KILL AGAIN!
STOP IT!
AHHHHH!
HEY, RADMULLER!

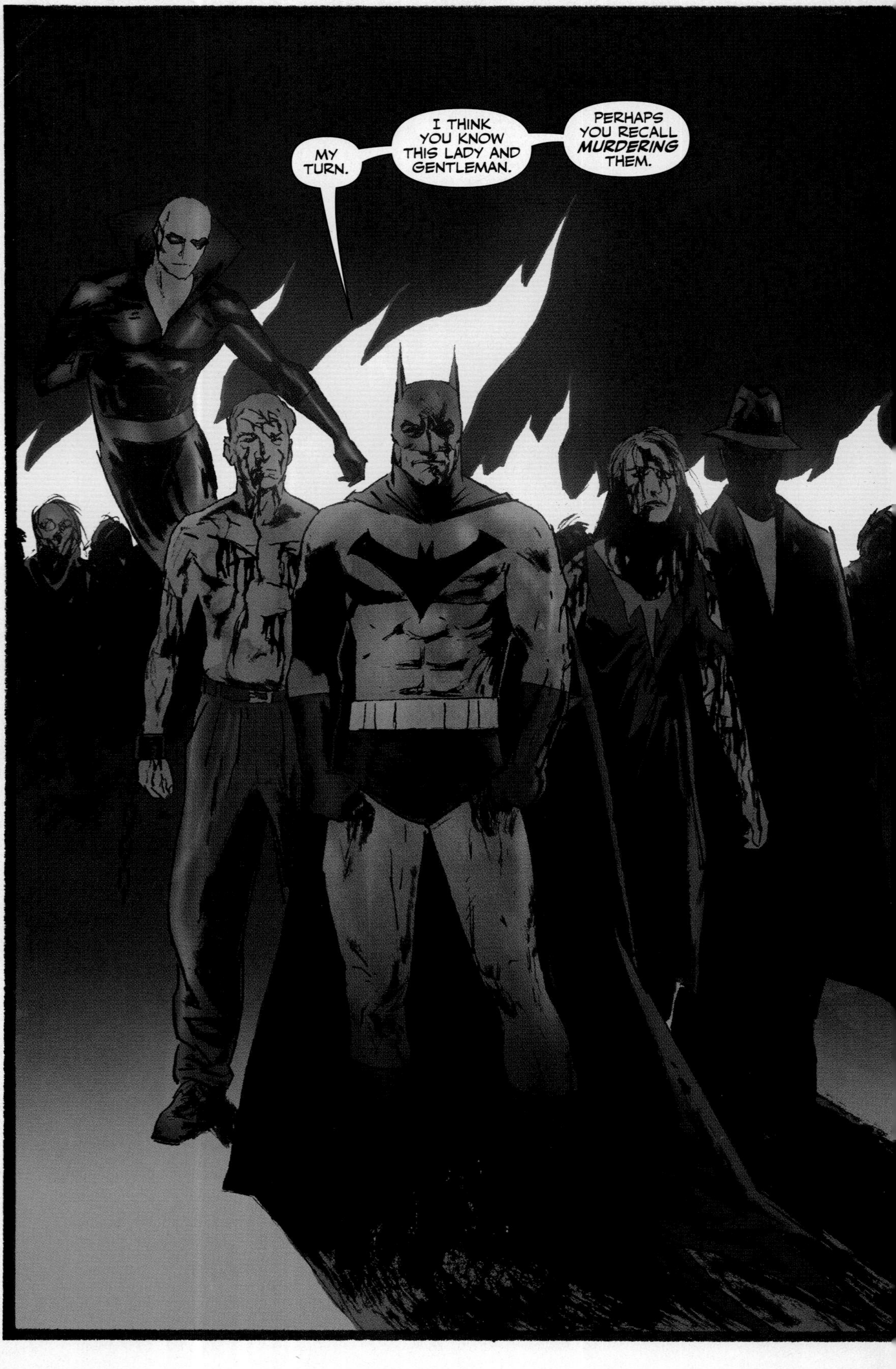
MY TURN.
I THINK YOU KNOW THIS LADY AND GENTLEMAN.
PERHAPS YOU RECALL *MURDERING* THEM.

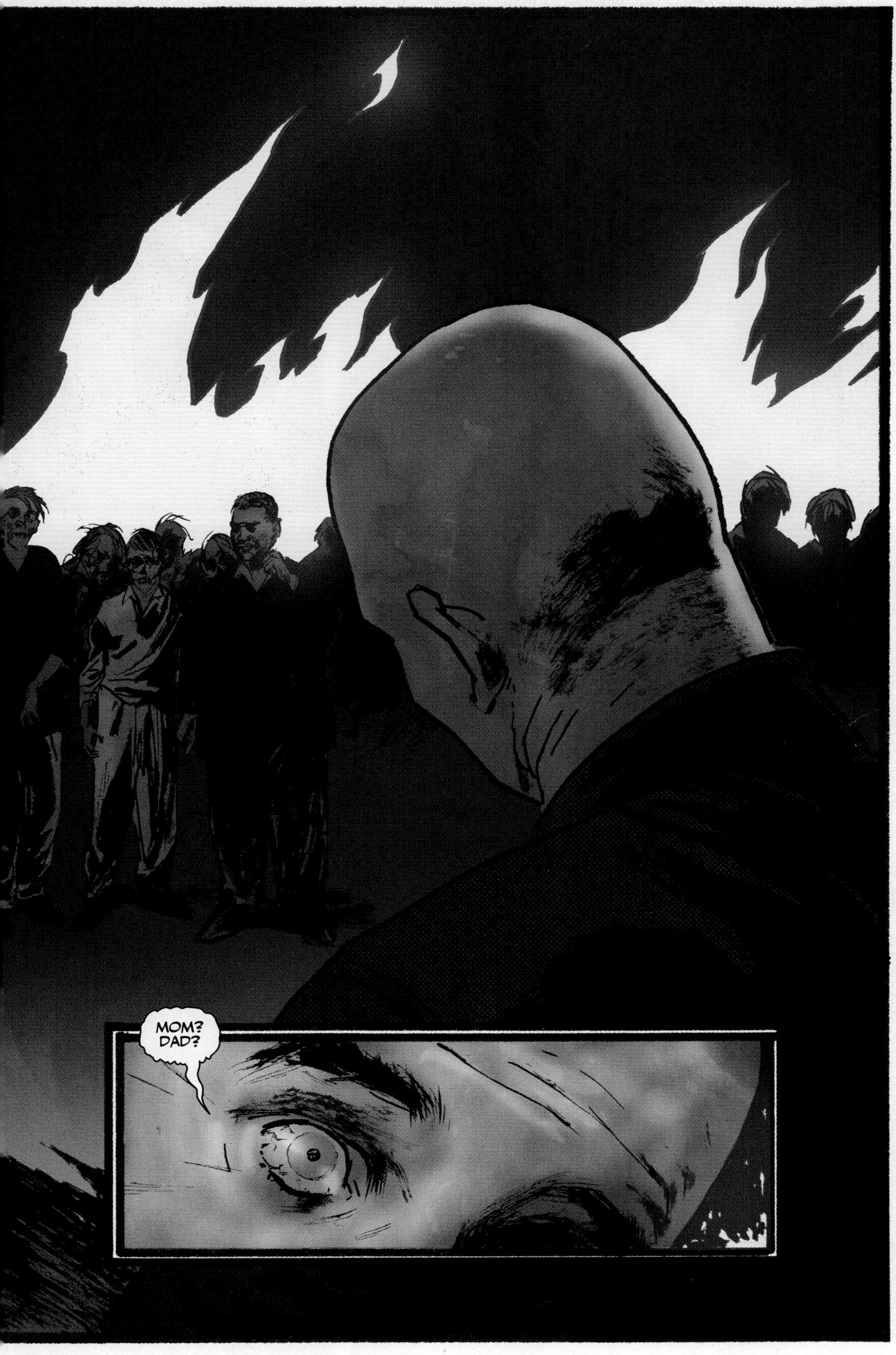
MOM?
DAD?

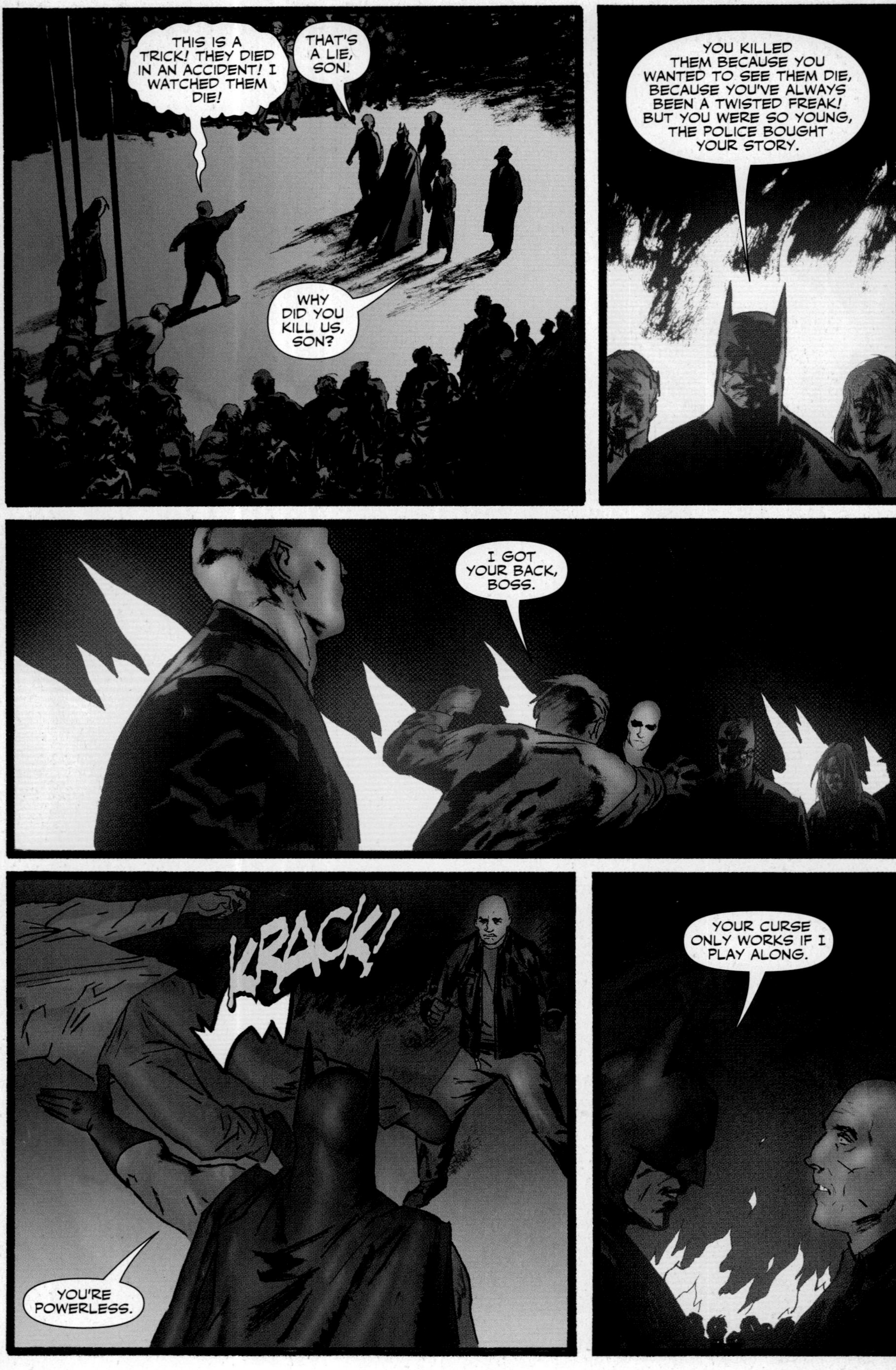
THIS IS A TRICK! THEY DIED IN AN ACCIDENT! I WATCHED THEM DIE!
THAT'S A LIE, SON.
WHY DID YOU KILL US, SON?
YOU KILLED THEM BECAUSE YOU WANTED TO SEE THEM DIE, BECAUSE YOU'VE ALWAYS BEEN A TWISTED FREAK! BUT YOU WERE SO YOUNG, THE POLICE BOUGHT YOUR STORY.
I GOT YOUR BACK, BOSS.
KRACK!
YOU'RE POWERLESS.
YOUR CURSE ONLY WORKS IF I PLAY ALONG.

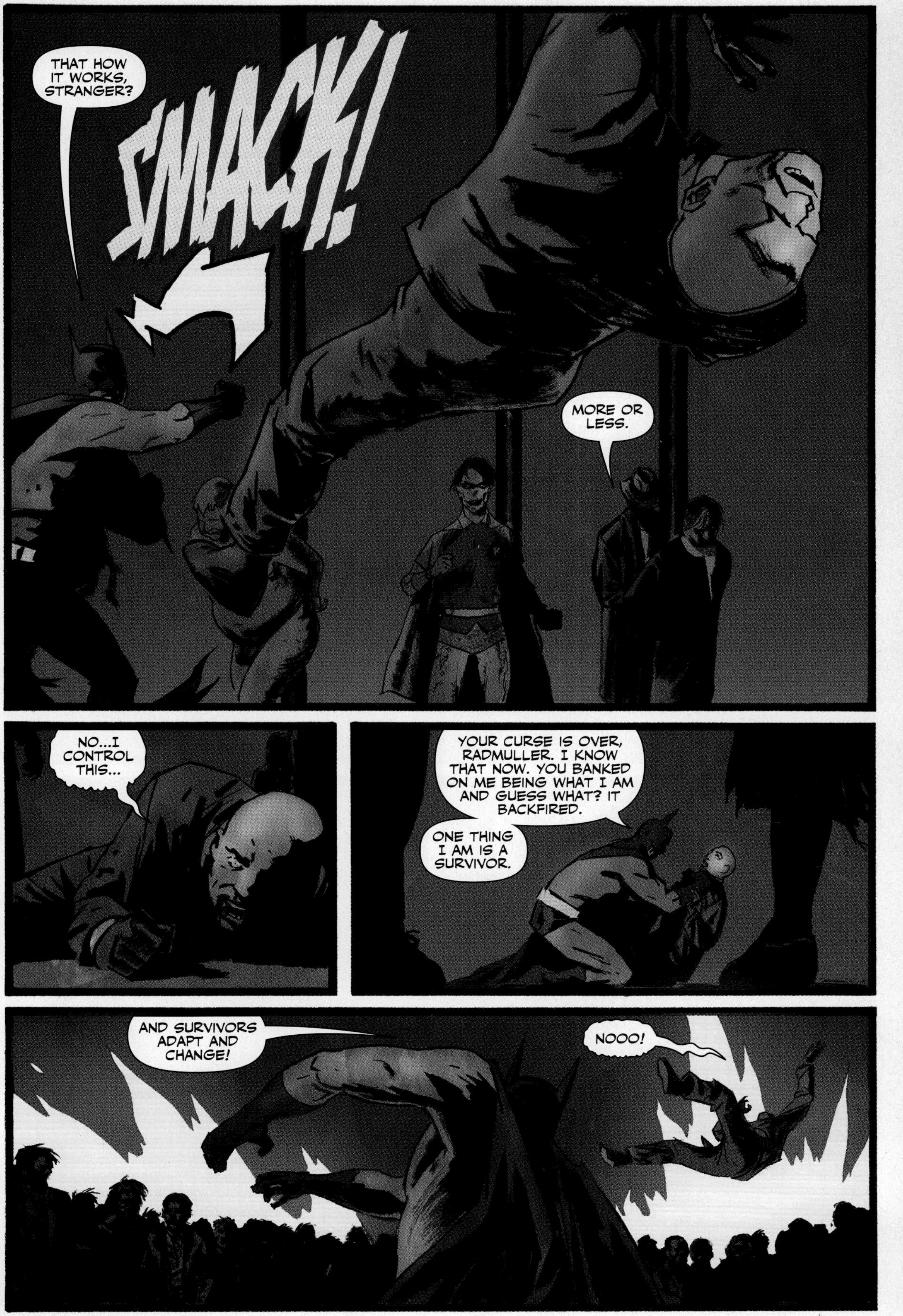
THAT HOW IT WORKS, STRANGER?
SMACK!
MORE OR LESS.
NO...I CONTROL THIS...
YOUR CURSE IS OVER, RADMULLER. I KNOW THAT NOW. YOU BANKED ON ME BEING WHAT I AM AND GUESS WHAT? IT BACKFIRED.
ONE THING I AM IS A SURVIVOR.
AND SURVIVORS ADAPT AND CHANGE!
NOOO!

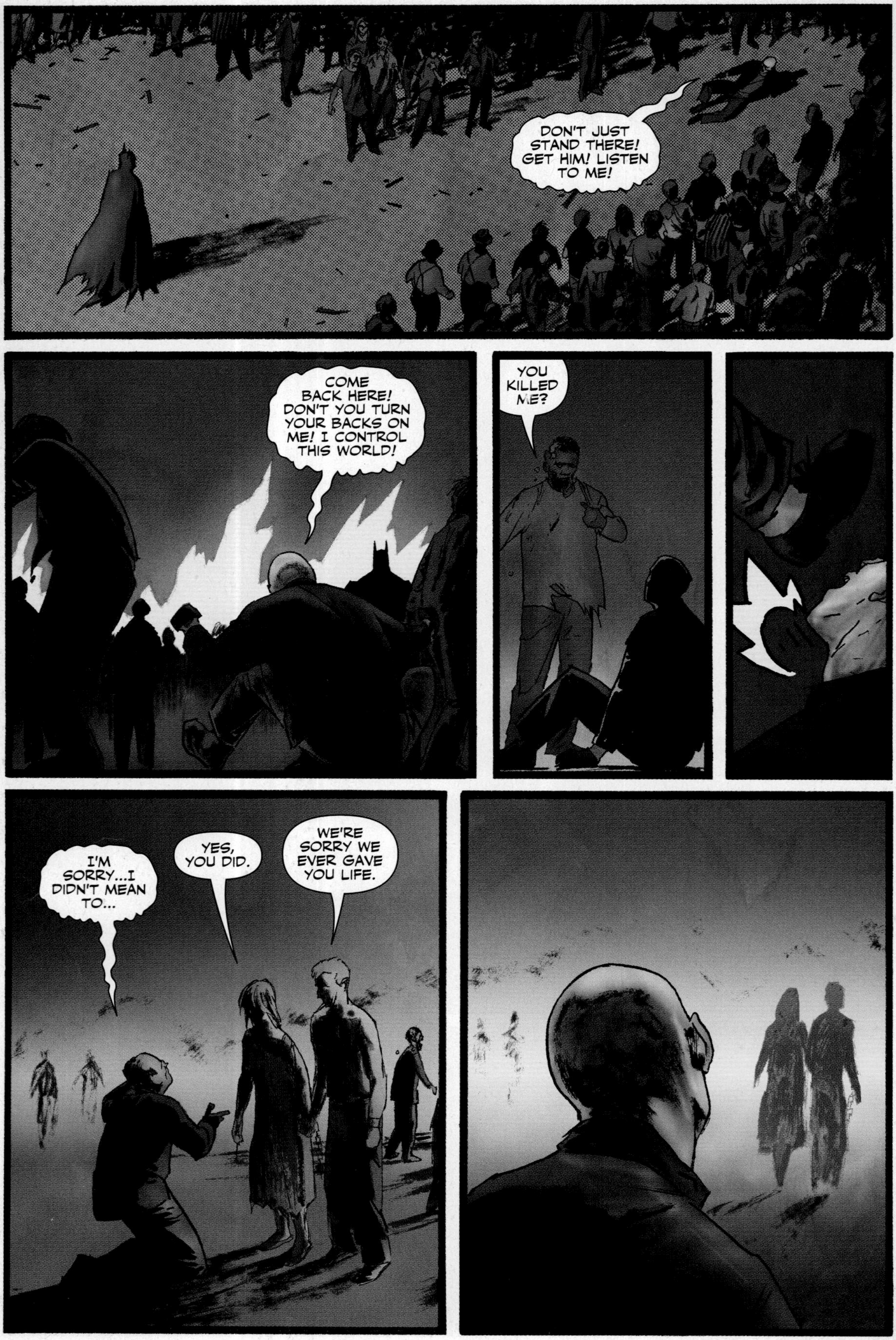
DON'T JUST STAND THERE! GET HIM! LISTEN TO ME!
COME BACK HERE! DON'T YOU TURN YOUR BACKS ON ME! I CONTROL THIS WORLD!
YOU KILLED ME?
I'M SORRY...I DIDN'T MEAN TO...
YES, YOU DID.
WE'RE SORRY WE EVER GAVE YOU LIFE.

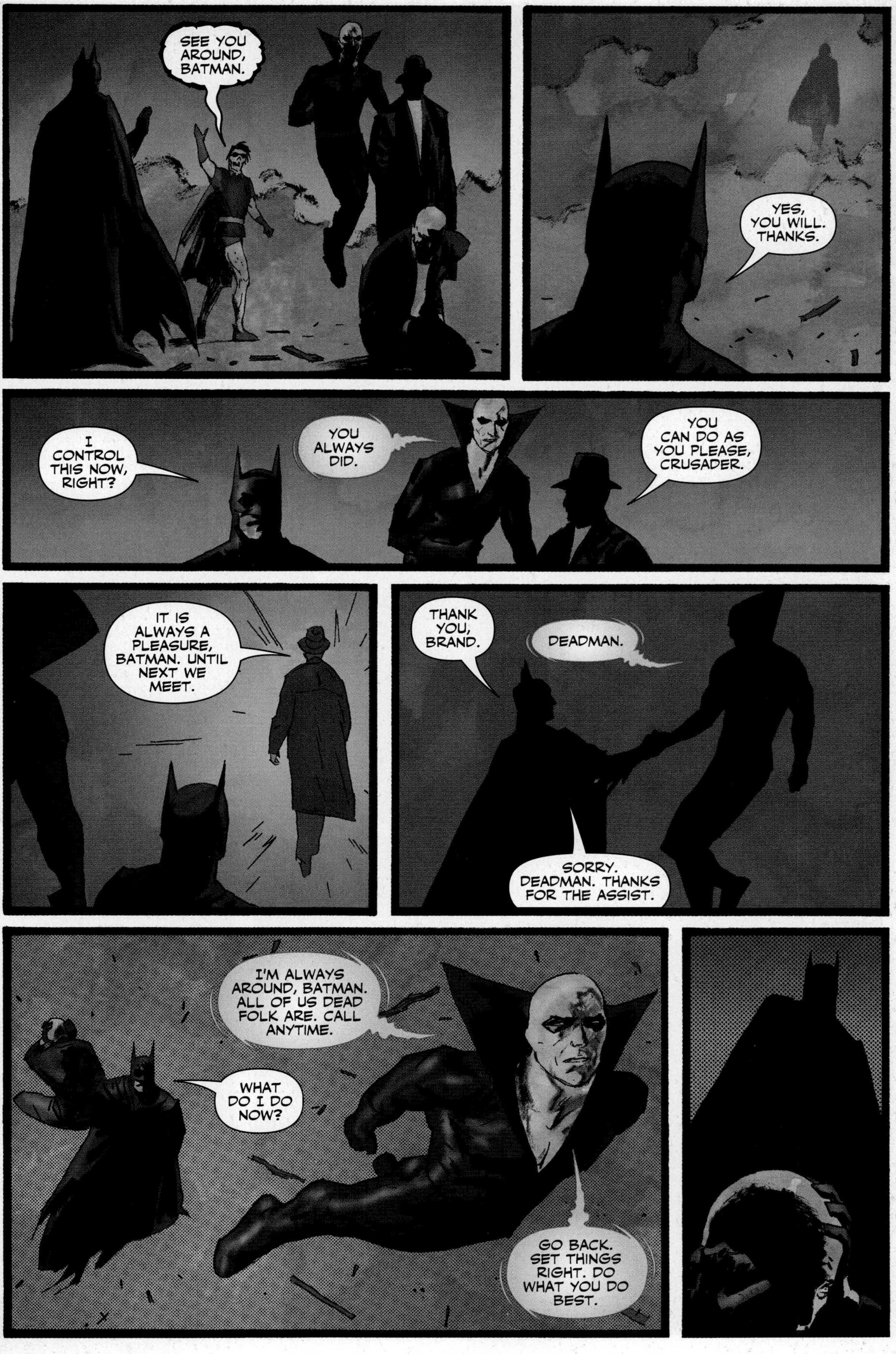
SEE YOU AROUND, BATMAN.
YES, YOU WILL. THANKS.
I CONTROL THIS NOW, RIGHT?
YOU ALWAYS DID.
YOU CAN DO AS YOU PLEASE, CRUSADER.
IT IS ALWAYS A PLEASURE, BATMAN. UNTIL NEXT WE MEET.
THANK YOU, BRAND.
DEADMAN.
SORRY. DEADMAN. THANKS FOR THE ASSIST.
I'M ALWAYS AROUND, BATMAN. ALL OF US DEAD FOLK ARE. CALL ANYTIME.
WHAT DO I DO NOW?
GO BACK. SET THINGS RIGHT. DO WHAT YOU DO BEST.

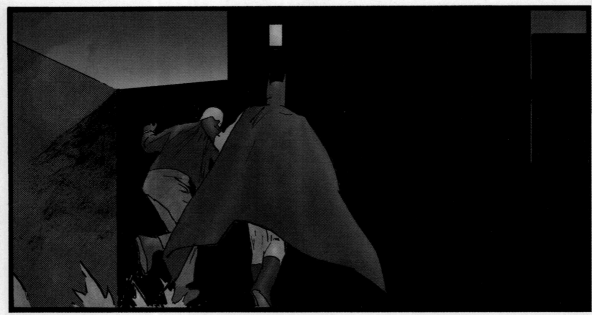

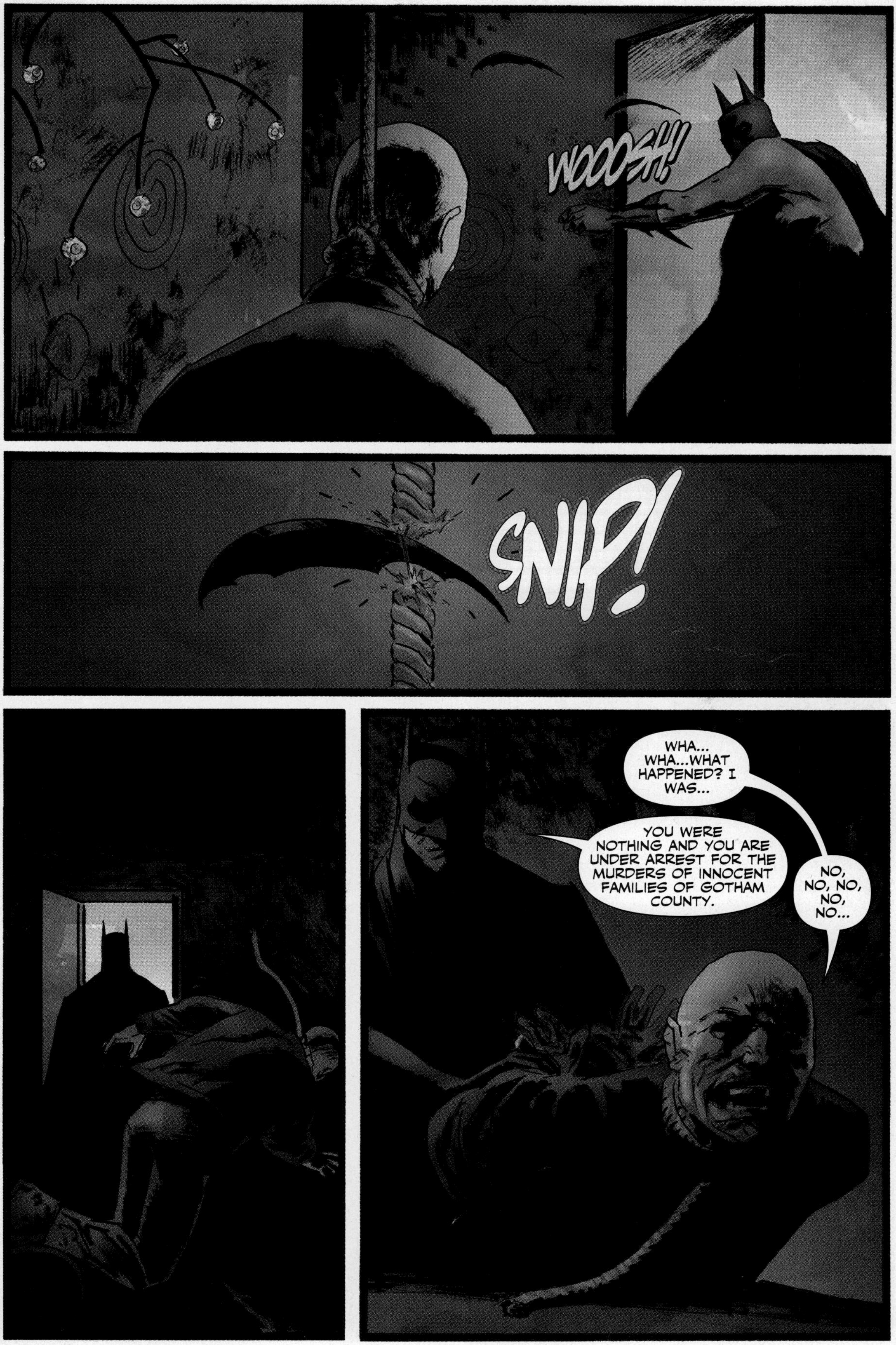
WOOOSH!!
SNIP!
WHA... WHA...WHAT HAPPENED? I WAS...
YOU WERE NOTHING AND YOU ARE UNDER ARREST FOR THE MURDERS OF INNOCENT FAMILIES OF GOTHAM COUNTY.
NO, NO, NO, NO, NO...

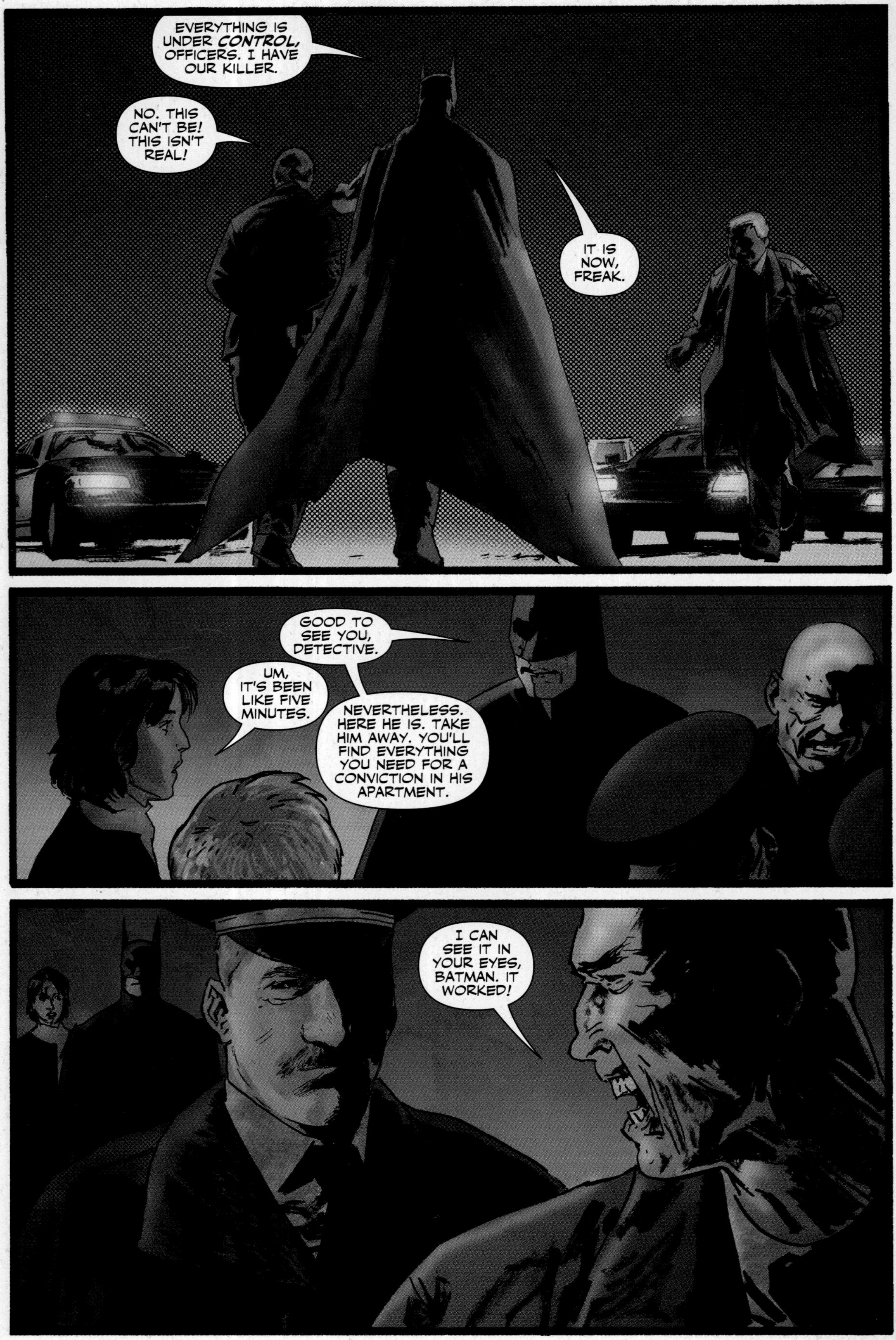
EVERYTHING IS UNDER CONTROL, OFFICERS. I HAVE OUR KILLER.
NO. THIS CAN'T BE! THIS ISN'T REAL!
IT IS NOW, FREAK.
GOOD TO SEE YOU, DETECTIVE.
UM, IT'S BEEN LIKE FIVE MINUTES.
NEVERTHELESS. HERE HE IS. TAKE HIM AWAY. YOU'LL FIND EVERYTHING YOU NEED FOR A CONVICTION IN HIS APARTMENT.
I CAN SEE IT IN YOUR EYES, BATMAN. IT WORKED!

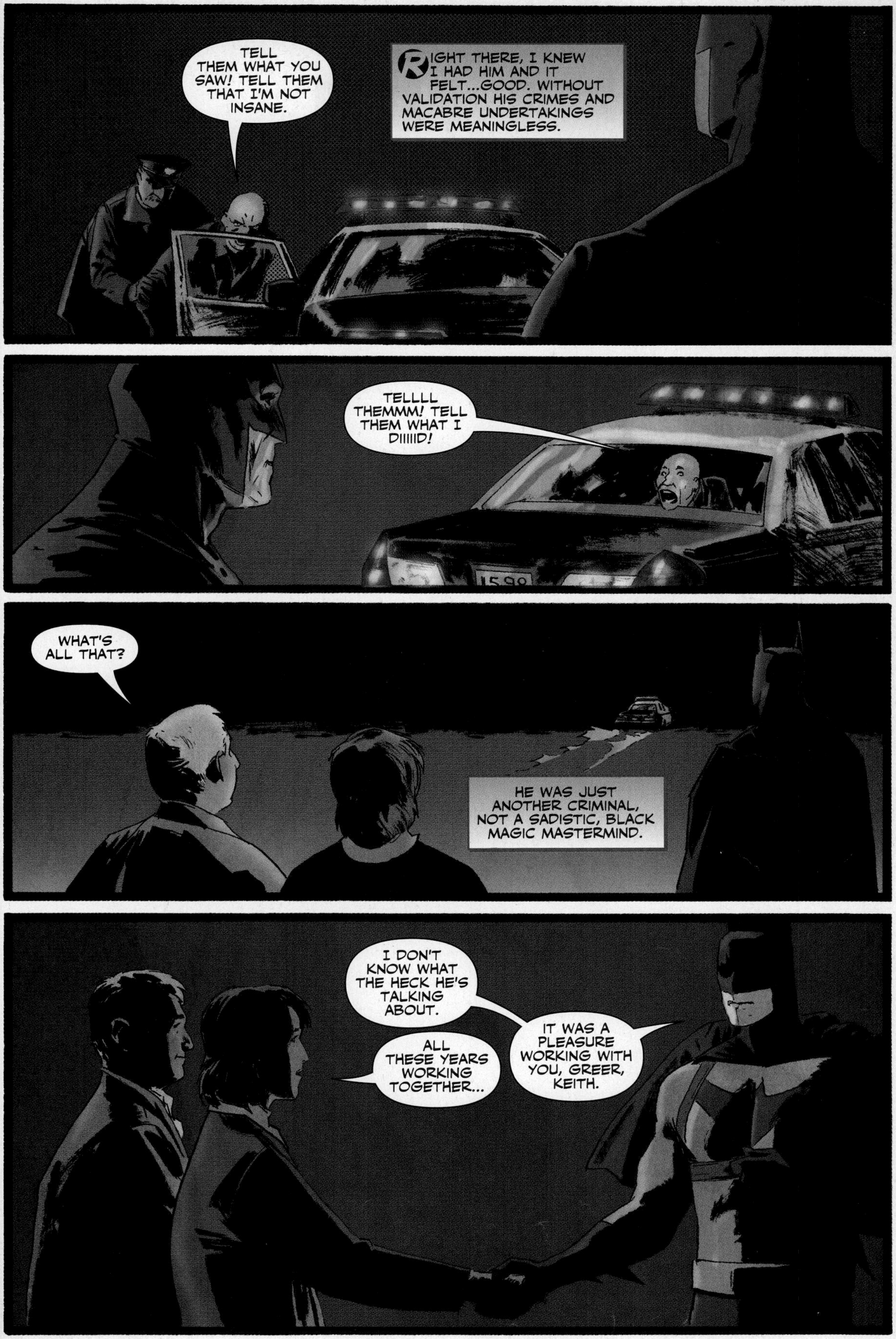
TELL THEM WHAT YOU SAW! TELL THEM THAT I'M NOT INSANE.
RIGHT THERE, I KNEW I HAD HIM AND IT FELT...GOOD. WITHOUT VALIDATION HIS CRIMES AND MACABRE UNDERTAKINGS WERE MEANINGLESS.
TELLLL THEMMM! TELL THEM WHAT I DIIIIID!
WHAT'S ALL THAT?
HE WAS JUST ANOTHER CRIMINAL, NOT A SADISTIC, BLACK MAGIC MASTERMIND.
I DON'T KNOW WHAT THE HECK HE'S TALKING ABOUT.
IT WAS A PLEASURE WORKING WITH YOU, GREER, KEITH.
ALL THESE YEARS WORKING TOGETHER...

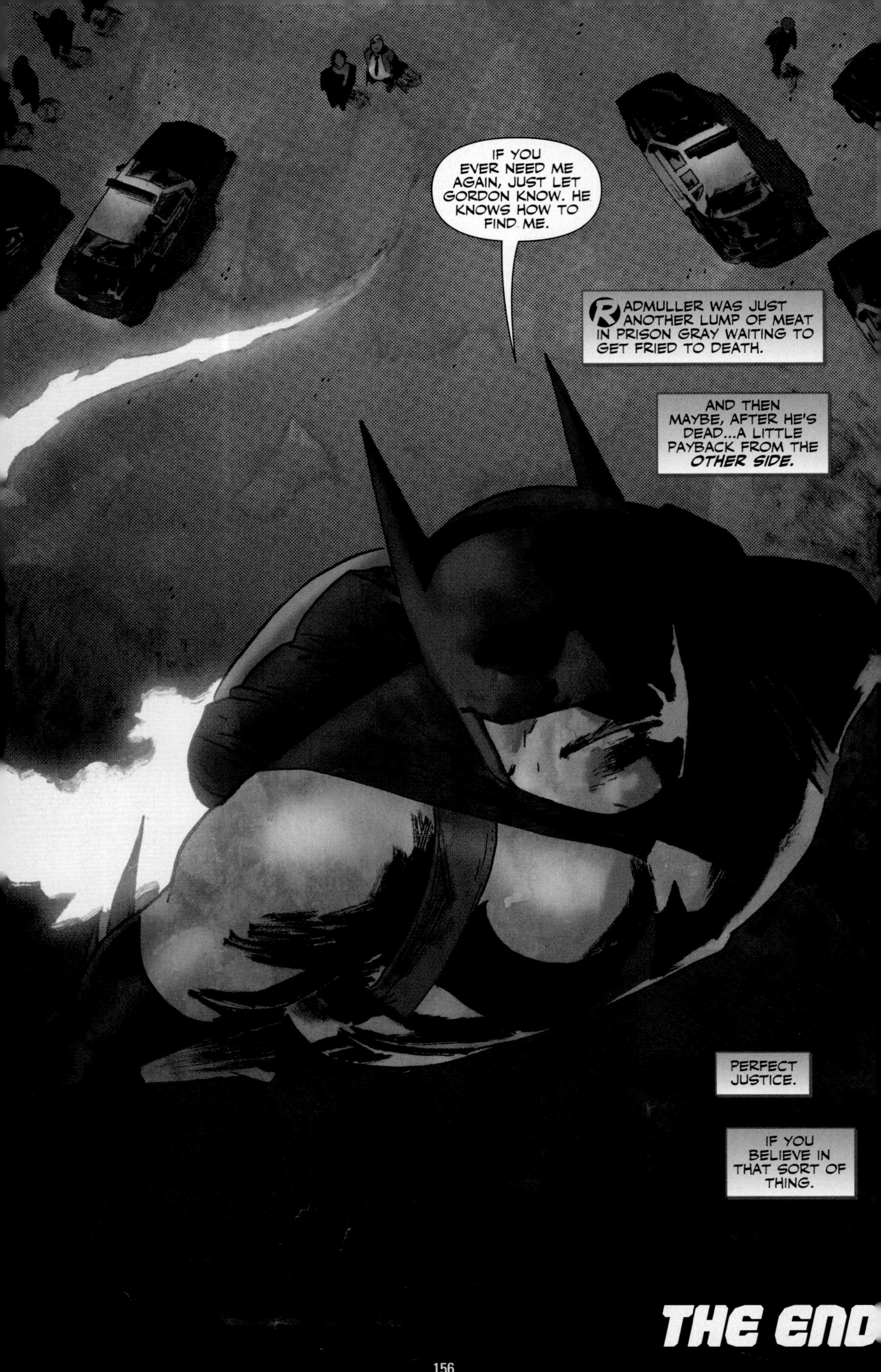
IF YOU EVER NEED ME AGAIN, JUST LET GORDON KNOW. HE KNOWS HOW TO FIND ME.
RADMULLER WAS JUST ANOTHER LUMP OF MEAT IN PRISON GRAY WAITING TO GET FRIED TO DEATH.
AND THEN MAYBE, AFTER HE'S DEAD...A LITTLE PAYBACK FROM THE OTHER SIDE.
PERFECT JUSTICE.
IF YOU BELIEVE IN THAT SORT OF THING.
THE END

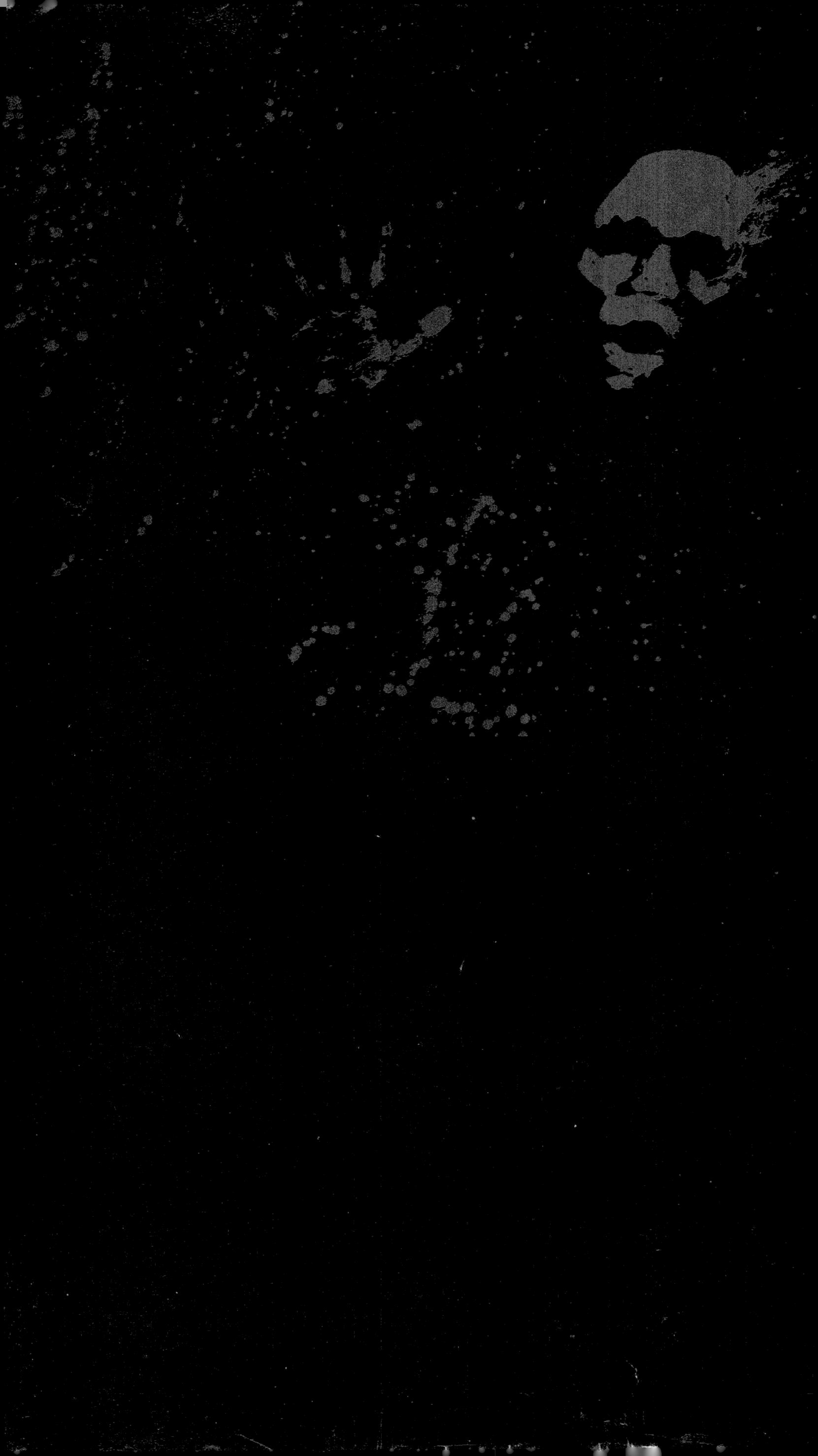

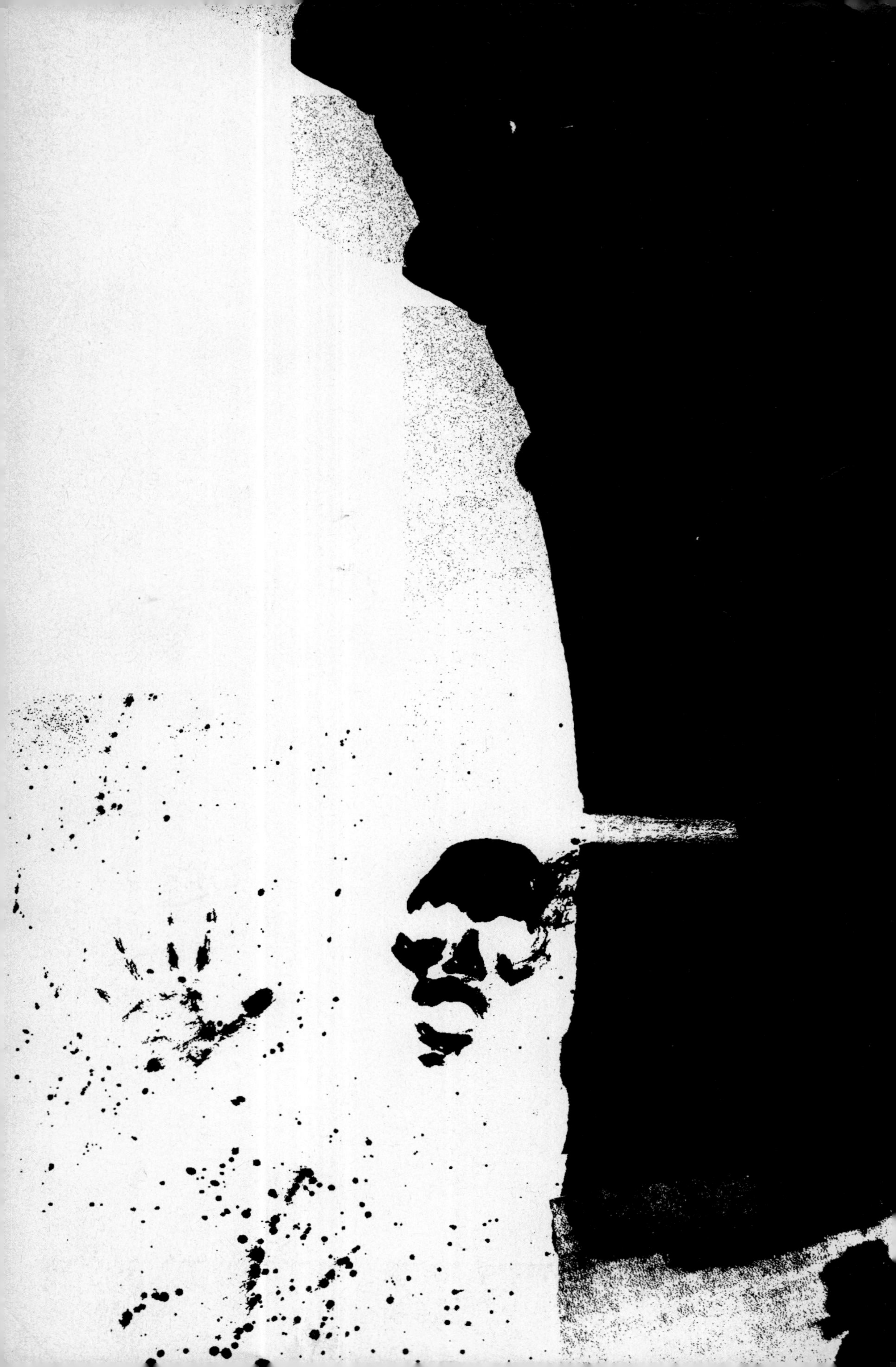

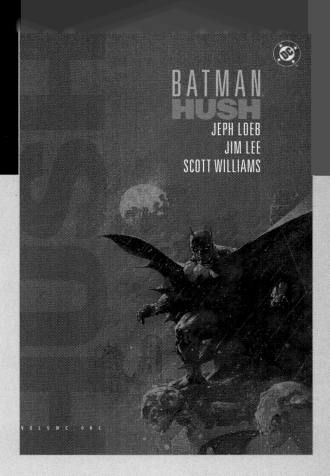

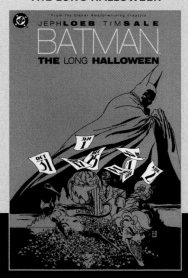